MW01129932

For a free catalogue of Feral House books, send SASE to:

Feral House
PO Box 3466
Portland, OR 97208

THE MAKING OF A SERIAL KILLER

THE REAL STORY
OF THE GAINESVILLE STUDENT MURDERS
IN THE KILLER'S OWN WORDS

DANNY ROLLING & SONDRA LONDON

INTRODUCTION BY COLIN WILSON

FERAL HOUSE

THE MAKING OF A SERIAL KILLER

THE REAL STORY OF THE GAINESVILLE STUDENT MURDERS IN THE KILLER'S OWN WORDS

DANNY ROLLING & SONDRA LONDON

INTRODUCTION BY COLIN WILSON

WARNING: EXPLICIT VIOLENCE
For Mature Adults Only

Portions of *The Making of a Serial Killer* were previously copyrighted in four volumes of *The Rolling Papers.* (c) 1992, 1993, 1994 by Sondra London
Excerpts have appeared in *Knockin' on Joe*, Nemesis Books (London, England, 1993), *The Globe*, and *The National Examiner.*

This First Special Limited Edition of *The Making of a Serial Killer* is published by FERAL HOUSE BOOKS Spring 1996

DANNY ROLLING DOES NOT PROFIT FROM THIS BOOK.

CONTENTS

CHAPTER 5

A Real Killer

CHAPTER 6

They Called Him Psycho

CHAPTER 7

Getting Babes

CHAPTER 8

Possessed by the Reaper

CHAPTER 9

No Place Left to Run

CHAPTER 10

The Last Dance

APPENDICES

INTRODUCTION

BY COLIN WILSON

In late August, 1990, both *Time* and *Newsweek* carried the story of the slaughter of four women and a man on the Gainesville campus, in Florida. In fact, it is infrequent for either magazine to carry stories about American murders in their European edition, and the fact that they did was a sign of how far the five murders had shocked America.

I had just finished writing — in collaboration with Donald Seaman — a book called *The Serial Killers,* and the last major American case I had dealt with had been the murders of the serial killer Leonard Lake, in California, which had come to light after Lake's suicide in 1985. In fact, as far as I can remember, this was the last occasion when *Time* and *Newsweek* had given wide coverage to an American case. For this reason, I paid particular attention to the reports from Gainesville — a campus where I had once lectured. Then, as the weeks and moths went by with no further reports, I assumed that the killer had escaped. In fact, no one knew that he had been arrested ten days after the murders.

It was some time before I learned what had actually happened. This came about in 1993, through reading Sondra London's book *Knockin' on Joe,* a remarkable and intimate study of serial killers, including Carl Panzram, Gerard Schaefer and Ottis Toole (the partner-in-crime of Henry Lee Lucas). I had never heard of Danny Rolling, but from this I learned that at that time, he stood accused of the Gainesville murders.

It seemed that Danny Rolling had written to Sondra London from prison in June, 1992, addressing her as "Madame Sondra, Media Queen." He was serving life for armed robbery, and had just been charged with the Gainesville murders. By Christmas of that year, Sondra London and Danny Rolling had decided they were in love. Finally she was allowed to visit him one time at Florida State Prison. The meeting apparently confirmed their feelings for one another. There was an instant and powerful physical attraction. Soon after this, they announced that they were engaged.

This announcement, in February of 1993, was featured in newspapers next to a story claiming that Danny Rolling had confessed to the Gainesville murders to a fellow inmate, Robert Fieldmore Lewis. The local media assumed — understandably — that Sondra was only pretending to be in love with Danny to get his story.

Sondra's title "Media Queen" had been acquired in 1989, when she launched a publishing company of that name, to bring out a private edition of a book called *Killer Fiction* by Gerard Schaefer, who was serving life for killing two teenage girls in Florida. (An augmented trade edition of *Killer Fiction* will be published in Fall, 1996, by Feral House.) Oddly enough, Schaefer had been Sondra's first lover. They had met when Schaefer was 18 and Sondra a year younger. But Sondra was shaken by his admission of the sinister and violent impulses he experienced towards women, and walked out on him. In fact, Schaefer's sexual fantasies were all concerned with humiliating women and with hanging them. *Killer Fiction* includes sketches of women in their underwear standing on gallows.

On July 22, 1972, about seven years after their breakup, Gerard Schaefer was arrested for abducting two teenage girls, tying them to trees, and terrorizing them. By some fluke, both escaped. Upon being arrested, Schaefer was fired from his job as a sheriff's deputy, and then, regrettably, bailed. Before he was incarcerated for six months in the following December, he had murdered at least two more teenage girls, Georgia Jessup and Susan Place. (In fact, it later became clear that he had used this brief freedom to murder at least five.) On September 27, 1972, Schaefer had turned up at Susan's home, and later had taken the two girls off in his car, telling

Susan's mother they were "going to the beach to play guitar." They never returned home.

But Susan's mother had been suspicious of this smiling man who, at 26, was so much older than her teenage daughter, and noted down the number of the license plate on his car. She managed to get one of the digits wrong, and an innocent man was interviewed by the police. But driving through Martin County, Florida, she noticed that all of the license plates there began with 42 — the local prefix she had recalled as being the first numbers on the license plate. The car proved to belong to Gerard Schaefer, who was in jail for abducting the two girls. A glance at his photograph told her that this was the man who had gone to the beach with her daughter. Some time after that, the dismembered remains of Susan Place and Georgia Jessup were found in nearby woods. A search of Schaefer's room at his mother's house in Ft. Lauderdale revealed many items (including teeth) belonging to a number of girls who had vanished.

Schaefer received two life terms for these two murders, but police suspect that the true number of victims was around 34. (Schaefer himself later told Sondra London the number was upwards of 80.)

Though Sondra was shocked at the thought that she had lost her virginity to a serial killer, her curiosity led her to write to him in prison. He replied, and in 1990 she went to see him. He showed her the "stories" he was writing — sadistic fantasies about raping and murdering women — and gave her permission to publish some of them. And so *Killer Fiction* appeared, in a desktop edition priced at $18.00. I bought my copy from a crime bookseller in New Jersey. It was only later, through Paul Woods, the British publisher of *Knockin' on Joe,* that I made Sondra's acquaintance.

Gerard Schaefer, in fact, must be one of the most disgusting serial killers of all time, although he consistently denied being a serial killer, and even tried suing me once for referring to him as one. (The judge threw it out.) His "killer fiction," and his even more explicit secret letters to Sondra, make it clear that all his fantasies involved cruelty. He liked terrifying his victims, and he particularly enjoyed having two girls at his mercy, so he could make each one beg him to kill the other one first. He finally died in prison in December of 1995, hacked to death by another prisoner.

All this, then, makes it clear why Sondra London was uniquely qualified to present the memoirs of another confessed serial killer.

Danny Rolling is clearly a different kind of person from Gerard Schaefer. His crimes are horrific, but the lack the sheer sadistic evil of Schaefer's. It is not my intention to make any excuses for Danny Rolling, for as a student of criminology, that is hardly my business. Yet one thing seems clear: that while Schaefer reveled in his sadistic fantasies, accepting them totally and unquestioningly, Danny Rolling has always been more of a Jekyll and Hyde, a man who struck many who knew him well as sensitive, decent and arguably talented, and who was possessed periodically by an immense violence. Schaefer's work has literally dozens of passages like this:

I kicked her in the stomach and she doubled up. "Teach you to bite my dick, bitch!" Bloody vomit spewed up from her gut and splashed from her mouth...

Danny Rolling, I think, would find this as revolting as most people do.

Sondra's account of Rolling in *Knockin' on Joe* makes it clear that from the beginning, he was fated to be a dropout from the society that the rest of us take for granted. Many criminals claim that their fathers are to blame, but in the case of Danny Rolling, this is undoubtedly true. His father, as this book will make clear, was a brutal domestic tyrant. The first time Danny dared to argue with him, his father threw him on the floor, handcuffed him, and sent for a squad car to take his son to jail; Danny spent two weeks in there. It is hard to understand such men, whose aim seems to be to crush the ego of their children and wives, rather than, like most fathers, doing their best to nurture a sense of security and self-confidence. Danny offers some insight in the sections of this book following "My Father the Hero," so one can try and work out the answers for oneself.

In a letter to me, Danny described how his father had once made a scene at the checkout of the supermarket, raving and shouting until the manager came and told him that if he didn't calm down, he would have to leave. Unimpressed, James Rolling asked the manager if he knew who he was talking to — that he was a police sergeant. All this fuss, Danny recounts, was due to the fact that Danny's mother had picked out the wrong brand of chewing tobacco for her husband. It is easy to see why his children found life with James Rolling intolerable.

It must be admitted that Rolling Senior had one good reason for feeling furious with his son. When Danny was a child, a friend introduced him to voyeurism. They would watch a young cheerleader undressing and bathing. Finally, they got caught at it, and it became general knowledge that Danny Rolling was a peeping Tom. For a father who had been a war hero, and who was now a member of the police force, it must have been a keen humiliation. The habit stayed with Danny his whole life.

What is clear is that the sense of insecurity in his home life led Danny to rebellion. If he had been of more malleable material, he would have been crushed, and become merely a social inadequate. In fact, he was born a fairly dominant person (one of the dominant five percent), and he was also talented, as his writing, his songs and artwork reveal. Such people tend to rebel against bullying.

My own situation bore some relation to Rolling's, for my father was an irritable, short-tempered man, and if anyone had asked me as a child if I loved him, I would have answered with astonishment, "Of course not!" The astonishment would have been due to the fact that I somehow took it for granted that no one loved their fathers. Mothers were for loving, fathers were for fearing — or at least being nervous about. Yet now it seems to me totally obvious that children — particularly boys — need a father to love; to begin with, they need him as a role model. (All this has been expressed with exemplary force and clarity in Robert Bly's *Iron John.)*

Now in my case, it may have been just as well that I felt totally detached from my father. I must emphasize that I didn't hate him, as Danny hated James Harold Rolling. I just didn't care much about him. Dad was not a reader, and he had no interest in ideas, so it would have been a catastrophe for me to take him as a role model. But when, at the age of ten, I became fascinated by chemistry, and then by astronomy and physics, I suddenly had a purpose in life. Things were still difficult. When I left school at 16, I went to work in a factory for 48 hours a week, and hated it as much as Dickens had hated the blacking factory, or Wells the drapery emporium. But by then I knew I wanted to be a writer, not a scientist, and it took eight years before I succeeded in getting my first book — *The Outsider* — published. It had been a hard struggle, and I frequently plunged into total discouragement — particularly when a typescript was rejected. But I recognize that if, on top of my other problems, I had had to deal with a father like James Rolling, I would almost certainly never have made the breakthrough. And I might now well be dead, from one of the illnesses that arise from sheer resentment and frustration.

Danny had another problem I didn't have. He was living in a drug culture. I was never tempted to take drugs, probably because they were not available after the Second World War when I was a teenager. Danny was downright unlucky. He enjoyed the Air Force, but just before he was due to be shipped to Vietnam, he was arrested for drugs, sent to the stockade, and discharged. His father was furious and disappointed, and things went from bad to worse. After a religious conversion, he married a fellow member of the Pentecostal Church. But he claims that she was sexually frigid, and when police caught Danny peering in through a window at a woman undressing, the marriage went into decline. She finally left him, and then divorced him. He took it very hard.

From then on, it was all downhill. In the misery and resentment of being served his divorce papers, he committed his first rape. Filled with remorse, he decided to go and apologize the next day, placing his future in his victim's hands. But he saw a threatening male coming out of her front door, and ran away. Soon after that he committed his first armed robbery.

Soon he was in prison — and this, it seemed to me, was the real turning point. The violence shocked him. He came close to being gang-raped in the shower by a crowd of black prisoners. Interracial violence was endemic. One white was killed by three blacks simply because he was white; then two months later the murdered prisoner's brother stabbed to death two of the killers.

Free once more, Danny's problem now was a compulsion to commit rape. As he points out, the difference between the rapist and the "normal male" is very small indeed. He references a study where a hundred college men, asked if they would rape a pretty girl if they were sure they could get away with it, replied yes. Yet in his description of a rape, in the section "You Don't Have to Do This," it is obvious that, in spite of being a peeping Tom, he was still a long way from being a Ted Bundy. According to his own account, he treated the girl like a human being, and only broke his promise to the extent of having an orgasm inside of her instead of withdrawing. Clearly, he was still a human being.

Yet his problem, obviously, was that he was fast losing all respect for himself. After another period in prison, even more degrading than the others, he seems to have committed his first multicide — a treble murder of a girl named Julie Grissom, her 8-year-old nephew, and her father. It was the day after he had been fired from a job, and again the cause seems to have been a fury of resentment.

He does not confess to this murder in the present book. But he does not deny it, either. Robert Fieldmore Lewis claims that Danny Rolling confessed to it in prison.

By now, Danny had become convinced that he had at least two alter-egos, one called Ennad, who was a rapist and a robber but not a killer, and one called Gemini, a demonic entity who thirsted for blood. Yet clearly, he was not entirely in Gemini's power, for during the course of an intended rape-murder, he realized that there was a baby lying in a crib, watching him with innocent curiosity. He allowed his intended victim to escape.

A few months before the Gainesville murders, a violent quarrel with his father ended with James Rolling trying to shoot him, and Danny shooting his father and leaving him for dead. In fact, James Rolling recovered, minus the use of one eye and one ear.

Danny Rolling was now on the run. Another rape attempt ended in sudden remorse. In another, the girl suddenly showed herself willing, and after it was over, drank a beer with him.

After that, he went to Gainesville, and committed the five murders that caused hundreds of students to flee the campus in terror. They are described in this book in such detail that there would be no point in even summarizing them.

After that, he left Gainesville and went back to armed robbery. Within ten days he was caught after robbing a grocery store in a town 40 miles south of Gainesville.

It was not until January of 1991 that the murder investigation reached the point of drawing his blood. When DNA testing identified him as the man who had raped three of the four women in Gainesville before killing them, he was promptly identified as the prime suspect, but it was not until November 11, 1991 that he was formally charged with the five murders and three rapes.

What finally made him decide to confess to the murders is another story. But at any rate, he did plead guilty to the crimes at his trial in February of 1994. He had already been given four life sentences plus 170 years for the armed robberies, but this time he received seven more life sentences, 100 more years, and five death penalties.

And that, it would seem, is all there is to say about it. His criminal career seems easy enough to understand. It began with the voyeurism in childhood, watching the cheerleader get undressed. Ted Bundy's career of murder started in exactly the same way. The poor relationship with his father led to social maladjustment, as well as inability to control his rage and resentment. The rest followed naturally — his first rape, his first armed robbery, his first prison sentence…

Yet Danny Rolling believes there was another cause: that he was periodically "possessed" — either by a darker side of his own personality, or by an evil spirit. In this book he tells how, lying in bed with his wife Omatha, the room filled with an evil presence. In a letter to me, he tells of another frightening encounter, when he was in solitary confinement:

I was resting on my iron bunk when this thing that appeared like a gargoyle pounced on my chest, pinning me to the mattress. It had both claws pressing against my shoulders…

It released its grip on one of my shoulders and clawed open my mouth, snaking a foot-long slimy tongue down my throat. I couldn't breathe… I was suffocating, and I began to struggle. I managed to push the thing far enough away from my face to get that horrible tongue out of my windpipe. It sneered and spat, "How does it feel to kiss a snail?" I screamed and it just disappeared.

This sounds, of course, like a bad nightmare, and that may well be all that it was. Yet it seems to me possible that Danny Rolling is dealing with something more than that.

In 1980, I began to write a book about poltergeists. I had been interested in the paranormal for ten years or more, since being commissioned to write a book called *The Occult*. My approach was rationalistic. I believed in poltergeists, but was convinced that they were due to spontaneous psychokinesis, or "mind over matter," mostly on the part of emotionally disturbed teenagers. But as I studied case after case for my new book, I gradually became convinced that they were nothing of the sort — that they were, indeed, disembodied entities — that is, "spirits." There seemed to be little doubt that many of them were highly unpleasant — not just disembodied juvenile delinquents, like poltergeists, but entities capable of inspiring criminal violence.

There was no abrupt change of viewpoint; I did not suddenly become a "spiritualist." But I came to accept that spirits could wander in and out of a human being as easily as a tramp can wander in and out of an empty house whose doors have all been left open. However, according to the authorities on this subject — men such as Allan Kardec and Carl Wickland — such spirits cannot obtain much influence over a person unless the individual happens to be on their "wave length." So in a sense, any such possession takes place by some form of mutual consent.

I have been struck by how many criminals come to believe that they have been possessed by some unpleasant entity. Ted Bundy said he felt like a vampire, and referred to his violent alter-ego as "the hunchback." The Yorkshire Ripper thought he was possessed by the Devil. Little by little, I have become willing to entertain the hypothesis that some criminals are possessed by demonic entities — that once they have been accustomed to being swayed by negative emotions, they have opened themselves to the possibility of being influenced by some of the nastier denizens of the "spirit world." It is only a hypothesis, a suspicion that creeps into my mind again and again, reading about serial killers like Ted Bundy and Pee Wee Gaskins. I have been particularly struck that men who start out as rapists, simply enjoying "stealing" sex without the other person's consent, often drift into the most appalling sadism. In the most recent serial murder case in England, the builder Fred West, who began simply as a man who thought about nothing but sex (due, I suspect, to an accident that caused brain damage) ended by torturing girls before he killed them, and only having sex with them once they were dead.

So I am perfectly willing to entertain the hypothesis that Danny Rolling was possessed by the entity he calls Gemini. He claims that Gemini unlocked the door of Christina Powell and Sonja Larson's apartment, so that he could enter. And detectives who saw the bookcase he moved in Christa Hoyt's apartment were convinced that two men must have been involved, since it was too heavy for one man to carry.

But is possession by spirits really a reality, or merely a manner of speaking, a kind of shorthand for a psychological condition we do not yet understand, like multiple personality?

When I was speaking to an audience in Marion, near Boston, Massachusetts, in 1995, the psychiatrist Stanislav Grof was one of my fellow lecturers. After a panel discussion about criminal psychosis, I asked him whether he had ever seen any evidence of possession. In reply, he told the following story, which can also be found in his book *The Adventure of Self-Discovery*.

In the Maryland Psychiatric Research Center, he encountered a girl called Flora, who had a criminal record. She had been imprisoned for driving the getaway car in a robbery in which a watchman was murdered. After leaving prison, she had become a multiple drug addict and alcoholic, and had been imprisoned again for accidentally wounding a girlfriend when cleaning a gun under the influence of heroin. Now she was suffering from a multitude of psychiatric problems, including suicidal violence.

Grof was treating patients with the psychedelic drug LSD, and decided — after much hesitation — to try this. During the first two sessions there was only minimal progress. But at the third session, she began to complain of facial cramps. Suddenly, her face froze into a "mask of evil," and a deep male voice came from her mouth, declaring that it was "the devil." He ordered Grof to stay away from Flora, declaring that she belonged to him, and that he would punish anyone who tried to take her away. He then began to threaten Grof, describing in detail what would happen to Grof and his colleagues if he persisted. What worried Grof was that "the devil" seemed to know all kinds of personal details about himself and his colleagues that Flora could not possibly have known.

Although he began to experience panic, Grof forced himself to take Flora's hand — which had twisted like a claw — and held it for the next two hours, while calming himself and envisaging a capsule of light embracing them both. After what seemed the longest two hours he had ever spent, her hand relaxed. When she "awoke," she had no memory of what had taken place. From that point on, Flora began to improve, until she was discharged, joined a religious group, and took a normal job.

Grof retains an open mind. But he is still puzzled about how "the devil" came to know so much about his personal life and that of his friends. It is easy to believe that the entity Grof encountered was a genuine "evil spirit." And I find it just as easy to believe that the same hypothesis may explain some of the mystery of Danny Rolling.

AUTHOR'S NOTE
BY SONDRA LONDON

It has taken three and a half years to complete the story of how Danny Rolling became a serial killer. During that time, as he underwent the process of presenting the various facets of his personality to me, he developed insight into the pathology that had controlled and baffled him his whole life. By the time the book was finished, he was no longer overwhelmed by the dark forces that had driven him in the past. He continues to struggle to overcome his tendency to fragment into incomplete personalities under stress. To the extent that he has learned to distinguish his own different voices, and to allow himself to express those thoughts and emotions that had been forbidden, his core personality has become more diffuse, and arguably, more healthy. All he ever wanted was to "just be Danny," and be loved and accepted, without having to keep his most crucial secrets hidden in the darkness.

My nonjudgmental approach, tempered with my prior experience with serial killers, encouraged him to gradually trust me enough to reveal himself more and more. He could not understand himself, but he could tell me bits and pieces of his story and then as if waking from a dream, turn to me and ask, "What were my words?" Seeing his true self mirrored in my eyes, he began for the first time to come to grips with the disturbed emotions and traumatic memories that had been controlling him from his unconscious mind.

If writing about the fatal process, if drawing its imagery, has not entirely demystified it, at least it has brought it down a notch from the realm of the utterly incomprehensible. Danny had always run from the knowledge of what was going on in his own mind, until he found himself at that ultimate dead end in the house of steel and stone at the end of Murder Road — where he ran into me.

I had my doubts at the beginning. When Danny first started writing to me, he had zero self-esteem, and only a desperately spurious sense of self-confidence. He had been alone with his secrets his entire life. He was not proud of what he had become. He was very much aware of me as a female from the beginning. Even before our relationship became more personal, he was in a courtship mode, wanting to please me. But this was a whole new situation. He had always had to fabricate a presentable front to be accepted, but now the only way he could capture the attention of this female was to candidly examine his weaknesses and failures, and reveal what was wrong with him. He wanted to open up to me, but he really didn't know how. He wanted me to know all about him, but he was intimidated by what he felt to be my superior writing skills. "When it comes to writing, baby, you're like a Porsche," he wrote. "I'm more like a go-cart."

Once Danny Rolling became involved in the interactive process of accounting for his life and crimes, he was surprised at the quality of what he was able to compose. The creativity he has exhibited for me had been obscured, repressed by the weight of layers of self-hatred he had accumulated since birth. The grime of those layers of anger, fear and hatred could only be washed away by tears of genuine remorse, followed by forgiveness, sympathy, encouragement, and love.

It was considerably difficult for me to persevere with studying this complex and troubled man under the given conditions, until together, we could reach the point where he was able to ask himself: "Why, Danny, why did you kill those beautiful people?" Although he wanted to confess, the manner in which it was done became a matter of great concern to all parties.

It's one thing for an author to stand back at a safe distance and compose a fictionalized account of a seriously disturbed, recently apprehended serial rapist and murderer. It's another thing to actually get involved with such an individual in real life. Having stayed the course, I can now say that it is a path even angels should fear to tread. State's attorneys and prison authorities have attempted to defeat our purpose. Family members and friends on both sides have pressured us to cease and desist. Rival journalists have been at their wits' end to steal our story, even going so far as having thousands of pages of my correspondence released, so they could be incorporated into their own stories. Victims' families who had sold the rights to their stories publicly threatened to kill me if I sold our story.

Nor has it been easy for Danny Rolling to keep pressing onward with the task at hand, long after being served notice by the State of Florida that he would not be allowed to divert any of the profits from publishing his story to his brother, Kevin, as he had originally intended — at least until the United States Supreme Court affirms the decision they made in 1991 that the so-called Son of Sam laws are unconstitutional. When Danny saw the State intended to prevent him from telling his story by hijacking the proceeds from the publication of any accounts of crimes that he might write in the future, he voluntarily relinquished all of his rights and assigned them to me. State of Florida v. Rolling, London, et al., a civil suit intended to block the publication of his confessions, is entering its third year of litigation at the time of publication of this book.

I remain confident that some day the egregiousness of this unconstitutional action against Danny Rolling and myself will be affirmed, and through due process, my lawyer will see that my fee is returned, setting an important legal precedent about freedom of speech along the way. Meanwhile, having to fight for the right to write does have that proverbial "chilling effect" that would have provided the decisive disincentive, if our motivation had only been financial gain. Given the conditions under which we have had to work, there have been many times when it seemed impossible for one or the other of us to continue. Still, we managed to press forward toward the goal that has bound us together, ever since the summer of 1992, when Danny asked me to help him explain himself to the world.

As we composed bits and pieces of this story, I compiled them into a series of scrapbooks called *The Rolling Papers,* which became an impressionistic kaleidoscopic self-portrait comprising all of our graphic and written material in the order of its composition. Along the meandering course of its development, I periodically copyrighted it to protect it from being raided, a fear that was not unjustified, as it eventually did occur.

In 1994, after Danny completed his murder confessions, the material previously compiled in *The Rolling Papers* was revised, finally emerging after another year's work as *The Making of a Serial Killer.* The considerable drama surrounding our personal and professional relationship falls outside the scope of this book, as my own account of the Rolling case appears separately in *All the Fallen Angels.* There is also a more imaginative work in progress, a series of fables written and illustrated by Danny Rolling on Death Row, collected under the title *Legends of the Black Marsh.*

In *The Making of a Serial Killer,* I have focused on delivering the promise of the title, by staying within the framework of Danny's point of view, and including only material that contributes to the overall understanding of how a little boy from a law-abiding Christian home could grow up to become his own worst nightmare.

Throughout his entire life, Danny has had to deal with the destructive impulses and behavior arising from the troubled parts of his mind that at times become so vividly differentiated that he appears to actually become another person. While the psychiatrists who examined him for court carefully skirted the "multiple personality disorder" diagnosis for his damaged psyche, instead they concluded that he suffered from a half-dozen noxious syndromes, from "borderline personality disorder" to a form of dissociation known as "possession disorder."

In writing about his life and crimes, the way he expresses himself varies widely. He is not consciously trying to convey an impression of dissociation. He is still experiencing shifts in behavior and perception. He just writes from wherever he may be, and whatever phase he is in at the moment shapes the style of his story as it unfolds. The book was written over a period of three and a half years, and the man who started out in 1992 writing about his last arrest was not the same one who wrote about the murders in the summer of 1994. It should come as no surprise that a man who could attend church seven days a week in the daylight and rape and rob and stab strangers to death in the night might be capable of quite a range of literary styles as well.

In trying to clarify the confusion of his own mind, he has given names to the two main alter-egos he has experienced. As I have come to know them, the one he calls Danny is his own natural original self — gentle, artistic, bright, polite and devout. But although the original Danny has many fine innate qualities, he would never become a man. At a very young age, as he puts it, "something died." Because the Danny side of him would always be immature and inadequate in many ways, the Ennad side developed into all that Danny could never be. Ennad is daring, sexually aggressive — a thrill-seeking scofflaw and a stand-up convict. While Danny Rolling is comfortable with these two aspects of his makeup, Gemini, on the other hand, dismays and frightens him.

He describes a serious struggle with rapidly alternating personalities in "Close Call," an account of an attempted murder in Colorado that Gemini was in the midst of perpetrating when a shocked Danny recoiled from the attack, apologized to the victim and urged her to run for her life from the murder demon that still fought to control him.

The people he robbed after the shootout with his father described him as a "Jekyll and Hyde," telling People magazine, "He would turn sweet and put the gun down, then he would get mad over something and pick it up."

In this book I have standardized the shifting and blending of many different voices of Danny Rolling into three type styles. Predominantly, we have the straight narrative text, where Danny Rolling relates his own experiences, speaking of himself as he most often does, in the third person.

The straight narrative text is also used for those portions of the story that were written by myself, relating material revealed at trial, including statements made by his relatives and friends, psychiatrists, and the people he socialized with in Sarasota, Florida, right before the murders.

In describing the abuse he suffered as a child, it is of considerable significance that his own memory of the most traumatic events was blocked. When he wrote "Nightmare on Canal Street," a year before he heard his childhood described by family and friends at trial, he could remember nothing at all before the age of eight. The more serious abuse, such as being handcuffed and beaten with his father's police belt, remained buried in his memory until revived by testimony. Of course, he still has no conscious memory of the numerous incidents of witnessed spousal abuse when his mother was carrying him, or his traumatic forceps delivery, or being kicked across the room as an infant. The descriptions of his childhood included here, then, include both his own memories and those recounted at trial.

Secondarily, but growing more predominant toward the end, are the indented sections where the author steps out of the narrative mode and turns toward the audience; you encounter the man himself, sitting on Death Row today in Starke, Florida, speaking directly to you.

Awww, come on, guys... there's nothing wrong with me that a good piece of pussy and a fifth of tequila wouldn't cure.

And finally, we have the versification that runs through everything Danny Rolling writes. Granted, it is a bit unsettling to have your hard-core crime scenes laced with chants from Spirits of the Night. But that's the way it really is. This propensity for rhyming and emoting is an essential component of Danny's makeup. Hearing or dreaming up these little snatches of song is similar to his visual artwork, in that it is one of the ways he experiences a form of dissociation. A tendency toward schizophrenia runs in his family as well, and that may account for some of Danny's rhyming, sing-song voices. Gemini likes to versify, but Danny does too.

The use of three alternating type styles provides a fair approximation of what the mind of this serial killer is really like. At times, one style will cut in on the other, or even take issue with an opposing point of view. Other times, you can see one identity through the eyes of another.

Danny's out, I'm in... Danny's out, I'm in...
Let's go hunting... my hopeless friend

While I have noticed clearly differentiated, recognizable personalities, there have also been overlapping and merging of these, as well as the forming and reforming of minor, transitional splinter personalities with names ranging from Cowboy and Michael Kennedy to Maniac and Max Man.

My challenge as his coauthor was to preserve the unique multiplicity of these voices, without either skewing the overall impression by failing to incorporate all parts, or confusing the reader with an unmanageable array of voices. The stylistic mutability of the text is really another manifestation of what this book is all about.

While the bulk of *The Making of a Serial Killer* was written by Danny Rolling, it has been my responsibility to edit and polish the fragments, arranging and composing them to enhance the narrative flow of the story. While more aggressive editorial intervention was necessary in his early efforts, by the time he wrote about the murders, his skills had matured to the point that the three chapters relating the Gainesville murders could be published word for word, verbatim, exactly as he wrote them. He did say that he put these three chapters through at least five drafts each before sending them to me.

There was a lot more to it than just writing, though. This has been an intensely personal encounter. I have instructed and inspired Danny; probed and cajoled him; encouraged and sympathized with him; provoked him and given him my love. I have explored with him his deepest and strangest secrets, and while there is still much I do not know about this darkly fascinating man, he thanks me for helping him put together the broken pieces of his mind and tells me, "You are the only one who ever really knew me at all."

In the family portrait, I am wearing a gray and white striped jacket. Mom is trying to force a smile. Kevin manages one... I do not... and Dad stares straight ahead cold as ice.

Photo by Sondra London

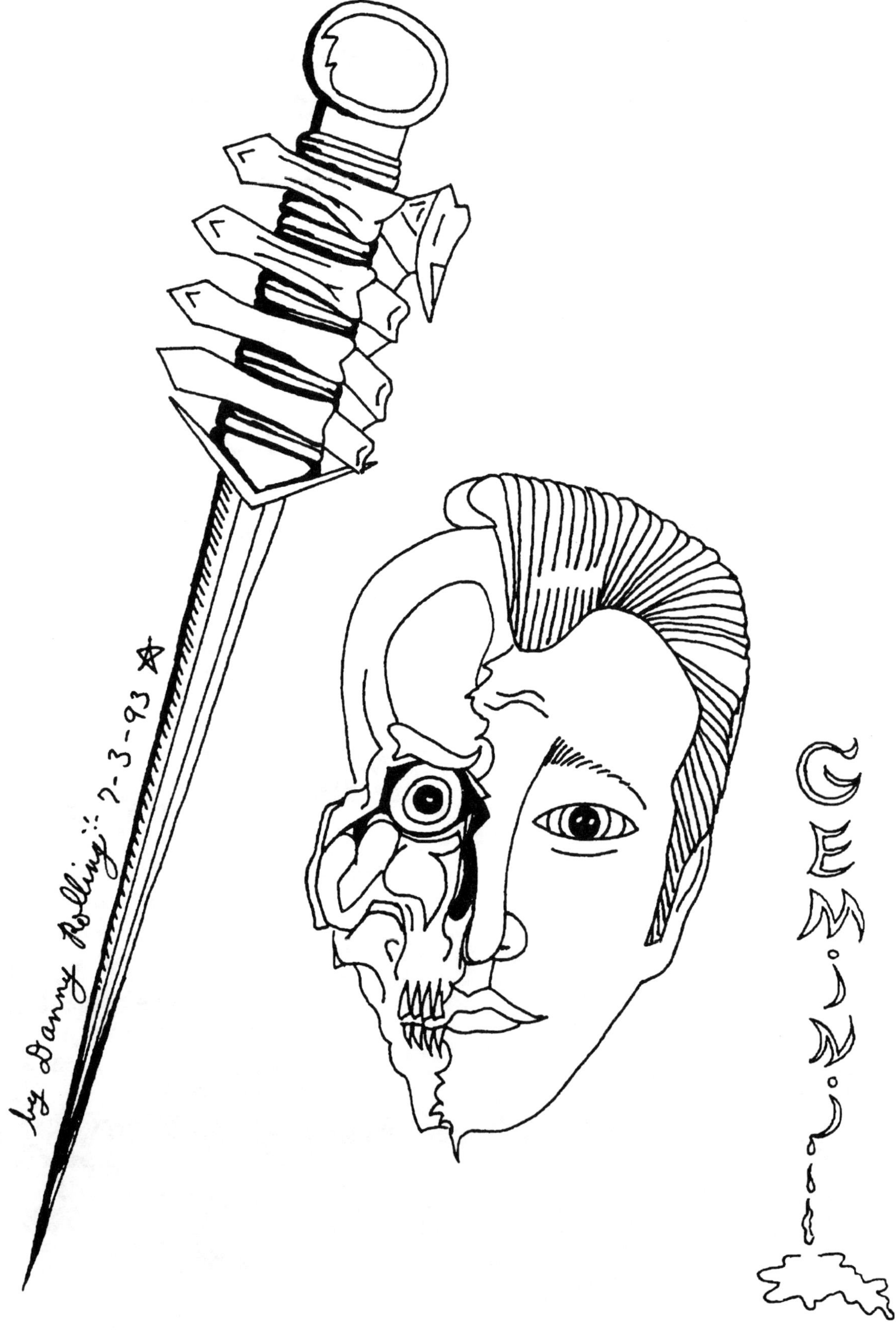
by Danny Rolling 7-3-93
GEMINI

PREFACE

BY DANNY ROLLING

Last Words of a Condemned Man

What you are about to read is a true tale of great loss and horror beyond what nightmares are made of. That loss behooves me to confess my sins before God and man by telling the story of what happened those tragic nights in Gainesville, Florida, as close to the actual events as my memory serves me to convey.

The writing was difficult for me because regardless of what has been said or believed, I am not proud of what I have done. Terrors upon terrors have befallen me, and I boast not of the suffering I have caused, because I do feel regret and compassion for those that remain. It was tempting to dress up the story, in respect to the deceased and their loved ones, but if I am to lay my soul bare before you — the reader — I must speak truly.

Dear reader friend, hear the declaration of this condemned man: There are forces that move in this world, forces you rarely see with the natural eye, because they are supernatural beings. Every now and then, a soul is born with eyes capable of seeing into that realm that goes beyond imagination. I have seen supernatural beings of darkness reaching for me. Oh God, they never stop reaching for all of us. They want our minds so they can destroy the creation of God.

As a child, my self-esteem was broken down. As a result, there was an opening in my mind — a crack, if you will. I've always been sensitive to the spirit world. I know when a demon is peering out of a dark corner, as well as I know when angels of great beauty and power are hovering near. In the course of my life I have yielded to both powers, and there is only one conclusion: Right and good always follow the heavenly. Wrong and evil produce nothing but HELL.

If you are one who hears the night calling and cannot resist its seducing, find you a place to pray and ask our Lord and Savior Jesus Christ to help you overcome these evil spirits that roam the darkness in search of a soul to devour.

To the Victims' Families

Christina Powell... Sonja Larson... Christa Hoyt... Manuel Taboada and Tracy Paules. I'm sure they were fine people and did not deserve the treatment they received at my hand. My tears pale in comparison to their suffering. If only it had never happened. I cannot go back and undo what was done. If only I could, I would give back what I took.

I know, I know. My tears mean nothing to you, and after you read this book, if you choose to do so, you will hate me even more.

It is in my heart to ask your forgiveness, but how can you forgive such an injustice? I only know I am deeply sorry for what happened. Words alone could never express my remorse.

I have prayed for you, that the good Lord will help you get on with your lives. Such is the plight of the living.

Perhaps on the day of my execution or death you will lay down your hatred and bury your anger with me.

Sincerely – Danny Rolling

CHAPTER 1
THE BLOODY TASK OF MURDER

The Arrival

The Grim Reaper came calling on the little college town, not on the wings of some terrible strange bird, but on the screaming wheels of man's invention.

The silver and black Greyhound swung into the station like a rolling coffin. A fugitive from justice stepped lightly off, carrying a navy blue sports bag filled with tomorrow's pain. A man driven by the winds of destiny, his name was Danny Rolling.

Standing there in the station, he appeared to be just another traveler weary from his journey. Why had he drifted into Gainesville? He wasn't a student. He was a traveler whose mind's eye viewed the world in a different light. At times the path showed crystal clear, but other times pyrotechnic thunderclaps flashed jagged sabers of demonic impulses through the dark brooding clouds of his mind.

An actor of sorts, he was playing out his fantasies on the Stage of the Real. Like a fiery tumbleweed dancing about the hollow night, he was a puppet to the forces that moved him. Who or what pulls the strings when murder is the theme? The evil puppet-master was born long ago in a sewage-filled cell in a Mississippi prison. This dark figure from the nether world of his twisted mind was called GEMINI.

Many components comprised Danny Rolling's psyche. One of the personalities that rented a parking space in his subconscious was an outlaw named Ennad, otherwise known as Jesse Lang. Bold and courageous, he was a daring fool who tempted fate with a gun. Then there was Michael Kennedy, an alias Danny picked up from a Vietnam vet whose Social Security card he acquired in a midnight burglary. Now Danny, Ennad, Jesse, Michael, and the bloody one, Gemini, had come to town... and the play began to unfold.

The Williamsburg Village Apartments

It was August 23rd, a balmy afternoon in 1990. The Florida sky yawned and closed its one red eye behind the purple mask of encroaching night. As shadows pooled and crawled over the college town of Gainesville, with them came horror.

Christina Powell, 17, of Jacksonville and Sonja Larson, 18, of Deerfield Beach had just settled into their new home at the Williamsburg Village Apartments on S.W. 16th Street. They were young and attractive females with promising futures.

Fall classes would soon begin and the girls were giddy with excitement as they went about the chore of giving warmth and personality to a fresh apartment.

Dusk gave way to the reaching darkness. Not far away, the scene was of a different nature — male violent and out of control.

In a stand of timber behind Archer Road, the crickets rubbed their legs together like bows across violins. Another voice piped from the thickets bleeding in with the cricket's night song. 'Twas the voice of madness carried on the ageless wings of destiny, the eternal struggle between Good and Evil that has plagued mankind from the beginning of time.

Danny Rolling sat cross-legged Indian style within the folds of a tan one-man pup-tent listening to the night sounds.

Zzz-it... Zzz-it... Zzz-it...

"Man! Just listen to those crickets," he breathed as he pressed the RECORD button on a hand-held stereo tape recorder and spoke into its internal mike. It was a farewell statement to his family in Shreveport, Louisiana, ending ominously, "Whelp! I got something I gotta do."

Christina and Sonja grew weary just past the witching hour and took to their beds, Christina on the couch in the living room and Sonja in the upstairs bedroom. They slept as innocent babes, peaceful and beautiful, unaware of the danger that lurked beyond their vision of dreams.

Zzz-it... Zzz-it... come Danneee...
It's time... come...
Taste the sweet dew of the night.

The man wandered from shadow to shadow draped in Ninja black — searching, listening, his senses extended like antennas.

He stole a black bicycle from behind a house trailer and raced off into the arms of darkness. Only an occasional streetlight gave a glimpse of the elusive ripper on wheels, speeding through the night.

Something magical occurs when the bell tolls the dead of night — the hour spirits leave their underworld holds to play pranks on the unsuspecting surface dwellers. The air becomes heavy with sweet smells of the earth and a mist blankets everything with a glistening sheen.

'Twas this ungodly hour Gemini emerged thirsting for blood — and he would not be denied. Not this night.

The darkly clad man was lost, but what did it matter? Any place was the place, when Gemini summoned. Danny's troubled mind couldn't resist its seducing urgings and the night embraced him as a friend.

Gripping handlebars of the aluminum steed, he bulldogged the bike into a hospital emergency entrance.

"Yeeeee-hi!" he screamed, startling a small group of nurses breaking on benches near the front entrance.

"Hey! Look at that! I wonder what he's up to?" a nurse questioned one of the others.

It was a strange sight indeed that came and went in a blink and was gone.

A policeman sitting in his cruiser noticed a white male glide past the nurses and exit into the dark street.

Routinely, the officer investigated and pulled the biker over to the curb. He didn't get out because the man exhibited no suspicious demeanor. Instead, he just rolled down the window and inquired, "Where's your light?"

"What — what light, officer?"

"In this town, you are required by law to have a light while operating any vehicle — even a bicycle — after dark."

"Oh! I didn't know. I just moved here to attend college this semester."

"Where are you going?" he probed, eyeing the bulging dark blue sports bag belted to the subject's side.

"I was invited to a party at the University Inn and I got lost."

"Well, you're a ways from there, but if you..." and he gave directions. "Now you get a light for that, you hear?"

"I will, officer. Thanks!" And the cop drove off unsuspecting.

The situation had been extremely dangerous. The officer had no idea what he was dealing with. If he had, he would have handled the encounter differently.

The blue hip bag the cop was obviously curious about hid tools of death.

The confrontation ended without incident and the countdown to a bloodbath that could have been avoided then and there, had that cop been a bit more thorough, was only minutes away.

Empty, dimly lit streets led the man to the Williamsburg Village Apartments. He left the bike leaning against an apartment wall near the entrance and eased around back.

Shadows of the 4-story complex towered overhead, like a gray castle in the mist.

Breathing deeply, he paused, unzipped the bag, removed a brown ski mask and pulled it over his head, hiding his identity.

Then he drew out a pair of leather sports gloves and slipped them on over his large hands. They felt cool and smooth, even comforting.

"Which one?" He whispered, gazing up at the window lights piercing the night like little lighthouses warning wayward ships to steer clear of the rocks.

There was a shift in thought as an evil wind rustled through the trees and Gemini surfaced.

Climb the stairs... Dannnneeee...
Climb on... child of the night so hollow...
I will lead... you will follow...

So up he went, until he stood on the deck of Apartment #113.

Time: 3:00 o'clock A.M., August 24, 1990.

"This one?"

Yes, Danny, this one.

And he tried the door. It was locked tight. He paused, unzipped the bag and drew out a heavy-duty screwdriver and a Mini-Mag penlight. He twisted it to life and stuck it butt-first into his mouth, pointing the beam at its intended target — the frame around the lock — and began to pry.

It would not budge. Frustrated but determined, he removed the penlight from his mouth and wedged it in the waistband of his pants.

"Gemini, if you want this to happen? Open the door. Show me your power."

He tried again. Still it refused to cooperate. He tugged and pushed but… nothing.

It stood defiant.

It's one thing to break into a dwelling and another entirely to gain access quietly to an occupied apartment in the dead of night, when every sound is amplified by the lack of resonance.

"Gemini, show me your magic. Open this damn door!"

He tried again, twisted the door knob, and it turned easily in his hand as the door opened.

Surprised and amazed, the masked man fished out a razor-sharp Ka-Bar Marine fighting knife and a roll of gray duct tape. Then he replaced the screwdriver and unbuckled the waist bag containing a loaded Taurus 9mm pistol, leaving it on the railing of the deck.

In the glow of light spilling through the doorway, the man tore two strips of tape about 6" in length from the roll, pressed them together side by side, stuck them to his bare left arm just above the elbow, and passed through the gaping door, closing it behind him silently.

The apartment was still as a grave. Only the low hmmm of the refrigerator and hssss of the air conditioner betrayed any presence other than the intruder.

The deranged man moved stealthily through the kitchen into the living room gripping the Ka-Bar, and found Christina Powell sleeping on the sofa against the wall. She was dreaming the sweet dreams of the young, unaware of the Evil hovering over her rest.

He watched her chest rise and fall, not disturbing her as she slept. Then he turned his attention to the stairs leading to the fourth floor bedroom. Each step he crept was taken with care.

As he ascended the staircase like a tiger creeping through bamboo in search of prey, a board creaked!

He froze, heart pounding in his ears, and looked over his shoulder at Christina to see if she stirred. She drew a deep breath and raised her arm over her chest resting it there, but she did not awake. The madman continued his climb.

Sonja Larson slept peacefully, swept away on the clouds of that world called dreams, as the Dark Presence invaded her tranquillity.

The masked man drew the penlight from his waistband and turned its face sending energy to the elements, casting a narrow beam of light. The beam played about the dark room and found Sonja's pretty face, but did not wake her. The man placed the light butt-first into his mouth to free his hands for the bloody task of murder.

Then… the Evil filled the room with terror that cut through the land of dreams like hot bolts of blue lightning!

The intruder peeled the duct tape from his arm and placed it in his left hand, adhesive side up. Then the moment had come. Eternity opened its jaws and snatched another soul from the Land of the Living.

The killer bent over Sonja and with one swift move pressed the duct tape over the sleeping damsel's mouth, at the same time stabbing her in the upper right chest.

The blade sunk to the hilt as Sonja tried to scream, but the hand and tape pressed over her mouth only allowed a muffled cry to escape from her lips.

Her eyes bulged in shock! She tried to struggle and kick at her attacker, but this only brought a frenzy of stabbings — blade and bone — blood spurting and splashing on the two embracing in the Dance of Death.

It lasted only seconds, but just before she found blissful unconsciousness, Gemini whispered close to her ear, "I'll come back for you after you're dead." Then he watched curiously at the approaching moment of death to see how it would go.

Sonja stared unbelieving into the eyes of the Nightmare draining life from her, and with a gurgle of blood the light left her lovely eyes.

The blood-drenched killer stood and crept from the room in silence. He descended the staircase carefully, and paused by Christina, still sleeping. He bent over her and pressed his hand over her mouth, then snarled as her eyes popped open with fright!

"Don't fight me! If you do, you're dead."

The awakened girl went rigid and tried to scream, then went limp as a rag doll under her attacker's cruel hands.

"Now listen, little girl! If you behave, I won't hurt you. Promise to be a good little girl?"

"Mmm-hm," she nodded through his hand.

"If you scream or try to do anything stupid, see this knife?" He brandished the large menacing blade near her face.

"Mmm-hm," she nodded again, looking at the bloody Ka-Bar threatening her. Then the masked man removed his hand.

"Where's Sonja?"

"Don't you worry about her. My partner is up there with her. She is being a good girl. You better do the same."

"All right."

And he dragged her off the sofa onto the carpet, rolled her over on her stomach and bound her hands behind her back with tape as she lay passive.

"Good girl," he soothed, stroking her soft hair.

"Get up!" She did, with some assistance, and stood shivering before the bloody horror holding her hostage.

"Stand up straight! That's my girl — daddy's sweet little girl," and he began to fondle her breasts through her nightshirt, watching the response in her doll-like eyes.

"Let's take a look at whatcha got." He tore off her t-shirt — RIP-TEAR — and her shoulders were bare, revealing a tan lace bra.

"Nice bra." He cut the straps, unhooked the fastener, and the bra fell away. Milky white breasts wiggled free of their restraints, much to the rapist's delight!

"Yes! Pretty, pretty titties," and he grabbed a handful, sucking on her nipple.

"Now, let's take a look at that pussy," and her panties were peeled off. She was completely naked now, trembling with paralyzing fear.

"Let's go into the kitchen," and she was pulled by the arm.

"Get down on your knees." She did.

"Open your mouth and stick out your tongue." She obeyed.

The rapist stripped off his pants and stroked himself to life only inches from the kneeling girl's face, pumping blood into his swelling rod with his right hand while presenting the Ka-Bar with the left.

"You better make me like it, do you hear?"

"You'll like it. I — I promise."

"If you bite me, I'll stab you to death, understand?"

"You'll like it, promise."

"Cross your heart and hope to die?"

"Cross my heart."

"Good girl," and he rubbed the helmet of his swollen dick over her face and into her waiting mouth. She gagged as he worked deeper and deeper down her throat, but she tried to please.

"That's good. Now get up and hop on the table." She tried, but couldn't because her bound hands left her off-balance. So the man lifted her and placed her butt on the edge of the table.

"Have you ever been raped before?"

"Yes."

"Really?"

"Uh-huh," her last words.

"Tell me about it." But she just went silent.

"Well, that's all right, cause I'm fixin' to do it again anyway. Now spread your legs. That's a good girl. Pretty pussy… yeah." And he raped her.

They went on like that for about fifteen minutes, her on the table with him between her legs, pawing and biting her breasts. Christina didn't say a word. She had become catatonic.

"Let's do it doggie-style." And he arranged two chairs by the edge of the table with her ass sticking up in the air, her head bowed and resting on the table top. She was entered from behind as he grabbed her hips, pounding her doggie-style. He grabbed a handful of her hair and reared her head back like he was riding a horse and her hair was the reins.

"Yeeeee-HI! You once-a-month bleeding bitch! Give me that pussy!" And he spanked her buttocks until they bruised as he humped her in that fashion.

"Oh yeah! I'm gonna… gonna cum… ahhhhh!" And he emptied himself into her.

"Come on." And she was led back to the living room.

"Lay down." She did, and her mouth was sealed with duct tape. Then she was rolled over onto her stomach.

19

Time seems to stand still just before Death comes, releasing a soul to eternity.

Gemini struck! Christina was stabbed five times in the back as she lay on the carpet.

Pop-thud… pop-thud… pop-thud… pop-pop.

And the knife was left lodged in her back. She hung onto life, refusing to die. Gasps of air whistled through gaping holes in her back as streams of blood poured over her sides.

This went on for three minutes, her there on the floor wheezing with the Ka-Bar protruding from her back like an odd appendage. Then the Demon knelt and drew the large killing knife from the bloody flesh where it was buried.

The clock stopped and the sands of life ran out as her spirit hovered above the body for a moment and then flew to its maker.

But the Creature's lust was not yet quenched. Up the staircase he bounded to Sonja's room! He grabbed her by the ankles and pulled her to the edge of the bed. Her nightshirt bunched up around her armpits, exposing knife wounds to her bare chest and breasts. The duct tape was peeled from her lifeless lips and her mouth plopped open. It was filled with blood.

Then her powder-blue-and-pink teddy bear print panties were removed and her legs spread wide. They yielded like old boards. Rigor mortis had already seized the carcass.

She was too bloody to rape. It was a ghastly sight of pure horror — her precious life snuffed out, cruelly and tragically. She was left in that undignified manner.

The Demon descended the staircase and turned his attention back to Christina. He grabbed her by the ankles and dragged her over by the sofa. He peeled the tape from her wrists, rolled her over on her back, and stripped the tape from her mouth.

"Party time, my pretty," and he raped her lifeless body, chewing on her nipples like a mad dog gnaws a bone. She had become a human doll being toyed with by a monster of hideous unreason.

After his climax what happened next was a blank to Danny until later that day. The movie reel turning in his head just went blank, and he found himself standing before the refrigerator eating an apple, then a banana, and then he left.

He retrieved the sports bag left on the railing of the deck, bounded down the stairs, and ran.

He threw the portions of used tape in the dumpster out front (mustn't leave evidence) and hopped on the bike. As he did so, a young man delivering newspapers rounded the corner. The two men eyed each other, then went their separate ways — the boy to deliver his papers, the man to his destiny.

It was 11:00 o'clock A.M., the 24th day of August, 1990.

Danny was peddling his bike along a Gainesville street when he felt the urge to check the sports bag belted to his side. Fishing around examining its contents, he found the Taurus, the Ka-Bar, the gloves, and… "What's this?" he murmured, and held up a clear plastic sandwich baggie to the blue sky.

"Oh my God! No!" It contained Christina Powell's nipples.

Danny became ill; he felt like throwing up right then and there on the street. Instead he threw the baggie with the nipples into the open maw of a street gutter, as if the rains could wash away the blood from his hands.

Ah, but alas. Cain slew Abel and asked, "Am I my brother's keeper?" But his brother's blood cried up from the earth and the Maker of All Things heard… He heard.

by Danny Rolling 4-23-93

CHAPTER 2
SOMETHING DIED

A Murderer I Became

When I was just a boy, from time to time our family visited a fishing camp on Lake Bistanoe. I would sneak away in the dead of night, slipping behind the cottage, where the tree frogs and crickets sang their night songs, down the winding path sparkling with lightning bugs, leading the way to my secret fishing place.

The old wooden pier would creak and groan under my footfalls as I tiptoed wide-eyed with wonder to the pier. In my left hand I would hold a Zebco 33 rod and reel and a tackle box full of lures. In my right, a flashlight.

Magical moments of discovery they were. Lake Bistanoe became spooky after dark, especially for a mere boy alone at the end of a long wooden pier jutting between the dark cypress trees covered with moss.

Fishing at night is a world apart from daylight hours. The darkness surrounds you, touching you with the damp mist rising from the lake's surface. I would shine the light into the watery depths illuminating that mysterious liquid world, drawing fish to its source. Off in the distance, I'd hear an old owl announce its presence, hooting through the marsh, perhaps searching for a field mouse or mole on the shore. I can still hear the sound of that old 33 casting and reeling — zzz… plop… click… urrr… urrr — and then sometimes I'd even get a tug and a splash and a FISH!

Sitting there alone in the glow of the Eveready under a blanket of stars, my mind was searching for the meaning of it all. Gazing at the millions of stars winking overhead, the universe seemed so vast and I, the lad, so small amongst the bodies of Heaven.

How beautiful and peaceful those moments were. Never in my wildest childhood dreams did I imagine that tender, loving child of years gone by would one day become a MURDERER. Ah but alas, a murderer I became.

What forces in nature could mold an innocent child into a monster so hideous society couldn't bear the weight of his evil deeds? Nature doesn't breed criminals. People spawn the violence that corrupts even nature.

We all live… we all love… we all die…
But none of us can do these for another.
No, we all live… right or wrong,
We all love… our own,
And we all die… alone.
For life is like a rose
Whose petals reach for the sky
But so easily
It is crushed.

Gargoyle of Heaven

A child filled with wonder and mischief lay atop the double-bunks in his small childhood bedroom, with the reprint of Custer's Last Stand hanging on the wall.

In his dream, the child was asleep, when a blinding flash of blue light pierced his mind and he awoke, still within his dream. Amazed and curious as children will be, he wanted to know the origin of that blue light that outshone the sun.

As he jumped down from the top berth onto the bare tile floor, the wild Indian warriors that stood over the fallen Union soldiers were taking their scalps with their sharp knives. They seemed to be watching the boy as they always did, and General Custer stood his ground in his tan buckskins, firing his pistols madly as his world came down around him.

Scampering quickly to the window to investigate the strange light, he searched the sky for the phenomenon immediately obvious to the casual eye. It filled the whole sky! Beyond explanation, beyond belief, there in the horizon stood an immense city of golden clear glass. From left to right, heaven to earth, as far as the eye could see it stood regal and strong.

"Wow! Mom! Dad! You gotta come take a look at this!" he shouted with all the force his young lungs could muster. Then it dawned on him — it was quiet. Not just quiet — totally still, the absence of all sounds.

A great fear fell on the child, and he began to run throughout the house in search of his mother and father. They were not to be found, and neither was anyone else. He was alone — totally alone.

He burst out the front door, letting it slam behind him with a WHAM! Standing there in the front yard of his father's house, he looked the neighborhood over good and proper. No one, not a soul in sight. Not a dog, not a cat, not a bird, not even a fly — nothing. Only the wind softly whispering.

Come to me... little one...
Come and see... your destiny...

The child was filled with a longing to flee, to escape the madness of it all. Running across the street, he beat on a neighbor's door, but no one answered. He tried the door. It was open. He entered and searched for someone — anyone — but there was no one. The same occurred at the next house, and the house after that. There was no one anywhere.

The answer must be in that gigantic city of golden glass, he thought, as he pointed his finger in the direction he sought. "I will go and see this sight," he said. But no one heard him.

Taking the keys from a neighbor's kitchen table, he started up their black '57 Chevy and plotted a course for the glowing crystal city of gold. His driving skills were not well-developed, but he knew how to drive well enough to make his way through town, then out onto the highway.

He drove for hours and the shining structure seemed ever beyond reach, like a mirage on the hot desert sands — but was it really? The closer he got, the higher it loomed. It was dazzlingly huge!

Thorns began to crawl up onto the highway. As he continued, they began to choke off the artery in which he traveled, until proceeding by automobile became impossible. He was forced to leave the '57 Chevy and continue afoot. Soon the thorns left only a narrow twisting path. He marched silently, contemplating the events behind him and beyond.

Finally the thorns — monstrous things they were, with vines as thick as tree trunks and thorns as long and sharp as spears — were barring his way entirely.

With great effort, he climbed and crawled — pricked, cut and bleeding — through the thicket into an opening that surrounded the heavenly dome. From here, he could see there were people inside. Exhausted, he stumbled across the field of freshly-trimmed green grass.

Ah, but alas. When he got within twenty feet of the great dome of glass he bumped into an invisible barrier, a force field. He stood there in his dream, dumbfounded by what he saw.

Inside there were great waterfalls, beautiful blue, clear pools, white unicorns, stately peacocks, a lion as tame as a pussycat. The people all were young and naked as a jaybird's behind. Innocent, like children, they danced around happily amongst the lions-and-tigers-and-bears with no fear.

Then he found a small opening in the force field with his hands, and squeezed through. It was even more beautiful inside! Great colorful flowers as big as pillows were everywhere and the fragrant smells of paradise filled the air.

The place had many levels, and there were clear tubes here and there throughout the city. All you had to do to ascend to an upper level was to step into one of these elevators, and a gush of fresh air would gently lift you.

As he stood before one of these tubes gazing at it in wonder, a beautiful naked young woman with sandy blonde hair came up to him and spoke in a voice with no emotion, like she was being told what to say and was merely repeating a message: "You don't belong here."

The boy puzzled over this, looking at his Levis and tennis shoes, thinking it was because he was clothed and everybody else was running around in their birthday suits. She read his thoughts and shook her head saying, "No. He wants to see you." And with that, she looked upward.

He shuddered at the thought. A shiver ran up his spine, cooling his brain. Was he insane?

She motioned for him to step into the glass tube, but he refused. It had no floor, and when he looked down the long shaft, he saw boiling flames. Still, she urged him on until at last he stepped in, and immediately he was whisked away. Up! Up! Up! He soared until he reached the highest level.

He stood before a massive ancient door bearing a big ugly gargoyle knocker with a brass ring through its nose. It sat there staring at him. He was afraid to touch it, but he knew he must. So he gently grabbed the polished brass ring and banged it, announcing his presence. The sound of the metal fittings coming together echoed behind the door, as it was opened by two 9-foot tall angels dressed in white flowing robes.

The room was enormous, and the floor was covered with puffy white clouds. In the middle of the vast chamber rose a staircase that led straight to the Throne of God. And He in all his majesty and glory sat upon the Divine Chair, looking down at him.

The boy could not look upon him. Instead, he fell on his face, trembling before his Maker. There was silence for what seemed an eternity, as if he were being examined. Then the Forever Almighty spoke:

"My child, you have two choices. You can spend eternity outside the protection of these walls beyond the Holy City, where you will be the only living creature, completely alone, forever alone — or you can spend eternity here with me, and be my Doorknocker."

Another appointed soul appeared from the air-lifted elevator and stood before the massive ancient door.

As the child sat there perched upon the Door of God, this soul grabbed his brass nose-ring and banged it upon his chest.

And the door opened as before.

The Best Dog Ever

December 25, 1959, 1:00 A.M. One cold snowy winter's night an event that escaped the eyes of a busy uncaring world began to unfold. A creature into the darkness was thrown — just a little white and brown lump of warmth, abandoned to die in the wet snow, but destined to become one hell of a dog. The cold December snow would not claim this rejected mongrel, this pup with the heart of a lion who refused to give up or give in to an early cruel fate.

James Rolling, Shreveport patrolman on duty that magical night known to all the world as Christmas Eve had no idea what he was about to find: a special Christmas present brought by a defiant young candle the freezing winter wind could not blow out. The patrolman pulled over his cruiser to investigate a bleak deserted area on the bad side of town. He turned on the searchlight and probed for mischief.

In the shadows all alone, a pup lay freezing, opened his little brown eyes, and saw the blue-white beacon piercing the darkness. He lifted his weak head and limped out of the rubble meant to be his grave. What spurs on such a pathetic creature, so alone and without hope? He had a longing for love so strong that everything gave way before it.

Perhaps an angel rode shotgun with Patrolman Rolling that night and saw the desire for life clinging in this fallen creature, had pity and gave it strength to push aside the chrome hubcaps and empty beer cans and crawl into the hearts of a policeman, his wife Claudia, and his two sons Danny and Kevin.

Officer Rolling got out of the warm cruiser to get a better look about the place. It began to snow again and he shrugged his shoulders against the chill. Satisfied there was no cause for alarm, he walked back to the idling patrol car, completely unaware of the drama played out between life and death in the freezing snow.

The officer got back into the '57 black and white Ford, closed the door, turned up the heat, switched off the searchlight, and sat there in the dark silence. He was lonely too, and wished he was home with his wife and boys, instead of prowling the lonely roads and back alleys that cold winter night. Then a weak, mournful cry for help reached out from the inhospitable darkness. James rolled down the window and keened in on the odd sound. There it was again! "Arf... arf..."

He flipped on the searchlight once more and swept the vacant lot with its knifing beam. Nothing? He opened the door and almost stepped on the little feller pleading to be rescued from the cold. Gently he

reached down and picked up the half-frozen puppy. "Well... what do we have here!" he asked. "Arf... arf... arrrffff..." whimpered the little tyke.

"Ha! Ha! OK, tonight's your night. I know two little boys who are just gonna love you!" And so the mutt found a home, and thus began the life and times of Rocky, the best damn dog ever!

Around the Rolling home, things were going to be different this Christmas. A new addition was about to join the family — and what a surprising little bundle of trouble and joy he turned out to be!

There were only a few simple presents under the Rollings' Christmas tree that year. Times were hard for everybody, but that didn't matter much, because those early difficult years held special moments like these. And as Danny and Kevin's mountain of a father stepped in from the cold with snow on his boots that Christmas morning, he smiled and said, "Come here, boys. I've got something to show you." He reached into his black leather jacket and pulled out the cutest little puppy you ever did see.

James knelt down and let the boys, wide-eyed with wonder, pet the pup. "He's just a puppy, and he's sick. But if you take good care of him, he'll grow up to be a big dog. Now you boys promise to be gentle with him?"

"Oh yes, Daddy! We promise!" the boys replied and with that, he handed the puppy over.

Danny held this living, breathing, wiggling creature in his tiny hands as it made a funny little grunt. Giggling, the two boys began to get acquainted with their new-found friend.

James said, "I think he's thirsty. Let's see if we can get him to drink some warm milk."

Claudia smiled and said, "I'll warm some up. He's so sweet, isn't he?"

The milk was warmed and a coffee saucer was set before the hungry critter and filled. Once his little cold black snout touched the warm milk, he lapped it up hungrily and didn't stop until it all disappeared. His little tummy swelled up so until he couldn't even move. Danny picked him up and he began that grunting sound again. "His stomach is hard as a rock!"

"Hard as a rock, huh?" said James. "Let's call him Rocky." And so that was to be his name for all eleven years of his life.

Now my friend, have you ever been invited over to someone's house for a visit, and observed the house dog as he jumped into the easy chair meant for you, and then refused to give it up? Your friend probably laughed and stated, "Oh, don't mind him. He thinks he's a person," and you looked at the hairy big-eyed mutt licking his lips as if to say, "That's absolutely right," and when you tried to move him he growled and looked all crazy.

Ha! Rocky wasn't like that at all. Nope, he was a true dog in the literal sense — a yard dog who looked like the cartoon personality Snoopy and lived in a dog house in the back yard, caught birds, pissed on everything, barked at kids taunting him on their way from school, and howled at the moon. Yeah, a real dog! The best damn dog ever.

One of his favorite things to do was to banzai the house when the back door was opened, and run through the house and out again, because he knew he wasn't allowed there. Still, he'd do it if he thought he could get away with it.

He also loved to play chase in the front yard and visit the bitch up the street on nights we would let him roam a bit. He was fast as lightning and slippery as quicksilver. The only time we could catch him was when he would let us, because he wanted to tussle around in the grass.

Man, what a dog! Yep, Rocky was one hell of a dog and my best friend. When no one would listen or understand me, and my heart was breaking over something, I'd make tracks for the tool shed in the back yard, my little sanctuary from the world.

Sitting there in the brown dirt, I'd begin to cry and old faithful Rocky would come to my side and cry with me. Rocky always understood. He would put his front paws in my lap, lick the tears off my face, look me in the eye, cock his head, and whimper. I'd pull him close and rock. Today, whenever I think of that dog, my heart still swells and squeezes out a tear for his memory.

One day, I walked home after school and found Rocky lying on his side by the kitchen door. I called his name, expecting him to jump up and bounce over to me, but all he could do was lift his head. I went to his side, knelt down, put my hand over his heart, and asked, "What's wrong, Rocky?" He looked up but couldn't see. He had gone blind in his last moments, but he knew it was me.

"Poor Rocky, poor boy," I said as he died. It seems to me looking back now, that Rocky had held on just long enough to say goodbye to me.

My Father the Hero

As I reflect on my childhood, some of the pieces of the puzzle come up missing, preventing a complete clear picture. However, even through the fog of my memory, there are moments that push aside the mist and present their ugly heads undeniable. And when the moment is seen through the confused, terror-stricken eyes of a child, total recall becomes a step into a dark and dusty closet where sleeping skeletons awake, shaking their long white fingers and crying, "Remember when?"

James Harold Rolling was a great man — a war hero with four bronze stars, a Purple Heart, a Silver Star, and a long list of commendations to his credit. In fact, he was the most decorated soldier of the Korean War from the whole State of Georgia, and he has the medals to prove it. A young man then, he had lived through many bloody battles in freezing snow-covered foxholes in Korea.

At one point his position was overrun by the Chinese-Korean Rock soldiers. While his fellow comrades-in-arms were being bayoneted to death around him, James opened up with his Browning Automatic Rifle, spitting molten death on the advancing enemy. A soldier friend just inches from his position in the same iced-over muddy hole took a Chinese bullet through the left eye, splattering his blood and brains all over my dad. He was horrified, but he continued to blaze his B.A.R. in the face of the enemy until his last bullet was spent. Then he had to fight them hand to hand, bayonet to bayonet.

One dark cold night, he and several other Special Forces personnel donned in slicker suits and flippers were lowered over the side of a destroyer and placed in rubber rafts. They quickly and quietly paddled out across the shark-invested treacherous waters. Their mission, to swim around in the murky depths, hand-tagging live mines so the gunboats could blow them out of the water, making way for a break-of-day assault on a major beachhead the next morning. A frogman near James was feeling around blindly in the frigid black waters when suddenly… Ka-BOOM! Splash!

The mysterious sea gave up its deadly secret, as the man unluckily touched a mine, detonating it. James swam over to the injured sailor, only to find him bobbing about with a blank expression on his gap-mouthed face. When James touched the sailor, he toppled over in the water, revealing what the blast had done. It blew him in two at the waist.

James single-handedly spearheaded a daring do-or-die charge down a barren hill after a green lieutenant fresh out of the academy led his platoon into an ambush. They were being picked off one at a time, pinned down on top of that hill. There was no cover and the shaken lieutenant cried out, "Men! It's no use. We've got to surrender or die!"

In classic Audie Murphy style, James Harold Rolling stood up amongst a hail of bullets and slugged the officer in the kisser, breaking his jaw and knocking him out cold. Then he heaved the unconscious lieutenant over his left shoulder and with his B.A.R. in his right hand and a blaze in his eyes, he shouted, "Boys! I don't know about you… but I ain't dyin' in no stinkin' prisoner of war camp! I'm goin' home!" And he stormed down the hill firing at the enemy, as the whole platoon rallied behind him. Out of the sixty brave men that charged down that bloody hill, only 13 survived to tell the tale. James Harold Rolling was one of them.

After the conflict, at the hearing his superiors didn't know whether to court-martial him or pin a medal on him. They chose to reward his courage rather than punish his folly… and so breathed the HERO.

But even with all his good qualities, James had a dark side, one he only shared with those closest to him. When it came to the woman who loved him and the sons who adored him, he had little patience or understanding.

Yes, James Harold Rolling has done great and mighty deeds. He was a fighting man who served honorably in the United States Navy, a civil servant of 22 years on the Shreveport Police Department, well-respected and admired by his fellow men in blue. Ah, but alas. Over the years, he has earned the earmarks of a man who because of his bullheaded stubbornness, has known great pain and personal tragedy.

Today he is a pitiful man who limps with a cane,

blind in one eye and deaf in one ear — all because the demons of his childhood and that terrible Korean War haunted him one too many times until he took a gun to that notion, only to have the bullets bounce back in his own face, humbling the fierce warrior.

And so, my reader friend, I open the door to the Rolling house, inviting you inside. As you peer into my life, please don't hold my father too harshly in your thoughts. The war had turned him into a battle-crazed killer, and the pressures of a policeman's duties combined with raising a family only fueled the fires of his disagreeable, often cruel disposition.

My dad was two people to me. There was the image of the policeman, the retired lieutenant, looked up to by everyone for 22 years… and I can still see that shining badge. But when he came home and the uniform came off, Dad became someone else. I do not believe he could control his explosive temper. His own childhood was a bitter one, in which he was forced to work in the cotton fields by my overbearing grandfather Homer Rolling.

At a tender age, my father witnessed a most gruesome murder. He was sitting with his grandmother at the dinner table one day when before his unbelieving eyes, he saw her husband slip up behind her and run the butcher knife across her throat.

Pop's granddaddy died in prison.

Never Will I Be Proud

As James Harold's mother, Mrs. Cavis Rolling, described her grandson, "Danny's a good boy. He's just like the clouds in the sky. Some days it's shining and some days it's stormy and raining. Danny changes just like the clouds, and nobody knows why."

"Danny was abused from the day he was born," Claudia Rolling wrote in a letter to the court. "My husband was jealous of him. He never wanted me to hold him or show love in him. He was told from the time he could understand that he would be dead or in jail before he reached the age of 15."

Claudia's sister Agnes Mitchell said, "Danny grew up knowing he was not loved or wanted by his father. He was told all his life he was stupid and no good." Neighbor Bernadine Holder said, "He has a father who hates him! Danny's father wants him dead."

It was a troubled pregnancy followed by a difficult birth. While she was carrying Danny, Claudia was bullied, choked and pushed down a flight of stairs by her husband. "It was a forceps delivery, and it made each side of his head poke out," said Claudia. "It terrified me, but the doctor told me that it wasn't but broken veins. He said it would go away, and it did — after about a year."

Agnes was at the hospital when Danny was born. When James Harold Rolling saw his firstborn son, he told her, "This kid is not coming home with us, I guess you know that. Claudia is not grown-up enough to take care of no child, so it's not coming home with us. We don't need any kids in our house. Your mama's going to have to take care of this baby."

"Look at him," urged Agnes. "He is a beautiful little boy. You should be real proud of him."

"Never," declared the new father. "Never will I ever be proud of him. As far as I'm concerned that's Claudia's boy, that's not my son."

"James always acted like even though he was a baby, that he should have all the answers and know exactly how to act," said Claudia. "I don't recall that he ever really hit him until Danny was crawling and he never really crawled. He sat on his little backside and put one leg underneath and pushed with the other leg and James didn't like that. To him I think it looked crippling or something, and with my husband, everything has to be perfect."

One day when Danny was six or seven months old Claudia asked Agnes to come and take her with her clothes to her mother's because she didn't have a way to do laundry. "I had already put one load of the clothes in the car," said Agnes, "when all of a sudden, James just busted in the front door and said 'What do you think you're doing? What are you doing here?' I told him that Claudia had told me to come and pick up the wash. And he said, 'The best thing for you to do is to leave out.' And Claudia said, 'This baby's got no more clean clothes and I have to wash.' He said, 'I'm the boss here and I take care of what's going on.' He kicked that baby and he slid halfway across the room. He landed on his side and hit the wall on the opposite side in the hall. I told him I was going to call the police. He drew a gun and ordered me out of the house. I picked the baby up and took my sister and put them in the car and took them to my parents."

"Yeeeah!" Claudia screeched with a wild faraway look on her tear-streaked face.

"Oh, Mommy! It's me, Danny! Can't you see me?"

"Yeeeah! Yeeeeah! Yeeeah!" His mother just kept screaming and screaming, as she clawed at the air. Like an animal in a trap, her mind had snapped. She didn't even recognize her own son.

When Claudia's sister Agnes came to the front door, James Harold pushed past her, saying, "You better go in there and take care of your sister, she's in the corner of the bathroom clean out of her mind."

"What have you done to her?"

"Not half what I'm going to do. You better get her out of here before I hurt her."

"Well, you get on out of here and leave her alone. Let me see if I can reason with her." And he got in his police car and left.

Agnes found Claudia in the bathroom with blood running down her arm. She grabbed her and hugged her. "Claudia, this is Agnes, everything's okay, everything's all right." Claudia looked wild, jerking and pointing at the razor in the sink.

Claudia was still screaming and writhing even after the ambulance driver arrived, but when he asked her what happened, she replied, "He attacked me, and the only thing I had to defend myself with was this newspaper."

After they got her on the stretcher, she said, "Agnes, get that razor blade and take it home with you. He put that in my hand and tried to force me to cut my wrist."

"Claudia, no! You're going to have to get out of this."

"I'm going to," she whispered.

As they wheeled her away, Danny and Kevin stood there helpless on the small porch. They watched through tear-flooded eyes as the red and white ambulance roared off down Canal Street. It was a long time before they saw their precious mother again. James had finally pushed her too far.

Danny wanted to shout at his father, to punch him, to hit him for how he bullied his dear mother. But he was just a little feller... and he was scared.

It seemed like a very long time that his mom was at the hospital, and little Danny asked his daddy every day, "When is Mommy coming home?"

After they took his mother away, something died in Danny's young mind, and as the days turned into weeks, something else began to take form, although he was too young to notice it at first. It came from the aching emptiness in his heart. He couldn't understand what had happened. And he never got an answer.

Flashbacks

James Rolling had flashbacks from the war. Once during the middle of the night, he broke out in a cold sweat and without realizing what he was doing, jumped up in the bed and grabbed Claudia by the throat, choking her until she turned blue and passed out! Thankfully, he came to his senses in time, but he almost killed her that night. As I sit here on Death Row contemplating my fate, I find myself having flashbacks of my own.

(At the grocery store) "Didn't I tell you to get me Red Man chewing tobacco? Not this Levi crap! That's what your Mama Mirdy likes, isn't it? Now go get what I told you," he would demand loud enough for everyone in the whole store to hear.

(At the restaurant) "Waiter! Didn't I tell you to bring me some more butter?"

"Yes, sir."

"Well? Where is it?"

"Right away, sir."

"You didn't have to be so rude, James."

"Don't tell me what to do, woman!" raising his voice and causing a scene. "I'm paying for this meal and if I want some more butter, I'm damn well entitled!"

(On vacation) "Didn't I tell you to keep an eye out for that turnoff? Damn it, Claudia! Why didn't you tell me?"

"I did, James, but..."

"But nothing!" he would growl with that mean look on his face. He would argue about some little thing for hours until the whole family would be driven to tears.

Whenever James Rolling would take his family out in public, he was prone to humiliating everyone, as it gave him a sense of power over them. Anything even remotely challenging James Rolling's sovereign rule would cause him to go off like nitro. He would not let any of Claudia's friends or family come visit, afraid they might poison her mind against him.

Danny and Kevin weren't allowed to have any friends over either. Until they were sixteen, they weren't allowed to date or choose their own clothes. They weren't even allowed to sit on the only couch in the house. That was his couch — the boys might get it dirty.

Nightmare on Canal Street

The older I got, the crazier my dad got.

Oh, I don't know. Maybe it was the other way around.

"When James corrected Danny, it was always harsh," said Claudia. "When he really did get after him, he got after him with a belt, and he left marks. But he hurt him other ways too. Sometimes he would put him up against the wall, and the marks of his fingers would be there. And he shook him a lot, and that sort of scared me, because I had read somewhere if you shake a person too hard it can do brain damage."

One night Danny and Kevin awoke to hear their mother's screams coming from the kitchen. They scampered from their room to find Claudia on the kitchen floor with James beating her.

"Daddy… Daddy… don't! Stop! Please, Daddy! Please!" The little boys tugged on their father's pants but he kept beating her. Finally, he stopped and walked out, leaving his wife and sons huddled together alone on the kitchen floor weeping.

Another time he pointed a gun at her and threatened to kill her. He would say, "Don't ever forget that my grandfather cut my grandmother's throat while she was eating."

"It almost seemed as if Danny did everything to draw attention to himself in front of his dad," said Claudia looking back years later. "It was almost as if he was saying, 'You won't hug me, so hit me — just recognize me in some way.' Kevin didn't do that. Kevin learned early to stay out of his way. He would just go somewhere where his daddy wasn't."

Danny tried to get close to his Dad. He would put his arms around him and say, "Daddy, tell me that you love me. Why do you hate me? Why don't you love me?"

"Get away from me, boy," James Harold would growl, shoving his son away. "Don't come in here with that sissy stuff. You're growing up to be a man. Men's not supposed to love other men. That's just way out there, and I'm not going to have you doing that."

Neither did he approve of the boys hugging their mother. "Women don't hug their children," he would say. "Don't kiss them. It looks bad."

In fact, Danny's father didn't believe in love at all. "That love stuff again," he'd say. "You people are crazy. Love is garbage. Love is when somebody wants to use you, they want something from you for nothing. There's no such thing as love."

Danny's Aunt Agnes said, "Danny was kindhearted, he was the most humble type of child. When he come to visit me, he would just throw his arms around me in a melting kind of feeling, and I would hug him and say, 'Danny, I love you,' and he'd look up at me and say, 'Do you? Do you really, Auntie? Do you really and truly? My daddy says there's no such thing as love.'

"I said, 'But there is.' So when he joined this church, this was a Pentecostal Church, he came to me one day and he says, 'Auntie, I know what you're talking about, love. I found a love that I never ever knew before.'

"And I said, 'Danny, I have told you and told you that there is love,' and he said, 'I know, Auntie, but my dad won't let us love.'"

Birthdays were never celebrated in the Rolling house, and even Christmas was a dismal affair because of the growling bear.

Christmas is supposed to be a time for families to grow close and spread some cheer, but not so in the little house on Canal Street. Claudia always tried to brighten up the house with a pretty decorated tree and nice little ornaments. "Maybe Christmas will be different this year, boys," she'd say hopefully. But it never failed. The bear would grumble and growl his way through the whole holiday season.

"What the hell are you doing?"

"Just fixin' up the tree, James."

"Didn't I tell you I want my supper at six? Damn it! I've got to work Christmas night so you can have a roof over your head and you can't even cook supper for me?"

"I'm sorry, James. I will."

If it wasn't this, it was that. But for some strange reason, Christmas for the Rollings was always a time of fear and bitter misgivings.

Dinner at the Rolling table was an emotionally tense event. "Don't talk at the table! Don't smack! Sit up straight or I'll knock you off that chair!" He would scream... then he'd smile. He would have his mouth full of food. It would be running down the sides of his face, and he'd be screaming at the boys that they weren't eating right and smacking his food in his mouth, as if to say, "See? I can do as I damn well please — but not you. You do as you're told or else." And "or else" happened all too often.

Danny didn't hold his utensils to suit his dad. James would take the fork out of his hand and say, "You hold it like a pencil, Danny, like a pencil."

"Don't breathe at the table," James Harold ordered one night, and the boys didn't. When their mother looked up, she saw their little faces turning blue. "Breathe, you can breathe at the table," Claudia assured them, but they weren't so sure.

The family dog wasn't even immune. James would storm into the house after a stressful day at the station, push the back door open and call, "Rocky! Rocky!" If the little feller didn't come to him right away, he would kick him around the yard or snatch him up by the scruff of his neck and beat him with his fist. How Danny and Kevin hated to see their pet treated so!

They remembered how James Harold had kicked their first puppy to death before their eyes because he had soiled the floor. He kept a trap baited for cats in his storage shed, and he'd shoot the captive animals to death with his service revolver, laughing as they thrashed about desperately trying to escape. The Rolling house was like that trap, baited with the food he put on the table, and just as deadly. It was James Harold's way or there was hell to pay.

If he was ever seen somewhere with Danny, James Harold acted ashamed, even embarrassed. He didn't want his boys to fit in at school. He made sure they didn't. He never attended a school function, even though the school house was just a couple of blocks away. The only time he showed interest in the boys was when he needed someone to take his frustrations out on.

James Harold would blindfold his sons at the dinner table or make them walk around wearing bags over their heads. He would put pots over their heads and make them sit in the hall. He had a spoon and he would touch each one on top of the head as he passed by. He'd tell people, "Those children are crazy, they're disobedient, they're just like their mother."

He locked them out of the house. He would beat them with his fists or with a rope or with his police belt. He would handcuff them or tie them up. When Danny was eight years old, his Aunt Agnes called the Chief of Police because Danny had called her crying his dad had beat him and he was going to run away. When Agnes came to the Rolling home to check on the boys, she found them tied to an iron pole, drenched with sweat in the sweltering heat of a Louisiana summer.

Agnes confronted James Harold and demanded he release the boys. "I'm going to call the police on you," she told him. "Let me take them to my mother's."

"They're old enough to be here by themselves, they don't need to be taken care of," he snapped. "Besides, your mother pets them and spoils them, so we're not going to let her keep them any more."

When Agnes called Mr. D'Artois, the Chief of Police in Shreveport, and reported what she had seen, he said, "Well, I'm sorry, he's a good officer for me. He does his duty here, and there's nothing I can do. It's a family affair."

The day before Danny and Kevin started junior high, James grabbed Danny by his hair. "Didn't I tell you to get a haircut?" No answer. "Didn't I?" He slammed his head against the wall. "Get your ass in the house." He pulled off his black leather service belt. "Take off your pants."

"I'll get a haircut, Daddy."

"It's too late for that! I told you to get one last week! Now drop 'em and bend over!"

(Whallop! Whallop! Whallop!) "I'll get a haircut, Daddy." (Whallop! Whallop! Whallop!) "I'll get a haircut."

After beating them both, their father sat them down on a stool in the back yard and shaved their heads. The next day they were the laughingstock of the whole school. They nicknamed Kevin "Cabbagehead" because his ears stuck out to there, and they called Danny "Sasquatch" or "Bigfoot."

Yeah... "There goes Cabbagehead and Sasquatch! Tee hee!" "Bald head!" "Ooooh, you've got cooties! Ha! Ha!"

As the boys grew older, it only got worse. Once when Danny was about 13, James Harold had ordered them to mow the lawn, and he said they didn't do it right. Danny's aunt Agnes walked in to find the boys handcuffed side-by-side together on the living room floor with James Harold on top of them. He had his knees right over their lungs, and the whole weight of his body was on them. Danny was about to pass out, and he was begging his dad, "Please, Daddy," he said, "I can't breathe, I can't breathe!"

Agnes said, "What in the world are you doing?" But James Harold just laughed a crazy kind of laugh, and wouldn't saying anything.

Another time a neighbor called Agnes and told her James Harold was beating the children with a rope. When Agnes got there, she found them handcuffed together with their hands behind them. James had left. Kevin told her that his dad got a call on the police radio. Agnes called the police and a patrolman came and unlocked the handcuffs.

Danny told his Aunt Agnes he wanted to kill himself. "I've already planned the way I'm going to do it," he said.

"Danny, why would you even want to do that, when there's other ways for you to protect yourself?"

"Auntie, my daddy hates me. I love him and I wish he would love me. What could I do to make him love me?"

"Danny, I can't answer that."

"Well, I'm just going to commit suicide. I've already got it fixed up the way I'm going to do it."

I Just Can't Make It

The constant ups and downs of the Rolling-coaster-ride commanded by Danny's split-personality father kept him emotionally torn apart. Different personalities were forming within his mind as far back as he could recall.

One summer night a friend named James Anderson came over to play. James Harold was at work, so it was OK. Otherwise, it wouldn't have been. Danny was about 13 or 14 and just beginning to get interested in girls. He knew they were different, he just didn't know how much. That night he got my first look at a naked girl.

James said, "Danny? Come here, I want to show you something," as he jumped over the fence into the neighbor's yard. Danny looked at James puzzled and asked, "What are you doing?"

"Come on, take a look at this," he answered, looking in the neighbor's bathroom window. Danny was curious, so he jumped over the fence himself. Little did he know how big a leap that would turn out to be.

Standing there in the dark, the glowing light that reached out from the window drew Danny into another world. She was beautiful, the cheerleader girl next door. What started out to be a childhood infatuation soon became an obsession, and Danny began walking the neighborhood in search of a new window to his fantasy.

One morning before sunrise, Danny got caught peeking in a neighbor's bathroom window. The girl's mother told his dad about it. He didn't believe her. It was the first time Danny got caught. Then he got caught at it a second time. This time James Harold sat him down and said, "Well, boy, the word's out. Now you've got to live with it."

One night James Harold came home early and caught Danny in the next door neighbor's yard peering in their window. He shouted, "Get your ass over here NOW!"

Danny jumped the fence back into his own yard, knowing what was about to happen. His dad threw him down on the ground, jumped on top of him, and began punching him in the face until he cut one of his knuckles on Danny's front teeth.

"Aahh! Look what you did!" James cried. "You cut my knuckle!" And he ran off into the house holding his hand, leaving his son crying on the ground with a busted lip, loosened teeth, and a bruised face.

All children are born with a sensitive nature, some more than others. Danny was sensitive to the point of pain. It seemed as though little Danny could feel the thoughts of others and all too often those thoughts spoke loudly in terms of rejection.

Danny felt outside the norm and his childhood reflected such. It came at him from all directions — home, school, the neighbors. He grew up fighting tooth and toenail emotions he couldn't control without a confidant. He tried to fit in at home, but James Harold made that impossible. He feared, loved and hated his father in a single breath. If he had a problem — and what child doesn't? — he learned early on not to share it with his dad.

Why should I? He doesn't give a damn how I feel! If I want to grow out my hair a bit? He sees to it I get a crew cut. If I want a certain type of jeans all the kids are wearing? He makes sure I wear something I can't stand. I can't have my friends over. And to top things off, I have this ever-growing problem that just keeps growing ever more serious as I grow taller — peeking in windows.

"The word's out — now you've got to live with it." But Danny couldn't live with it.

He couldn't take the peer rejection at school and the lack of love at home. They were at it almost every other day, and we're talking knockdown drag-out fights. James Harold beat Danny, beat Kevin, beat Claudia, beat the dog. Danny wanted to die, to run away from the entire scene.

He got a job at the Dairy Queen, right up the street. When he first asked if he take the job, James told him, "Yes, but the only way you can keep it is if you do not bring a bad grade home on your report card." So Danny dropped his head, because he knew he'd made a bad one already.

Claudia said, "James, it's only a few days to report card day, and if he's already made a bad grade, you shouldn't hold that against him."

"I said if he made a bad grade."

Sure enough, he brought home a bad grade, and James demanded, "Tell them you're done. You can't work anymore."

Danny wanted the job so bad. He busted out of the house into the backyard. James went right behind him, because you don't turn from James like that. You stay and you listen to whatever he has to say until he releases you. But this time Danny was too hurt and too angry to care.

James shoved Danny up against the toolshed. He drew back to hit him, but Danny moved, and James' hand went through the plate glass window.

Danny ran in the house, covered in blood. It was in his clothes, his hair, everywhere.

"Danny, my God!"

"It's okay, Mom. It's okay."

"Go in and clean up."

He locked himself in the bathroom and stood in front of the mirror crying. He thought his heart would break. He took a stick of his mom's red lipstick and scribbled on the mirror, "I TRIED — BUT I JUST CAN'T MAKE IT!"

Then he crawled out the window and ran away. But he had no place to go. So he ended up back at the little white house on Canal Street, and the cycle repeated itself.

Love that is really hate is the most painful thorn to bear.

"He was always trying to get rid of that person that his daddy made him believe he was," his mother said. "I could say 'Danny, I love you,' and he'd look at me and say, 'You love me, Mom?' And I'd say, 'Of course I love you, Danny.' And he would say, 'Why? What is there in me for anybody to love?' And he still does that."

As time went on and Danny grew into a man, he couldn't shake walking neighborhoods in the cool of the evening, looking in windows. The sun would go down and Danny couldn't help himself. The voices of the night seduced him and he could not resist. They were always calling him, urging him to walk picket fences like a cat. Thunderstorms, snowstorms, sleet and hail, sticky hot summer nights… he felt the dusk beckoning him to roam the dark and silent streets. Night after lonely night, he would spend hours glued to some damsel's window — watching, dreaming, and fantasizing about being on the other side of the glass.

He got to know families so well, he felt like they were his own family. And that was part of it. As a child, the warmth and love he failed to get at home was found in watching other families, and seeing how well they got along. It was a comfort to him.

In his own mind, he didn't see any real wrong in what he did when the sun went down. That was the thrill of it — being there in the dark, watching the others who fit in where he never felt wanted or needed. So he wandered in the shadows where his secret self was welcome as-is.

The conflict came in the morning when the sunshine spilled across the land. Then he had to look in the mirror, and he didn't like what he saw there. He needed help, but he refused to accept what he knew deep down inside, that things were getting darker and more confused. He was like a blank chalkboard for the spirits of the night to write upon.

So, as you can see, I was living a double life as far back as thirteen years old. I knew I needed help. What I was doing was wrong, but who could I turn to? Certainly not my demanding dad — and some things a guy just can't discuss with his mom. It was a disgrace, and I hated it, but I couldn't help myself. Mom begged dad to get me some help. Instead he bullied me, and the girls at school began giggling and making jokes in the cafeteria. So the problem only grew as I grew. And one day, it became bigger than me.

Voyeurism for me began as a mere curiosity. The female form was a beautiful mystery and very exciting to look on. At the first stage of adolescence, I made the connection by peering in windows and masturbating while watching lovely ladies do their thing.

Eventually, the pretty butterfly that fluttered across my genitals metamorphosed into a dominant beast of lust. As I developed into a man, the secret behavior developed into a personality with an identity all its own, that finally took on the face of murder.

Run, Danny, Run

Danny learned early to find his own way to escape from the painful reality that imprisoned him. In 1994, when he admitted committing five of the most gruesome murders in criminal history, he told the judge, "Your honor, I've been running all my life, whether from problems at home or with the law, or from myself."

One day James Harold caught Danny with James Anderson on top of Sunset Acres Elementary throwing those pebbles they spread over tarred rooftops. They weren't hurting anything, just being boys.

James Harold flipped out! He was fuming. Danny was afraid his dad was going to beat him silly. So he took off and spent most of the night in a field by the railroad tracks adjacent to Oak Terrace Junior High. It was the first time he had run away from home.

It got so cold he was forced to seek shelter. He went to the 24-hour laundromat where his mom washed clothes. Finally he got warm, but he still couldn't sleep.

Eventually he started to walk home, but a patrol car cruising the beat pulled over and asked him what he was doing and who he was.

Danny tried to lie his way out of it, but one of the cops asked, "You're James Harold's son, aren't you?" The tired and hungry boy fessed up. It was about 3:00 A.M. when they took him home.

When the tormented child couldn't use his legs to get him out of his daddy's reach, he did his running within his own mind. Bright and creative, he did well in school until the third grade. "Danny was sick almost that whole year," said his mother. "I wish I had those pictures to show you. He was like a skeleton. It was his tonsils. Dr. Strain said we can't take them out until we build him up, and he was out a lot that year. His teacher would leave his work and then pick it up. But he missed out on too much, and she said she could pass Danny on the grades he had, but it wouldn't be good for him because he really hadn't accomplished that much that year. She suggested holding him back, and we did. Because of Danny's personality and talents and his difficulty in just regular school things like math, reading, that kind of thing, she suggested that we get counseling for him and also channel his talents so that when he was grown, he could have some sort of livelihood."

But counseling for Danny was never made available. James Harold wouldn't hear of it. "Everything I ever did in our marriage, I got permission," said his mother. "When I would ask James he'd say no, there's nothing wrong with him, he's just mean."

"Just as I suspected. This no-count kid of mine failed again," said James. "You failed! You got to do the third grade again. You'll be in the same grade with your baby brother. You didn't study, you didn't do your work, you're a failure."

In the long lonely days at home that year, Danny first began to use the artistic talent he shared with his mom to create his own world.

As a child, my dad made me feel inadequate and odd. I grew up turning my mind off to what was happening around me, because I was forced to endure painful experiences I could not tolerate. The stress never let up. In order to survive, I distanced myself from the suffering and sought a fantasy world to escape to.

My heroes lived and breathed in Marvel Comics — characters such as The Silver Surfer, The Fantastic Four, Spiderman, The X-Men and Daredevil — all became real to me in a child's imagination. I couldn't wait to get my hands on the next month's copy. I spent hours drawing Spiderman and Silver Surfer in different poses.

"Danny would talk about visions of demons," said his cousin Chuck Strozier. "People in his dreams beating him, going through a gauntlet of people striking him with sticks, torturing him, demons going at him. He'd draw pictures of them. Describe them to me."

Then he found another creative way to run from the demons haunting him. The man later known as "The Singing Serial Killer" was 15 years old when he became a guitar-slinger.

I got a Silvertone for Christmas and I taught myself to play. When I grew older, I never learned other people's songs, I only sang my own. Except for a couple like "Rocky Top," "Got So Far to Go," and "Katie Joe," I don't play anything but Danny Rolling tunes. I guess that kinda makes me an enigma.

Louisiana Law

This is "Louisiana Law," the first song I wrote when I was 15 years old, my life's story told:

Looking through the bars in my window...
I've been here for so very long...
I've lost count of time...
Workin' in a field one morning...
I found my chance to leave...
And Louisiana's after me...
For the things I've done...
And she's surely gonna find me...
If I don't keep on the run

Ah, walkin' down the railroad tracks...
Ah, searchin' for a train...
I hitched a ride to New Orleans...
Took me a day or so
Found me an old tin shack...
No one lives there any more...
What's that I hear?
Ah, hound dogs a-howlin'
People callin' out my name...

Suddenly! Red lights a-flashin'...
People poundin' on my door
I grab my shotgun and start a-blastin'...
Holes through the door!
Bullets coming through the walls...
They've opened up on me...
And Louisiana's after me...
For the things I've done
Now she's surely found me...
No place left to run.

A Bitter Seed

If you want to know what prison does to a man, just look at me. I've done time in six southern states: Louisiana, Georgia, Alabama, Mississippi, Texas, and now Florida. I've been on chain-gangs, road-gangs, solitary confinement, and now Death Row, and each has its own distinct flavor. Although anyone would just as soon forget the joint, you never do. The culture shock of it changes you forever, branding you an outcast.

Danny was first locked up when he was 16. As teenagers will experiment, he had his first taste of alcohol on February 17, 1971..

He had always been highly imaginative. It was how he vented his frustration and pain. One sunny

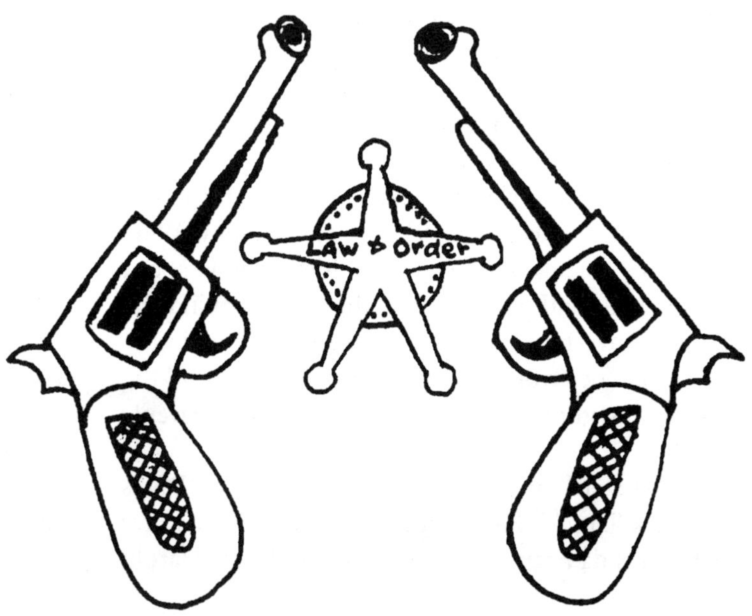

winter's day, he went searching for adventure in the woods behind the old Sunset Drive-In.

With his bows and arrows in hand, he became an Indian hunter in quest of the Great White Buffalo — although the prey were merely rabbits and snakes, and any other critter that had the misfortune of ending up at the other end of his arrow. This day, he had seen only a couple of rabbits, become bored, and started to turn over things looking for snakes.

He came upon a piece of tin. "I'll betcha there's a big one under there!" he said in anticipation. He flipped it over and jumped back. A big black snake curled up ready to strike in defense. Immediately he pulled an arrow from its quiver, notched it, drew it back, aimed, and let it fly, pinning the venomous vermin to the bare earth.

As Danny watched in amazement, the snake writhing and biting the wooden thorn embedded through its scaly hide, he heard a boisterous laugh. He turned and saw a white-bearded old man sitting on the steps of his one-room rickety shack. All about his feet, ten mongrel dogs were barking and dancing about wildly.

The old man motioned for the boy to come over. He did so with caution — the dogs snarling and baring their yellow fangs. The old gentleman shouted, "Behave now!" and the dogs cowed down.

He told Danny to step into his shack and take his .22 caliber pistol from his pillow and kill the snake. As Danny stood over the snake, he took aim and blew its head off. He brought the smoking gun back to the old man and he chuckled, "Good shot, boy."

They became good friends and on weekends and after school, Danny would clean out his old shack that would become full of empty beer cans and wine bottles. You see, the old man was a wino.

One day after cleaning out the shack, Danny was given half a gallon of Italian Swiss Colony Wine Muscatel — real rotgut stuff. He drank it all in about 30 minutes, and passed out in the weeds behind the Sunset Drive-In while the sun was shining high in the sky. When he awoke, the stars were twinkling and the moon was grinning down at him from its heavenly perch.

"Oh shit!" he said, struggling to his feet. "Dad's gonna kill me!" He staggered home only minutes before his dad came home from work. James Harold was still in his police uniform when he stormed in and found his son sitting in his easy chair watching TV.

"You drunken bum! Here I am working my ass off night and day to give you a place to stay and just look at you! You're a disgrace!"

Danny jumped up and yelled, "I'm not afraid of you, old man!" He had never talked back to his dad, because he was scared of him, but the alcohol gave him courage. "Leave me alone!" he shouted, and — CRASH! — jammed his fist through the window.

Father and son scuffled. Danny broke away and dashed toward the kitchen where Claudia was washing dishes. James grabbed Danny, slammed him onto the floor and rolled him over on his stomach. With textbook procedure, Officer Rolling slapped the handcuffs on his young son.

Then he got Headquarters on the phone and called for a squad car. The minutes ticked by as Danny lay there handcuffed on the floor, and before long before the car pulled up in front and two men in blue approached the house.

"Is this the problem?"

"You see it is."

"Well, son, we've got a place for you."

As they escorted him out the door, Danny surprised them by breaking free of their grip and making a mad dash for it. But he stumbled over the curb and came crashing down on the pavement, skinning his arms and face. They yanked him up and threw him in the squad car, and carried him directly to juvey jail.

This was a turning point in my life. I had never been around kids like that before, and I got into a fight the first day. I stayed locked up in The Hole most of the time I was there. I remember how hurt and betrayed I felt. I couldn't deal with the confinement. I was bitter and confused. I mean, if you can't trust your own father, who can you trust? That's when I began to talk to myself.

I sat in The Hole remembering how I would look up to my daddy for love and support, only to get pushed away or smashed into the wall, as if I was to blame for all his burdens. My whole life, I saw the hatred for me burning in my father's eyes. That look, and all that went with it, pierced my soul and killed parts of me. And so the other parts began to take their place, to compensate for what was dead inside me.

You see, I had multiple personalities at a very young age. I would go off to myself and just change over. It was a defense, the only way I could deal with the pain and confusion in my life.

Two weeks later when Danny was released, on the way home he gave his dad an ultimatum. "Either you sign for me to enlist in the Navy when I turn 17 or I'm gonna run away and you'll never see me again." By the look on Danny's face, James knew he meant it, so he told his son he could go.

Danny's scores on the Navy enlistment test were a few points shy of passing, so he tried the Air Force battery and passed with flying colors.

He joined the military to get away from his bullying father, only to find himself in a world he knew nothing about, a world that one day would swallow him up and spit him out again, a bitter seed upon troubled ground.

/// The Dirty Deal \\\

The deepest wound doesn't originate from weapons of forged steel
But, heart to heart comes the dirty deal

by Danny Rolling 1-17-95 ★

ROLLING TUNES
★ 1-21-93 :: Rolling

CHAPTER 3
DRUGS, SEX, & CLOSE ENCOUNTERS

Purple Haze Daze

June 28, 1971. Danny entered Lackland Air Force Base in Texas at the tender age of 17 — immature, basically a child in a man's world.

He completed basic training, which consisted of training in combat first aid, hand-to-hand combat, book work, and marching everywhere screaming and yelling like somebody had kicked you in the ass. Ha! Sometimes they did.

Airman Rolling was bright and good-looking. He was proud to be an American and to serve his country. After basic he got his first stripe.

His first duty base was Homestead AFB in Florida, where he was placed in the Strategic Air Command (SAC) as a Security Police officer, guarding B-52 nuclear bombers and KC-135 tankers. Rain or shine, he walked around the big birds slinging a fully-loaded M-16. He soon got his second stripe and became Airman First Class Rolling. His badge represented the very essence of pride.

While I was at Homestead, I was introduced to the wonderful (yeah, sure!) world of drugs.

I can't tell you how much acid I did in the military. That's like asking a wino how many beers he drank in his whole lifetime. I don't know... it's hard to remember. I've done at least a hundred trips. I've tried it all... purple haze, orange wedge, blotter, Mr. Natural, windowpane, orange sunshine, chocolate mescaline... Once I zombied out on PCP, and for eight hours I went blind and couldn't even talk. But that was nothing compared to the two hits of purple haze I did on my very first trip. It was a gas.

The place, the Sportatorium in Miami, Florida. The event, a rock concert starring famed lead guitarist Alvin Lee and the band Ten Years After. The time, sundown.

Young hippies gathered like vultures swooping in on carrion, as hot rods jostled for parking spots. A fire engine red 4-on-the-floor Dodge Duster 340 with 3/4 racing cam wheeled onto the crowded dirt parking lot, powered down, rumbled into a slot, braked, and came to an abrupt halt bathed in a cloud of dust. On the 8-track blasted "Nights in White Satin" by The Moody Blues.

Airman First Class Danny Rolling white-knuckled the Hurst shifter on the floor, found reverse, turned the key, and the rod died without a sputter. He reached across the two giggling teenage girls beside him and opened the door as a fine breath of red dust poured in.

"Let's go!"

Danny, Maggie and Wanda bailed out and joined the crazy caravan migrating towards the open gates of Miami's wildest concert hall. In the winter, the Sportatorium was used as a quarter-mile oval dirt track for motocross and stock car racing. During the rest of the year, it was converted into a massive concert hall, packing in as many as fifty thousand screaming maniacs.

Danny was eighteen. His girlfriend Maggie and her friend Wanda were both sixteen, and the trio of teenagers were about to attend their very first concert.

They waited impatiently with the rest of the ragtag gypsies to purchase tickets. When the first band cranked up, the line moved quickly. Excitement intensified as they bought their tickets and hurried inside.

The sweet, thick smell of burning marijuana greeted them as they entered the world of illicit drugs, booze and rock-&-roll.

Except for the stage and concession stands, the huge cavern was dark and filled with smoke. Bare steel beams rose from the floor behind the bleachers arching high overhead. Danny felt like he was being swallowed by some prehistoric whale.

Thousands of longhairs moved together in the darkness, a mass of blitzed mad hatters. A few crazed fans even climbed up the towering girders and hung from the rafters. The police stayed outside by the gates. They had better sense than to tangle with thousands of stoned freaks in the dark.

The trio wove through the crowd, spellbound by the excitement of the music. They found a spot midway up the bleachers as close to the front as possible, and Danny and Maggie sat close together holding hands, listening to the opening act.

A party joint the size of a zeppelin floated from hand to hand, passing right under Danny's nose.

"Hey, man! Pass that over here!"

"Sure, dude. Get high, brother, and pass it on," grinned the red-eyed longhair.

Danny Rolling was a Security Policeman. But when the uniform came off, he turned into a party animal, a real bogart when it came to drugs — especially ass-kick weed. He took a long deep toke... and then another... and another...

Shhhht! Ahhhh... Shhhht! Ahhhh...

"Killer! Here, Maggie, wanna toke?"

But she shook her head, so he passed the billowing plumes of smoke on down the line.

Reefer gives you the munchies and the cottonmouth, so it wasn't long before the airman needed something to wet his whistle.

"Maggie, I've got the munchies. I'm going for junk food and drinks. You and Wanda want something?"

"Yeah!" she smiled. "I'll have a Dr. Pepper and a bag of popcorn."

"Wanda?"

"I'll have the same," she shouted over the music.

"OK, be back in a little bit. You two stay put so we won't lose our seats."

He kissed Maggie, stood, and descended the bleachers into the maze of pulsing shadows. Pale faces emerged and disappeared in the darkness like a brood of vampire bats dangling from the roof of some ancient black cave.

As the airman drew closer to the concession stand, he saw a pair of blonde identical twin teenage girls dressed out in red and white tasseled cowgirl miniskirts and vests, with white Stetson hats, boots, holsters, and cap pistols. Side by side they stood, completely out of place amongst the crowd of hippies, freaks and fairies, posing and smiling like models in a commercial for some new super red lipstick.

Tack! Tack! Tack!

They blew the smoke from the barrels of their pearl-handled silver cap pistols. Danny watched their act for a moment then moved on.

"Purple haze! Purple haze for sale! Purple haze! Purple haze for sale!"

What was this? Right in the middle of the walk stood a curious figure in a swirling black cape with long hair tumbling from under a black top hat.

"Purple haze! Purple haze for sale!"

"Hey! How much?"

Two strychnine-dilated eyes blazed from beneath the top hat. "Go away, narc!" he snarled.

"Hey, man! I ain't no narc. My hair is short because I'm in the Air Force. They make us wear it this short."

"Are you sure? You ain't no narc?"

"Listen, dude, I'm tellin' ya I'm cool! So how much?"

"OK... two bucks," and the pusher reached into the folds of his cape and drew out a pillbox filled with magic, removed a single purple barrel-shaped pill, and placed it in the buyer's outstretched hand.

"Hey! Are you sure that's enough?"

"Oh yes! That's a four-way hit of pure purple haze. Break it up into two halves and it'll send two people to the moon."

"Sounds good to me!" Danny slapped two Washingtons in the pusher's hand and popped the purple tab into his mouth.

He brought the refreshments back to Maggie and Wanda, saying "Sorry it took so long. Man! This place is packed! Thirsty?"

"You bet!"

And they kicked back while the opening act got down and dirty. Grooving to the hot tunes, the snacks disappeared as an hour went by. Shouldn't something be happening by now? Danny had never tried LSD and he didn't know what to expect. GI friends had warned him not to experiment with the drug, but he had to find out for himself.

"Maggie, I've gotta use the head. You want something?"

"Nope, I'm fine."

"You, Wanda?"

"Uh-uh."

"Okey-dokey! Be back shortly."

But what was he really up to? His mission: to find that freak pushing the purple haze. Faces floated in the smoky gloom like ghouls dancing around a bubbling cauldron at a witch's mass, as the airman sought the peddler of twisted dreams.

The cowgirls were still in the same spot, posing and popping caps at the crowd.

Tack! Tack! Tack!

Come to find out, they were promoting Marlboro cigarettes, giggling and posing as they passed out the complimentary packs of smokes. Curiosity satisfied, he pressed on, searching for the top-hat hippie.

"Purple haze! Purple haze for sale! Purple haze! Purple haze for sale!"

There he was, rooted to the selfsame spot. Angry, Danny got in his face.

"Hey, man! Remember me?"

The hippie shook his head with a puzzled, spaced-out look.

"I bought a hit of acid from you over an hour and a half ago!"

The pusher shrugged his shoulders as if to say, "So what?"

"Well, I didn't get off! And I want my money back!"

Hazed eyes peered at the airman, unbelieving.

"Look, GI, tell you what I'll do," and he produced another tiny purple pill. "Open your hand."

He did, and the hallucinogenic pill fell into his palm.

"If this doesn't do the trick, I can't help you. Nobody can!" A big grin beamed across his starry-eyed face as the magic was passed.

"OK, dude," and he swallowed it instantly. "Thanks!" But the freak had already disappeared in the crowd.

The airman got another Dr. Pepper and beat it back to the girls in the bleachers. Maggie and Wanda had no idea what Danny had been up to, but soon enough they would find out.

The first band wrapped up their gig and the house lights blinked on. Everyone looked around at each other, freaking on how weird they all looked.

"Look at that dude!"

"What the hell is he doing?"

"Man is he spaced!" Dashing around and around an electrical scaffold by the stage, he was dancing with the devils of his warped mind. The tie-dyed freak would play ring around the scaffold for the entire concert.

After the brief intermission, the lights winked out and a voice boomed out over the humming amps. "And now! The band you've been waiting to see! Introducing... Alvin Lee... and Ten... Years... AFTER!"

As the musicians stepped on stage, the fans jumped to their feet and went crazy! They lit into "Going Home," the same tune they played at Woodstock. Strobes and multicolored lights flashed and pulsed to the music.

Danny rose to his feet so he could see better, when suddenly! Someone poked their finger in the spokes of the universe. Time slowed, sound became distorted, and a surge of energy elevated his heartbeat. His breathing became irregular as he blasted off on the rocket ship called lysergic acid diethylamide.

He took a deep breath, sat down, and almost passed out. Everything turned in circles. Colors exploded before his dilated eyes like Roman candle starbursts. A boiling pyrotechnic storm of rainbow lightning bolts swirled in kaleidoscopic patterns. One wave after another took him higher and higher, until he went over the edge.

"Danny? What's wrong?" asked Maggie, concerned.

"Aw, man! Am I trippin'! Whew! I dropped some acid... man!"

The concert was the best. Alvin Lee hit licks that bounced off the ceiling while Danny climbed higher and higher on the staircase of illusion, experiencing strange sights and sensations.

TRACERS: Distortions created by the effects of LSD.

STROBES: Flashes of light produced by large doses of LSD.

HALLUCINATIONS: Visions induced by lysergic acid diethylamide.

All these elements melted into one hell of a ride. Danny had bought his ticket, and now he had to hold on for dear life. All five senses were magnified tenfold. Overwhelmed, he started to feel nauseated.

"Maggie... I've gotta hit the latrine. You girls wait here."

When he stood, he tumbled over the couple seated in front of him.

"Hey, man! Watch it, will ya?!" The hippie screamed as Danny knocked his drink out of his hand.

"Sorry, man," Danny mumbled as he gathered himself and wobbled down the bleachers.

The crowd pulsed like demented damned spirits. Finally he found the bathroom and stumbled through the door.

"YEEK! Get out of here!"

"Oops! Sorry!"

He had entered the wrong bathroom and quickly dashed back out the door. He tried again. This time he read the sign very carefully. It said MEN. He pressed through and tripped on his own feet, sprawling across the blue tile floor.

"Man! Is he fucked up!"

"Hey, dude! Wish I had some of what you got!"

Disoriented and nauseated, he crawled to the far stall and vomited violently.

Urrr... ahhh... urrr... ahhh... ahhh!

The contents of his stomach now swam in the toilet. He sat there trying to compose himself as the blue tile floor moved, bubbling up around him until it filled the stall with spheres of rainbows, and he began to choke.

Whoa! Reflexes cast him out onto the floor with his pants around his ankles. Quickly, he rose, pulled up his pants, buckled his belt, and approached the sink.

The mirror presented itself, but the image staring back at him was anything but good old familiar Danny. It was a porous, glowing, red-eyed demon with skin that moved and breathed. He looked deep into the weaves of his overlapping multicolored skin, terrified and fascinated.

He began to recover from the nausea and tore his eyes away from the horrifying vision. After he felt better, he fought his way back through the crowd, but it took him almost an hour. Maggie was worried.

"Where were you?"

"I — I got lost. Man! Am I spaced! Where's Wanda?"

"She went looking for you. Are you all right?"

"I don't know. I'm really fucked up. I guess I'm all right. Wow! Look at that!" And he was off and flying again.

Ten Years After finished their last song and did two encores. As the house lights came up, Wanda came back from her search.

The crowd started to thin out, but Danny and the girls remained seated, observing the whole spectacle. The freak was still dancing round and round the scaffold, and they watched five security guards drag him away screaming. Wild!

Finally the trio found their way out into the parking lot and pure chaos.

Beep-beeeeep! Honk... honk... HONNNNK!

"Move your ass, muthafucka!"

Just as the trio strolled by, one bulky, tattooed, ugly guy got out of his Road Runner, stormed over to this couple blocking the flow of traffic, pulled the poor driver out of his blue doodlebug and beat the living shit out of him.

"This is nuts! Let's get the hell out of here!" They found the Duster, hopped in, and joined the mad exodus.

Florida highways are long and straight, but when seen under the influence of LSD, the roads take on a nature of their own, swaying, dipping, and writhing like venomous vipers.

"Maggie, am I driving OK? I mean, am I keeping it straight?"

"Yeah, but if you want, I'll drive."

"Nahhh! I'm fine." But he wasn't. And he almost got them all killed.

The Duster pulled up to a red light and came to a halt. A light breeze whispered through the open windows. Inside his enhanced mind, everything was alive, even the street lights. They swayed from side to side, strobing as the road pulsed and squirmed beneath them.

Danny's mouth was thick with saliva and he opened the door to spit on the road.

Haaa... putt... SPLAT!

The wad struck the asphalt like an atom bomb, exploding in rainbows of swirling, fractured color. Then it came back together... and grew legs... and started gigging about violently, humming a twisted bubble-gum tune.

Ah-ah... eee... eee! Ah-ah... eee... eee!

Wow! Danny forgot all about where he was. Time and space did not exist. Nothing did but the bizarre boogie before him.

Ah-ah... eee... eee! Ah-ah... eee... eee!

Way off in the distance, he thought he heard a horn barking. Maggie shook him and screamed, "The light's green! The light's green! What's wrong with you?"

Honk! Honk! HONNNNNK!

"Hey asshole! Get that bucket of bolts moving!" The voice of an angry motorist blared through the haze. Hallucinating, the airman slammed the door and floored it, burning rubber — but the light had already turned red.

A station-wagon with the right-of-way nearly T-boned the Duster in its right side.

Rrrrrrr!

Tires screeched in protest as the wagon locked up all fours, leaving skid marks in its wake as the Duster shot by with inches to spare.

Honk! Honk! HONNNNNK!

"Are you crazy?" The driver of the wagon spat and cursed before he sped away.

Danny pulled over onto the emergency lane and sat there for a minute. He took a deep breath and said calmly, "You better drive, Maggie. I'm freaked out."

Whew-WEE! Was Maggie relieved! So with her to his left and Wanda to his right, Danny rode off into the hazy crazy night.

"I'm thirsty! How's about we stop for burgers and cokes?"

"Yeah," replied Wanda while Maggie grew silent. She didn't do drugs. Oh, maybe she would take a sip or two of beer at a party, but LSD? No way! She was pissed off that her date was into such.

She pulled the Duster into a fast food joint, parked, got out and entered. As soon as the trio stepped inside, Danny noticed a big black State Trooper hunched over his table wolfing down a double cheeseburger. He looked up and stared directly at Danny.

PARANOIA! He felt it shoot through him like an electric shock. He just knew the cop suspected him to be high. He could almost hear him saying to himself, "Look at that one. Hmmm... he's on something. I'll hafta keep my eye on him."

They chose a table in the back as far from the Trooper as they could get. The waitress took their order and the girls went to the bathroom, leaving Danny alone. The Trooper was still eyeballing him suspiciously. Was he acting strange? Of course he was! Hell! He was tripping his brains out!

He looked down and saw a newspaper on the table. Funny, he hadn't noticed it before. He yanked it up and hid behind it so he wouldn't have to look at the Trooper observing him.

It turned out not to be a regular newspaper, but an underground paper called The Head. Danny lost himself in the cartoons and put the cop out of his mind. When the waitress brought their orders, he folded the paper and laid it back down.

As he paid the waitress, he glanced back down at the paper. To his horror, on the front page, a big black shiny .38 cal. special with a fat smoking joint protruding from its barrel jumped off the page. Printed above it, a huge black headline screamed, "KILLER WEED!"

He tore his eyes away from the threatening image and gazed around the restaurant. Suddenly the cop by the door turned into a big hairy gorilla in a Trooper's uniform. His glowing red eyes were fixed on Danny.

That was the last straw. He rose carefully, walked out, and piled into the back seat of the Duster.

The girls returned from the bathroom only to find Danny missing and the orders sitting on the table. They assumed he had visited the bathroom, but after fifteen minutes passed, Maggie became concerned and knocked on the men's room door.

"Danny? You in there?" No answer. So they gathered up the rest of their refreshments and made for the Duster. There they found Danny curled up in the back seat — far, far away. Completely out of his mind, he was lost in a world of flashing colors and distorted sounds.

The next thing he knew he was back at the barracks lying on his bunk in the dark listening to the paint drip off the walls and the lockers breathe.

Drip... drip... drip... SPLAT!

Oooooh... ahhhh... ooooh... ahhhhh...

He got up and made for the latrine. Standing before the sink, he tugged on the light chain. CLICK! A flood of brilliant light exploded into his twisted brain, turning into cartwheeling rainbows. Gradually, his vision returned and he washed his face. The water was cool, comforting, a stable link back to reality.

"Oh, man! How did I get back?" He couldn't remember.

Looking into the mirror, he was drawn into the reflection. Now he was on the other side looking back at himself. His face melted away, revealing a bleached bone-white skull with bulging eyes.

"Ahhhhhh!" He turned off the light and dashed back to his bunk, dove in, and curled up in the fetal position. Alone in the dark, he drifted off into a deep purple haze daze. No way in, no way out. Just...

Splat... splat...

Oooooh... ahhhh... ooooh... ahhhhh...

Not All Sugar and Spice

Danny's first sexual contact with a girl was not a good one. One Friday night he went off base and had one too many beers. As he was stumbling back to base, he came upon a fenced-in public pool and decided to take a midnight dip.

As he began to climb the chainlink fence, he heard a girl laughing. He jumped down and walked across the street to her house. This girl was sitting on the front porch. He asked her why she was laughing at him. She said with a Cuban accent, "The police drive by here all the time and you'll get busted if you try to go swimming after hours." They talked a little more. She asked him inside to her bedroom, and they did it.

The next morning Danny woke up with a bad taste in his mouth and the whole thing made him sick. She was not very clean, and it took a month to get the smell off him.

When I was young, my mama said, "Son,
Life's a hard row to hoe,
And there's some things you need to know.
Now little girls are not all sugar and spice,
So son, take your mama's advice.
Cause a broken heart's a hard thing to mend.
It's hard to put the pieces back together again.

Well, sittin' on my daddy's knee, he said, "Son,
I want you to listen to me.
You can cut your finger or skin your knee,
You know, it heals fairly easily.
But a broken heart's a hard thing to mend.
It's hard to put the pieces back together again.

Now, when Adam was given Eve, he said,
"I just don't need another mouth to feed."
Well, she just smiled and winked her eye.
She said, "Yeah, boy!
But I give ya whatcha need.
Cause a broken heart's a hard thing to mend."

Where the Waters Met

Danny was at a party out by the points in Homestead and there were these two good looking girls about 17 years old, one black, one white. Everybody at this party was doing orange sunshine acid and smoking weed. It was around 10:00 to 11:00 P.M. so the sun had long since checked out.

The two chicks freaked out. Apparently the guy who was selling the LSD turned the girls on to more than they could handle. They took off their shirts and went around topless. Soon all the guys were pawing them.

The party got even crazier. See, there were these canals that emptied out into the ocean on the points, and the two girls got totally naked and jumped into the canal. They splashed around for 10 to 15 minutes with their friends begging them to get out. It was deep and dangerous there. Everybody knew strange fish had been seen in that salt water canal.

The white girl was attacked by some kind of fish, maybe a shark. We never found out. I remember her screaming, "Help! Something is in here! It bit me! It's biting me! Yeeee-aaah!" We all thought she was just tripping, until a couple of dudes dove in and pulled her out screaming and bleeding. Her friends rushed her to the hospital.

The black girl didn't go with her friend. She was too zonked out. She just stumbled around for hours that night, naked, being passed from one guy to the next. It was sickening.

There is no doubt that girl never would have acted that way if she hadn't taken acid. That black chick was one classy looking gal, but after that night she lost it — BIG TIME.

It was a bad situation. Danny tried to help her put her clothes on and get her act together, but before he could assist, some guy grabbed her hand, and well... Danny was tripping himself. So he just let her go. He didn't get involved.

The girl had a BAD TRIP that night. Just before Danny left the scene, he bumped into her as he was leaving. She was out of her mind crying, "The spiders! The spiders! Get them off me!"

Sunset... where the waters met
Moon rises shining bright
Under the starlit night
Star falls
Into the ocean swell
Quickly! The glowing ember dies
Into dark waters sighs
Shark glides through the shallows
In search of unlucky fellows
The ocean hides its secrets deep
Where whales sing and crabs creep

Sunset... where the treetops met
Moon rises shining bright

Under the starlit night
Bats take wing
Into the cool night spring
Moth struggles
On a sticky string
Spider's web
Shimmering

Military Maryjane

As time went on, Danny was up for his third stripe when he received orders for Vietnam. Wow! Was he ever gung-ho! The thought of combat really made him stand tall and strut his stuff, until they called about a dozen of the guys into the briefing room and ran it down to them. They said, "Boys, one out of three of you are coming back in a body bag, one out of three will receive a crippling wound, and one out of three will come home whole." So much for his glorious image of Vietnam. Still, he was eager to go. They told him he was going to be placed in a tower filled with sandbags on the perimeter of some base outside Saigon.

When Danny told his dad, he was proud of him. Then, one fateful night, an MP friend Danny was buying drugs from was busted stumbling around the base spaced out on some killer LSD.

The Officer of Special Investigation (OSI) questioned him and threatened him with life imprisonment in Leavenworth, so he spilled his guts about a hundred or so cops and servicemen and women he had been dealing to on base. Danny happened to be in the bunch.

His orders were immediately canceled, and he was given an Article 15 for a trace amount of maryjane found in the bottom of his pants pocket. He was busted down to Airman Basic and thrown in the stockade for 30 days. To say the least, James Rolling was utterly outraged when the commander gave him a call informing him of his son's status.

Well, after they threw Danny in the stockade, they took away his stripes and canceled his Vietnam tour. After that they just kept stepping on his toes. He was given a second Article 15 for failure to obey a direct order (which he did obey). Another 30 days in the stockade.

About a month later, he was painting wooden stairs leading to the SAC trailer's command post. (One day he was ordered to paint them brown, the next day blue; don't even ask!) The first sergeant ordered him to double-time it back to the barracks and report to Lieutenant Blackwell. A light bulb went off in Danny's head after he heard that. Why would they be in such a hurry to get him back to the barracks to report? The only reason he could think of would be a death in the family... or else they had searched his room and found the baggie full of pot seeds he had been saving to start a garden. Danny suspected the latter to be the case.

So he hauled ass back to the barracks, in fact he ran the three mile distance with all his might. He didn't own a car and his blue and silver BSA 650 White Lightning motorcycle had been stolen. All he could think of was those seeds and the years he was going to spend in Leavenworth. If only he could get there before the OSI, perhaps he could get rid of the incriminating evidence.

When he finally stomped up to the barracks sweating golf balls in the hot Florida sun, his hopes vanished before his eyes as he discovered an armed MP sitting in a chair propped up against the door. He regarded Danny lightly as he approached.

"Say! I was ordered to report to Lieutenant Blackwell. What's going on?"

"The Lieutenant is in the dayroom waiting on you." And with that the MP ignored him. It looked bad for the old boy.

"Airman Rolling reporting as ordered, sir," he snapped to and saluted the brass.

"At ease, Airman. Sit down," the Lieutenant ordered flatly.

"Could you tell me what this is all about, sir?"

"You'll find out soon enough, young man."

And Danny was left to his own thoughts. The wheels in his head were turning full steam ahead. Ah! An idea!

"Sarge? Do you think it would be all right for me to go downstairs and get a Coke? I ran all the way over here and my throat is dry. Would you like one too?" he asked as sincerely as any innocent teenager could.

"Awright," he frowned, "but make it snappy."

"I'll make it snappy all right," Danny said as soon as the door to the stairwell closed behind him. He dashed down two flights of stairs, blasted through the laundry room spilling into the back 40, lifted himself up on the second story ledge, let himself into his room the usual alternate way (through the open window). Quickly and quietly, he removed the bag of seeds from his desk drawer and let himself out the way he came in, the whole while with the MP just outside his door.

He dropped down off the ledge to the green grass below, opened the baggie, and flung the little gray-green speckled seeds, scattering them all over the lawn. He tossed the baggie in the trash, walked over to the Coke machine and coined the Sergeant and himself a Coke, then strolled up the stairs whistling Dixie.

He handed the Sarge his cold Coke. Sarge nodded, then Danny sat himself down, popped the tab on the red can of fizzy, and watched the rest of Let's Make a Deal. Yeah!

The OSI's came marching in wearing their black suits and their usual dark cloud expressions.

"Are you Airman Rolling?"

"Yes sir."

"Come with us."

And Danny followed them to his room, with the MP still outside on guard. He knew what to expect next. They tore his room apart, and waited until the last thing to open his desk drawer to search for the bag of seeds they were expecting to find there.

Lo and behold, the item they sought had sprouted wings and flown away! They exchanged puzzled acknowledgments trying not to seem surprised. They dumped the contents of the drawer on his bunk and rummaged through the lot, then turned and looked at Airman Rolling with pure disgust. He tried not to smile, but he couldn't help it. He had to turn away to keep from laughing.

About sixty days later, all these little maryjane plants popped up on the back 40's lawn. They knew how they got there, but they couldn't prove it, so they had a detachment pull up the unlawful plants, and gave Danny 30 more days in the stockade.

After he did his time, he was transferred to another squadron, and not long after that he received his discharge: General Under Honorable Conditions.

Danny came home disgraced before his father, who did not want to receive his failure for a son.

Praise His Holy Name

It was midnight in Shreveport and the bowling alley had just closed. Fresh out of the United States Air Force, Danny was hitchhiking along Hearn Avenue, when a man called Brother Estes was moved by the spirit to offer him a ride. Danny accepted, and Brother Estes asked, "Where are you going?"

Danny told him where his grandfather Daddy Walter lived. At age 19 he wasn't getting along with his dad, as usual, so he was staying with his grandfather. It just so happened that one street over from where he was headed was Brother Estes' church, the United Pentecostal Church of Shreveport. They had to go right past it.

Funny, Danny had not noticed it before. As they passed by the neon-lit church, Brother Estes mentioned that he belonged to it. Danny said, "That's cool," and promptly directed him on down the road. For some reason, he overlooked the turn to Daddy Walter's house and they had to make the block again.

When they passed by the church a second time, Brother Estes asked Danny if he would like to come inside and pray with him. The idea gripped ahold of Danny and he readily agreed. That wonderful blessed night is something Danny will never forget. The place was dimly-lit, except for a big beautiful brass cross that was magnificently illuminated over the baptistery behind the pulpit. As they passed through the vestibule into the sanctuary, there were three men already there praying in tongues.

The way those men were praying, it was so strange and beautiful. Danny had never heard people pray like that, with such feeling and sincerity. He knelt there at the altar and prayed with the gentlemen who began weeping for his soul, and an unusual thing happened. Danny felt something he hadn't felt in years — peace, blessed peace that streamed down his face and wet the altar he knelt at.

Danny gave himself to Jesus Christ that night. The Lord touched Danny's troubled weary soul and calmed the raging sea of pain. Praise His Holy Name!

He who flung the stars
Into the heavens above
Created the mountains… the oceans…
The eagle… the dove
None greater than Thee, Oh Lord,
None greater than Thee

Angels bow before you
And fold their wings

Lift up their voice
And praise the King of Kings
None greater than Thee, Oh Lord,
None greater than Thee

Thou art the Alpha... Omega...
Beginning and the end.
At the sound of thy voice,
Peace bestills the mighty wind
None greater than Thee, Oh Lord,
None greater than Thee

The next day was Sunday, and Danny was baptized by Reverend Mike Hudspeth in the precious name of Jesus Christ. When he went under the water, its cool cleansing power washed away his sins by the blood of Our Lord and Savior Jesus Christ. Danny came up speaking in tongues and magnifying God! He had received the Promise and was filled with the Holy Ghost! He felt clean, pure, and accepted by God and man. His slate had been wiped clean and he walked in the newness of life!

As time went on, Danny became more and more involved in church activities. He drove the Sunday School bus that picked up the handicapped and the children for church. He visited the nursing homes and played his guitar for the old folks. He went with the youth to the square downtown under the Texas Street Bridge to sing hymns and pass out tracts.

"He played the Easter Bunny one year and he sang in the choir for a short spell," said Claudia Rolling. "He wanted to write music for the church, but the choir director told him that his music had no value. And that really upset him. They all knew that he could write music and sing, and he could draw anything, and I'm sure the members were aware of that, but I think what they really admired most in Danny was his kindness to the older people in the church and the little children. He liked to help them."

Danny went to church Wednesday, Thursday, Friday, Saturday and Sunday. And when he wasn't at church, he was about the neighborhood with his guitar in one hand and a Bible in the other. He would knock on doors and sing a song, then pass out a gospel tract and cordially invite them to church.

Angel & Dragon

Lord only knows, I'm a pitiful example of a Child of God. Nonetheless, a Christian I am, and a Christian I remain. My experience with Christ includes speaking in tongues, and I thank God that it does. To this day, I still speak in a heavenly tongue when the Holy Ghost blesses me so.

I've had numerous supernatural experiences. Some so haunting, they were actual visits from demons. Still, most have been beautiful moments with my Savior Jesus Christ. He is the author and finisher of my soul. He will not leave my soul to the demons that have haunted me all my life. The Lord Jesus knows I love him, and I am not ashamed to declare it.

On my knees today,
Before the Lord I do pray,
Make me over anew... for You.
If I fail to honor Thee,
Then chastise and humble me.
Make me over anew... for You.

And if my light flickers low,
Fill me up, Lord, that I may glow.
Make me over anew... for You.
Though my sins be scarlet red
Because of You, snow white instead.
Make me over anew... for You.

Yes, make me over anew,
That I might honor You.
Change this cup of clay
Into gold that I may
Honor You, Oh Lord, honor You.

The Best Years

Even though Danny's life was full, he felt something missing. So he asked God to send him a wife, and one was given to him. That's how he met Omatha on a Sunday night at the United Pentecostal Church of Shreveport. It was love at first sight, and they were married by Reverend Hudspeth four months later. A rather short engagement, but Danny was very much in love with her, and he couldn't wait to make her his wife.

September 6, 1974. There amongst burning

white candles and 600 friends and family members, Danny raised the veil from his new wife's face and kissed her gently on the lips. So Omatha Ann Halko became Omatha Rolling. "What God hath joined together, let no man cast asunder."

But their marriage was to be a bittersweet one, filled with moments of great joy and great disappointment, destined to end in divorce.

Omatha is an Indian name, and she possessed the beauty and charm of an Indian princess. Long waist-length auburn hair that held deep, rich colors of red and gold amongst the shiny black and brown, high cheekbones, blue eyes that could capture your very heart and soul. She stood erect and proud, a true beauty within and without.

Danny is a name derived from the Biblical name Daniel, which means "God is my Judge." He stood tall and slender, good-looking with brown hair, hazel eyes, and a sincere desire to succeed at his marriage and in his faith.

This was a marriage that could have been special and last a lifetime. Ah, but alas, as marriages go the way of the T-Rex, so went the Rollings'.

Danny was far from the perfect husband, and Omatha far from the perfect wife. Still, they had something special, and proof of that soon developed. Kiley Danielle was born to the Rollings a year later. She was a beautiful bundle of bright bubbly joy, a lovely child, good-natured and well-behaved, the apple of her daddy's eye.

For the first two years of that victorious church life, Danny was walking around in a halo of blessings. Everything was so right, so beautiful! They were the best years of his life. God was very merciful and kind to his humble servant Danny Rolling.

As time ticked on, the troubles crept back into his life. His relationship with Omatha became strained and distant. His prayer life and social life disintegrated, and once again he began to walk the streets at night.

Omatha was often frigid. Danny was crazy about sex, but it was just a duty to her. She didn't come on to it at all. Cold she was, didn't even like kissing. And when she would turn the cold shoulder to him, he would find relief standing in the rain outside some stranger's window, looking at some woman doing different things.

One night while his wife was pregnant with his daughter, she refused to satisfy him, so he ducked out into the night and the police caught him. When they found out his name, they looked at each other.

"So you're Lieutenant Rolling's boy?"

"Yes sir."

"Well, we're not going to run you in, but we are going to take you back to your apartment and tell your wife whatcha been up to out here," and that's what they did.

God… the shame of that night — my pregnant wife answering the door to see me between two policemen and them telling her I had been peeking in windows.

Sitting by the window, in an empty room.
Trying to get over these feelings, a little too soon.
I tried to call you, but you are never there.
Makes me wonder, if you ever cared.
And you finally hurt me more than I love you.

Visitors from Hell

One evening after church on a still warm July night, the first warning came on the wings of the night in the hands of a messenger from hell. The Rollings had just put their daughter into her crib in the nursery and lay themselves down for the night. Omatha fell quickly asleep, but Danny could find no peace. He tossed and turned, and gazed out the window into the illuminated street out front.

Suddenly! A cold violent wind blasted through the opened window, raising the ceiling-to-floor olive-colored curtains over a startled Danny! He wondered, had a tornado struck? Paralyzed with fear, he stared wide-eyed out the window as things flew around the room.

Then… there… outside the window… it came creeping down from the roof — a Shadow of Evil, demonic energy personified. It slipped under the window and poured into the room, slithered up the wall and gathered in the corner of the ceiling. The freezing wind howled as the Visitor from the underworld hovering above the bedded Rollings began to watch, to call, and to reach for Danny's soul.

He could feel its evil power. The hair on his arms and neck stood up as he watched the demon watching him. He tried to move, but was frozen in wonder and fear. He tried to speak, to wake his wife, but he could only moan. Finally his moaning awoke Omatha and she sat up in the bed terrified. "Danny! Danny! What's wrong? I'm scared! Something's wrong!" she cried, shaking Danny, who was in a trancelike state.

Danny could only moan and look astonished at the thing hovering above him. It could change shapes— hideous shapes of creatures never seen by mortal eyes, drawn up from hell's wells and filled with devil's yells. The thing held no light. It looked like if you put your hand into it, your hand would go somewhere and you would never see it again.

There in his bed, Danny struggled to gain release from the spell. Sweat poured down his desperate face, as he overcame his fear and willed himself to speak three names. The first name was a whisper forced from a forged will, the second, a triumph — and the third, a victory: "Jesus... Jesus... JESUS!"

After he shouted the Holy Name the third time, the dark demon immediately dashed out the window into the night. The curtains which were flapping wildly overhead settled down into their place, the wind ceased, and there was once again peace in the Rolling home. Danny turned and touched Omatha on her silky smooth shoulder, and said, "Don't worry, Omatha, we've got Jesus," and they both went to sleep undisturbed for the rest of the night.

The second warning came ghostly haunting from the grave of a forgotten cemetery hidden in the back roads of Mississippi.

Danny and Omatha had an argument because Danny wanted to go deer hunting, and Omatha said, "If you go, I won't be here when you get back." And so it was.

He had hunted all day without success, and came home to an empty apartment, and a note scribbled on the bathroom mirror with soap: "Danny, I love you, I've gone to my sister's." There in the silence of that moment, he packed his clothes and left.

He drove from Shreveport, Louisiana to Clearwater, Florida, got a job cleaning the oven in a little pastry shop during the day, and walked the lonely sands at night.

I stroll along the beach... I hear the seagulls cry.
They sail across the waves... nto a clear blue sky.
You know, the human heart...
is such a fragile thing.
Like the rain it weeps... like the wind it sings.
And you finally hurt me more than I love you.

Three weeks later he found himself under a table cleaning, and began to long for home. "Why did I leave?" he asked himself. He crawled out from under the table, jumped in his car, and headed for his wife and child in Shreveport.

That night he fell asleep at the wheel, and awoke just in time to prevent a nasty head-on collision. He then pulled into a small country town outside of Jacksonville, Mississippi, parked behind a little grocery store, and went to sleep.

Tap... tap... tap...

He was awake and disoriented with a light shining in his face. With his hand over his eyes, he rolled down the frost-heavy window to see who it was and what they wanted. There holding a long flashlight stood the sheriff and a deputy.

"Whatcha doing parked here?" said the Sheriff.

Danny replied, "I was just trying to make Shreveport by morning, and fell asleep at the wheel, so I pulled in here to get some shut-eye."

"Well, son, you can't stay here," said the Sheriff, shining the light around inside the car. "You'll have to find a rest spot down the road."

"OK, officer, thank you," said Danny, and he drove off sleepy-eyed into the dark.

He hadn't driven very far before he nodded off to sleep again, and drove off the highway. The whining of the tires on the shoulder of the road woke him with a start. His heart throbbing in his throat, he yanked the steering wheel hard left, and got it back on the highway. Then he pulled over and stopped.

"Whewww-WEE!" Danny said to himself. "I can't go another mile. I gotta find a place to rest."

A semi sped past, shaking the parked car. Its red tail lights hissed off into the night, and the highway swallowed it in the distance. He saw a side road up ahead and a dirt road that cut into a thick stand of pine.

"I'm in luck!" he thought, "I'll drive up that dirt road a ways and make sure it's no one's driveway then I can just sleep till noon." So he drove off the highway and turned up the dirt road. After he eased down the path a ways, he saw a light up ahead. "Ah, naw, it looks like someone must live up there."

Still he continued on until the path opened up into a clearing. There, like a ghost in the mist, stood an old-timey white one-room church, its steeple pointing a wooden finger towards the heavens, as a warning to trespassing sinners. A single utility pole with a light burning was grounded just behind the church, casting its shadow across the meadow. To the right was an ancient graveyard with an ironwork fence surrounding it.

Danny thought he was in luck when he turned around in the gravel driveway and parked it facing the way he came in. It was cold, freezing in fact. His breath fogged up the inside and the frost bit on the outside windows. He slept deeply.

Suddenly! For no apparent reason, he awoke abruptly from his exhausted sleep, feeling uneasy. Something was wrong — very wrong. That night Danny's guardian angel was at his assigned post, and tapped his shoulder, alerting him that Evil was about.

Danny put his hand on the frosty window and wiped the mist from it. As he looked into the rearview mirror, something began to stir amongst the tombstones and crosses in the old graveyard. Just a shadow at first, it stood up and headed for the ironwork gate. As it opened the gate, there was a screech of protest, and the Visitor passed through, then walked — no, it didn't walk — it floated across the mist-covered frozen ground.

Closer… closer it came, arm outstretched and pointing towards the parked car. It appeared to Danny to be a man — a tall, dark man wearing a wide-brim Quaker black hat, a knee-length coat, and gray slacks. He had no face, only darkness filled his ragged clothes.

Danny sat frozen to the spot, gripping the steering wheel tightly. The Vision crept up to the car and reached for him. He turned the ignition key and spewed gravel as he left in a hurry. He looked in the rearview mirror, and saw the Vision vanish in the mist that brought it.

Warnings… warnings from beyond.
Oh, if only young Danny
Could have seen the signs!

When he finally did get back to Shreveport, weary and worried, his fears were washed away, as his wife opened the door with an embarrassed smile. Life was good again for Danny Rolling, but only for a little while.

The Whispering Troll

One moment you are young
and full of innocent dreams.
The next moment you look into a mirror
to see eyes filled with years of pain
glaring back at you,
swimming in their own horror.

It begins at a tender age, with a sensitive, bright child eager to learn and be accepted. Something happens — some sort of abuse or tragedy that chisels away at the child's self-image. This fracture becomes a bleeding wound as the abuse continues and self-esteem is damaged.

Thus, a window develops in the young person's mind. That's when the murder demon enters and plants the seed of perversion, promising acceptance and relief. Over the years the seed grows along with the carrier, poking through one defense after another, until it becomes a terrible tree, capable of reaching down and gathering up unsuspecting souls into its cruel limbs.

Once it becomes an adult tree, the only way to cure what the infestation has done to the gentle, loving child of years gone by is to either trim away its branches — or cut it down. Either way the tree dies, and along with it, the person as well.

Haunted Tree

Job 14:7-10: For there is hope of a tree,
if it be cut down, that it will sprout again,
and that the tender branch thereof will not cease.
Though the root thereof was old in the earth,
and the stock thereof die in the ground,
yet through the scent of water it will bud,
and bring forth boughs like a plant.
But man dieth, and wasteth away;
yea, man giveth up the ghost,
and where is he?
What do I see in the tree?
Subconscious strongholds
Guard each secret discreetly.
Down twisting turning tendrils
Into the dark earth I descend
To face each elusive fiend or friend.
The root of the matter started helter-skelter.

51

What Have You Done?

Though the young sapling grew strong,
What went wrong?
Several elements would shape its destiny,
Altering development and splitting its nature
Through adversity.
Its roots sprout!
Leapfrogging pockets of clandestine shadow.
Hollowed be the heart of sorrow,
Filled with horrors bridging gaps
Between illusion and reality.
What evil possesses crooked limbs
Reaching in the dark?
One side — the love of light.
The other — terrible dread.
Tis a tree both alive
And dead.
Whispering leaves call, urging, "Come."
Adding to its total sum.
Wind, rain & lightning
Lashed at its very heart & soul
Carving a hollow where lurked
The whispering troll.

It wasn't long after the Visitor searched Danny out by that crumbling graveyard that another warning fell in his lap. That fateful day on a lonely stretch of Texas highway the Grim Reaper came shopping, and this time he would find the soul he sought. Like so many poor souls that have lost their lives to the cruel embrace of the concrete and twisting metal of America's highways, another life would be claimed unexpectedly.

Danny was transporting paper to printers in the tri-state area of Arkansas, Texas and Louisiana. His red and white International Lodestar thundered around the blind curve, topped the hill, and there it was: a grade with two bridges. A man pulling a double-wide house trailer had blocked the second bridge, backing up traffic in both lanes. Danny could hardly believe his eyes. He had been over this route countless times, and the blind curve and hill had never posed a problem before. Now a brown Dodge van was stopped directly in his path.

He stomped on the brake, but the weight of the truck pushed it 170 feet into its target, rubber burning and moaning on the hot asphalt. Like flashes from a high-speed camera, the van drew closer in microseconds.

"Oh, my God!" yelled Danny desperately, "I'm gonna hit 'im!" He turned the steering wheel to the left to avoid the collision, but to no avail. The big red truck clipped six inches off the brown van's rear bumper, shoving it into the station wagon in front of it, and catapulting it into the air.

The International had now come to a stop, and Danny could see the whole event close up. The van spun like a top and landed on its rear wheels. The back doors flew open and a woman burst from the van headlong, striking the asphalt with her head. She laid out on her back and didn't move.

Danny was stunned. "Oh God, this can't be happening!" he shouted, jumped from the truck and raced to the fallen woman's side. She lay on her back and Danny knelt down to see what he could do to help. But what he saw told him she was beyond the help of mortal man. The impact had burst open her head like an egg, and her blood ran down the grade towards the wrecked van.

Danny stood up and made for the van to see if

there was anyone else that needed help. As he walked up to the driver's side door, a man got out, dazed with a gash over his left eye, blood pouring over his face. He stumbled past Danny to check on his wife, who lay lifeless on the hot asphalt.

Danny wanted to reach out to the injured man and say, "Don't go back there, she's gone, there's nothing you can do." Ah, but alas. He just stood there while the man hurried by him.

The man knelt down by his fallen lifelong companion, and cried, "Oh, my baby… my poor baby." The whole scene cast a hopelessness that is all too familiar with roadside crashes — the smell of gasoline and blood, the victims weeping, the bystanders shaking their heads in sympathy.

The deceased woman's husband raised up from his loss, with tears and blood running down his face, and started for Danny, screaming, "You bastard! What have you done? What have you done?"

Two bystanders grabbed him and restrained him. Danny lowered his head, walked over to the bridge's guard rail, fell to his knees, put his head in his hands, and cried, "Poor lady… poor, poor lady…"

Danny wanted to escape the whole scene. There on his knees, hearing the cries of anguish and the wail of sirens approaching, the spokes of his universe broke and everything came tumbling in. His mind snapped there on the gritty bridge, and he felt himself shrinking, falling down a spiraling staircase into a dark quiet place. He heard one paramedic say to the other after taking his pulse, "He's going into shock," and then everything went black. He came to in the emergency room with a Pentecostal preacher praying over him.

For months after the accident, he couldn't shake it — the pale woman lying there on the gray asphalt, eyes forever fixed wide and glassy, jaw slack, mouth agape. Night after haunted night, he would awake in a cold sweat as her visage appeared in his dreams and her bloody husband pointed an accusing finger at him, screaming "You bastard! What have you done? What have you done?"

Here's Johnny

During this period, Omatha left me three times for her high-school sweetheart, John Lummus. I caught them together twice while Omatha and I were still married. The second time, I planned to blow them both away. I brought my .308 cal. Remington hunting rifle to rise to the occasion — but Kiley was with them. I couldn't do that in front of my own three and a half year-old bright-eyed little girl. So I settled for beating John Lummus' country ass. He got off light with just a busted lip and a black eye. Omatha wanted a divorce. I didn't, but I granted her one anyway.

What do you say to the one you love
When you know you hurt them
And you know you were wrong?
I need your love
Please don't take away your love

For a while things were good, and the calm lasted about six months. They were in debt and Danny had mortgaged his old beat-up Volkswagen Super Beetle to have money enough for a place to live.

Then the accident happened, and the strain of it took something out of Danny. His wife began to drift further from his touch. Omatha began visiting her sister on weekends and soon she was seeing John on the side. Then one evening after a hard day's work fighting the maddened highway, quite unexpectedly she broke it to Danny over dinner — which was served cold.

She spoke matter-of-factly. "Danny, my sister is coming to get Kiley and me in the morning."

"OK. You planning on staying the weekend again?"

"No. I'm leaving you."

"You're WHAT?" he shouted, pushing his plate away and jumping to his feet. "After all I'm doing to try and keep us together?"

"My dad will be here too," she said, looking frightened.

"Damn! I don't believe this!" Danny stormed over to his fear-stricken wife and flung her to the floor, jumped on top of her, grabbed a handful of long auburn hair and pounded the back of her head on the thick gold carpet. "You're going again? Why? Why are you doing this?"

He stood up and stalked out of the room, and returned carrying an armload of his wife's clothes. He threw them out into the hallway, picked Omatha up off the floor, and pushed her out with them, slamming the door behind her and locking it.

Omatha pounded on the door and shouted hysterically, "Danny, let me in! Let me in!"

Kiley came running into the living room looking wide-eyed and innocent with her index finger stuck in her mouth. She pointed towards the door and said, "Daddy, let Mommy in," and Danny's heart broke. He lowered his head and let Omatha back in the apartment.

The shouting match continued until a pounding on the door broke through the heated words. Danny snatched open the door to find one of the neighbors looking concerned and asking, "What's wrong here?"

"We're having a fight!" Danny screamed, and slammed the door in her face.

Omatha and Kiley went into the bedroom and Danny followed, totally upset and on edge now. He reached into the closet and pulled out his Super Single 12 gauge shotgun, loaded it, and pointed it at Omatha. Little Kiley cried, "Don't shoot Mommy! Daddy, stop!"

Danny lowered the long black-barreled shotgun and began to weep. Then he turned the gun on himself, pointed it in his face, cocked it and cried, "Is this what you want, Omatha?"

"No! No! Danny, don't!"

Danny stood there for a long tense moment, then eased the hammer forward and put away the gun.

That night they all slept in the same bed, but they were not together. The next morning Danny went to work, hoping they would be there when he got home. But that evening, he came home to an empty apartment. He sat at the dining room table looking across the trees into the blue horizon turning a deep purple, empty and at a loss.

I really didn't want to hurt her. I only thought... if I shook her up a bit? Maybe... just maybe? She wouldn't run out on me again. I was really upset. I mean, I took out a second mortgage on that ancient beat-up Volkswagen Beetle Bug. I had bills up to there to make a place for Omatha and Kiley to stay after Omatha left me the second time. And here she was saying adios again. And I knew it was John Lummus she was running to.

When you went away...
My world came tumblin' down.
Now, my life's a three-ring circus...
And I'm a lonely clown.
And you finally hurt me...
More than I love you.
Yes, you closed the door,...
And you said, "We are through,"
And you finally hurt me...
More than I love you.

Danny had to go. He packed a small bag and thumbed a ride to Huoma, Louisiana, where oil companies are based, and began a search for offshore employment at the shipyards, ending up on the doorstep of Briley Marine before the sun came up. He was dead tired and hadn't had anything to eat since he left Shreveport, but he was hopeful.

The sun popped up and with its warmth, arrived a tall, rough looking character.

"You lookin' for work, kid?"

Danny nodded.

"Well, we don't have any openings."

"Mister, I hitched down here all the way from Shreveport. My wife just left me for another man, and I haven't got any place to go or any future unless somebody gives me a break."

He looked Danny over. "Maybe...maybe today is your lucky day. Come on in my office and I'll make a few calls."

The office was small witha window overlooking the shipyard and docks. Pelicans danced in the early morning pale blue sky. Danny waited patiently fwhile the man picked up the phone and dialed.

"Hello, Baxter! How's it going? Uh-huh...OK... Say, listen, do you still need a deckhand for the Clifton Briley? Uh-huh...OK, talk to you later," and with that he hung up. "Like I said, kid, looks like today is your lucky day."

The Clifton Briley was a pretty red, white, and blue supply ship. Danny would never forget his first voyage, the smell of the salty ocean and dolphins playing tag with the bow of the boat. He was eager, a quick study, and a hard worker, and the captain soon trusted him enough to let him pilot the ship when they were out to sea. The food was excellent and the working conditions were good, but Danny found he would get seasick in stormy weather. he tried to overcome the nausea, but to no avail, and after sixty days he returned to Shreveport.

Later, the sea behind him, the old familiar pain

crept in again. He longed for his wife and child, and he sought them out.

John Lummus hadn't wasted any time moving in on them. He had rented a house trailer for them, and one Sunday morning Danny waited in his white F100 Ford pickup truck with his newly-bought 308 caliber hunting rifle, brokenhearted — and with murder on his mind.

Sure enough… "Heeeeere's Johnny!" Down the road he came with Omatha and Kiley in his big green truck. John pulled up into the driveway like he owned it. When Danny saw his daughter was with them, he knew he couldn't kill her mother before the child's eyes. So he got out of his truck and made for John.

Omatha and Kiley got out first on the right side. Danny stood waiting for John to get out on the left, and as soon as the door opened, Danny began punching John. He tried to get his hands on Danny, but he just ran into one fist after another. Thud! His eye swelled shut. Thud! Thud! His lip burst open, but he still kept charging. He grabbed Danny by the hair and almost broke his neck in his big pulp-wooder hands. Danny managed to break free and squared off, ready to continue.

John stood there not knowing what to do. Danny sensed this and asked, "Well, Johnny? You done?" John nodded and both men went inside. Omatha brought John a wet washcloth and cleaned him up, while Danny held his daughter and hugged her close.

"What do you want, Omatha?" he asked, bouncing Kiley on his knee.

"I want a divorce," she stated coldly.

"All right. You've got it."

Danny kissed Kiley goodbye and left, not having the heart to take his daughter from her mother.

Six months later, Danny's wife divorced him.

"Danny took his divorce very hard," said Claudia. "The Sheriff came to our door with the separation papers, and tried to hand them to Danny. Danny got a glance at them, and he started screaming and running around and around the house. I don't know how many times he ran around the house screaming, 'No, no, no! She's my wife… this can't happen… we can fix it — No, no, no!' We finally caught him and got him calmed down. And his daddy told him, 'You have to take the papers. And you have to sign them.' So he did."

Without you… what shall I do?
Cast my dreams into cold, cold streams?
Pluck the rose from my heart
And sadly depart?
If you run away…
What can I do? What can I say
To bring you back my way?

Without you… what shall I do?
Toss in my sleep… wake up and weep…
Into depression seep…
Off a jagged cliff leap?
Life ceases for me…
My mind's eye longs to see
The beauty and life that is you and me

The Starting Gun

The first rape I ever committed came as a direct result of rejection. When the sheriff served me with my divorce papers, I realized it was final. Omatha had divorced me and I was deeply wounded, dejected, angry, confused and depressed. The next night, I broke in on this gorgeous brunette college student and took out all my frustration and pain on her.

She was a delicious brunette discovered on a night patrol. He was searching the darkness for that portal to altered states of projected thought, and there she was — framed in the window of his fantasy. But this time Danny broke the ancient taboo, and progressed from fantasizing to bringing the dream to life.

"Why did Omatha leave me? Doesn't she know nobody could ever love her like I do? Nobody!" The disturbed man gritted his teeth, his fists balled up like hammers against his side. He was bitter and lost. Up one dark street and down another he wandered, through yards of people he didn't know, following the Spirits that led him, trying to find release.

Slipping from shadow to shadow, he came to a back yard he had visited a couple of times before. It was a warm night. Fall hadn't set in yet, and the front and rear doors were left open to allow the fresh air in. Only the screen doors were hooked shut.

Two college girls had recently rented the house — one a voluptuous brunette, the other a plump dishwater blonde. The beautiful brunette was on the living room couch studying. The Eyes were at the kitchen window watching.

Dannnnneeeee…

The gentle wind called ever so softly, just a whisper to his soul.

Take off your socks…
Put them on your hands…

He did, and slipped his Dingo boots back on.
Next?
Mask your identity…

"That's right, gotta hide my face. I only live three blocks away. Can't let her see who I am."

There was a large chamois cloth draped across the back of a metal chair on the porch. He picked up the 3-pronged gardening digger next to it and tore two holes in the cloth. Then he draped it over his head, lined up the holes and tied it in a knot behind his head.

Now unlatch the door…

"Ah, yes! I remember when my dad would lock me out of the house as a child, and I'd wedge a stick between the screen door and the frame and wiggle it up and down below the hook-latch until I tripped it."

Now he was ready. He gained entry and pressed through the utility room and the kitchen. He bounded into the living room, heart pounding.

The startled brunette sat stock-still as the masked stranger towered over her brandishing the digger like a miniature pitchfork.

"Whaaa — what do you want?" she asked, laying the textbook in her lap.

"Get up!" the intruder snarled. "Do as I say!"

He grabbed her by the arm, yanking her across the room. Books and reading glasses went one way, the woman the other.

Into the bedroom he dragged her, fighting all the way. But she did not scream. She was using all her energy to resist.

She broke free and hopped over the king-size bed in two hops. She pranced back and forth trying to get as far from her attacker as possible. But the tiger had its prey in sight and he could smell the pulse of sex running through her.

He dashed around the foot of the bed, but she jumped onto it. It was "Tag — you're it!" until the cat grew bored toying with his little mouse. He jumped onto the bed and flung her down.

"Ahhhhh! YEEEEE!" she screamed.

"Shut up!" Visions of Omatha flashed through his mind. "Shut up, I said! You do that again and I'll kill ya!"

The damsel grew silent.

"That's better! Look, I don't want to hurt you. So just behave yourself!" He turned her over on her belly and pulled her over the edge of the bed bent at the middle like she was praying. "Let's have a look atcha!"

"My — my roommate will be home soon!"

"You better hope she doesn't come home while I'm here, little girl. Now shut up and be still!" He pushed up her black sweater, bunching it up around her armpits, then pulled it over her shoulders and head.

Bare flesh bathed in the light pouring in from the hallway greeted his eager eyes. He tried to unsnap her bra, but he was so nervous, he couldn't do it at first. Finally he succeeded at the task and clumsily stripped the bra from her.

Pausing, he stroked the bare beauty of her shoulders as his swelling organ throbbed to life with unbridled desire. The moment lingered… and then he turned her over.

"Oh, what lovelies you have!" He pawed one plump breast, kneading it roughly. "Let's get your jeans off." And her pants were removed. When the panties hit the floor, that was the starting gun.

Standing there silhouetted by the hall light looking down at his pretty prize, he unbuttoned his 501 Levis.

"What are you staring at?" he grumbled. "Don't look at me!" He reached over and placed the sweater over her face.

"I can't breathe!"

"OK." He arranged it so it only covered her eyes. "Is that better?"

"Uh-huh."

Then he grabbed her legs and forced them open. Finding the moist center of pleasure, he slipped himself through her opening and ravaged her. It was over quickly.

The rapist put on his pants and scrambled out of

the house. He ran for two long blocks in a panic, still gripping the pitchfork digger. When he came to the big canal between Canal Street and West Canal, he threw the digger as far as he could — splash! — into the shallow, slimy green cold waters. Frantic and disoriented, he walked the last block to his house.

"Damn, Danny! Why did you do that? Stupid, stupid, stupid!" He looked up at the stars winking down on him and felt like everyone knew what he had done. The whole universe knew. His feet were on a path from which there was no return and no escape.

He couldn't sleep that night. The next day, he got up early to apologize to the woman and deliver himself into her hands. Whatever she chose to do with him would be fine. He was so miserable and ashamed he was beside himself. He didn't know what else to do except face it.

But it was not to be. As he made his way towards her, a big male exited her house and marched purposefully towards Danny. Whether the man was her father, her brother or her lover, Danny never found out. He did what he knew best. He ducked through a yard to the next block and ran away.

Like Jesse James

I wanted to be the direct opposite of my cop pop. That's how Ennad came to be everything my demanding father hated.

After the divorce, all the stops were yanked out and my emotions swirled down the funnel of despair. I was suicidal. I had to get relief somehow. I stole Dad's service revolver and came very close to blowing my brains out. I even went so far as to stick the barrel of the .38 caliber into my mouth and cock the hammer. I put my finger on the trigger and gazed into the starlit sky. My hand shook as the tears flowed down my face. But I just couldn't do it. I couldn't pull that trigger.

In my tortured state of mind, I thought, "OK, Danny. You can't do it yourself. So get someone else to end your miserable life for you."

I'll become an outlaw like Jesse James
I'll rob and steal till a bullet with my name
Sets my weary soul free.

She Doesn't Want to Know

Shortly after Omatha divorced me, my daughter Kiley, who was only 3-1/2 at the time, was lent to me one weekend. I hadn't seen her in about six months.

It was a wonderful visit. I took Kiley for a walk and showed her off to all my friends. She was so beautiful in her pink and white baby lace dress and white shoes. I held her in the crook of my right arm and she put her tiny arm around my neck. Father and daughter. God, I loved her. Still do.

I took her to the playground. I put her in a swing and gave her a push. She giggled and seemed to be enjoying herself. I loved her so much I thought my heart would explode!

I only had her for a couple of hours and then I had to let her go back to her mother a hundred miles away. I kissed her fat little cheek. She hugged my neck and the last picture in my memory is my mother leading her away by the hand. Kiley turned around and glanced back at me with those big blue wide-open eyes of hers. Then she put her index finger in her mouth and turned away. That's the last time I saw her.

It broke my heart in ways I couldn't even begin to understand. I was beside myself. I felt betrayed by Omatha. Each day that ticked off the calendar found me more depressed and angry. Yes, I was hurt and I was angry!

I love Kiley and she will always be part of my very heart. She doesn't remember looking up at me from her crib with those big blue eyes as I wept, praying that I would be the kind of father she deserved. No, she doesn't remember how I used to put her up on my shoulders and give her pony rides, holding on to her chubby little feet as she pulled my hair, giggling with glee. No, she only sees me as a distant dark figure she never knew and apparently doesn't want to know. I've written her several times, but my daughter chooses to reject her real father. If that's the way she wants it, I can't say I blame her, but I deeply regret it.

Always a Gentleman

"One day after he divorced, Danny asked me for a ride," said his Aunt Agnes. "And I asked him, 'Well, where are you going?' And he said, 'I'm dating this little girl.'

"Well, come to find out, her name was Mary Lynn, and she was just about 17 years old. She lived in Blanchard, Louisiana and she belonged to the Church of the Nazarene. That's the same denomination I belong to, and she knew some members in my family. At that time Danny was really involved in church work. She was a real pretty little blonde blue-eyed girl, and the family was a nice quiet family. Her mother and dad both worked, and she really cared about him. Well, he dated her several times, took her to church there at her church. I don't know where else they went. I know he had a few dates with her.

"I put him off at her house one day, and I said, 'Danny, you'll be there with her by yourself. Always remember to be a gentleman.' And he said, 'Auntie, I know where my place is.' But when his mother found out that Danny had been married and divorced, she wouldn't let her daughter see him any more. After they broke up, Mary Lynn asked me about him, and she made the remark, 'He was always a gentleman, I really cared about him.'"

A Close Encounter

Shortly after his divorce from Omatha, Danny had a close encounter of the scary kind. He had met this cute gal who worked for General Electric and made a date. It was to be quite an evening at her trailer out in the country. She had given him directions over the phone, and — you guessed it — he got lost and ended up driving down a long lonely dirt country road to nowhere.

The sun set and it got dark. Danny turned on the headlights so he could see. The radio was blasting. The dual spears of light cut through the night as the white Ford disappeared into the isolated deep bottom.

Finally he just stopped in frustration. He couldn't find the damn road she lived on and it was getting late.

Danny was just sitting there with pussy on his mind when the headlights began to flicker off and on and the radio did the same. Then the truck stalled and it wouldn't start again.

Sitting there in total darkness, Danny was puzzled. The truck had never acted like that before. Maybe it was out of gas? No. He had filled it up earlier that day. So what was going on? It made no sense. After a few minutes of whirring the starter, the truck cranked up with a roar. He turned it around and sped out of there lickety-split!

As he left the bottom, the radio and lights began to work properly as before. After he drove a short distance, he caught something unusual out of the corner of his left eye. He put the brakes on and backed up, with a swirl of dust dancing in the headlights and pouring into the cab through the opened window.

When he got back to the spot where he first glimpsed the object, he stopped to let the dust settle a bit before getting out. He opened the door and stood near the truck, but went no further. What he saw freaked him out BIG TIME!

There in an open field approximately 150 yards beyond a barbed-wire fence sat a huge glowing pulsating blue-white object with a rainbow-like ring pulsing around it. Danny started to jump the fence and check it out up close, but the prickling hairs on the back of his neck told him to get the hell out of there — FAST!

Danny made tracks for the highway and continued his quest for pussy. Now where the hell did that gal live? He shrugged off what he had seen as just a strange occurrence that must have a logical explanation.

He found a country store with a pay-phone out front and got new directions. Finally he found the chick's trailer.

After they had a couple of drinks, he casually mentioned that on the way over to her place, he might have seen a UFO.

She cocked her head to one side like a cockatoo and asked, "What time did you see it?"

"About 9:30 or 10:00."

She looked uneasy and said, "You may very well have seen one. Just an hour ago, my son and I were listening to the radio, and the DJ said he was getting calls from people saying they saw a UFO."

What an experience! Danny would never forget it, but he only mentioned it a couple of times because it gave folks the impression he was as nutty as a fruitcake.

Danny's Nuts

It was Saturday night in Shreveport, and Danny's nuts were Rolling around the skating rink.

Danny must have stuck out like a sore thumb — this 6'3" giant towering over the little kids scurrying around the rink. But even though he felt a little out of place, he loved to roller skate and he always looked out for the little fellas.

The teenagers had brought some of those multicolored wands you snap and they glow in the dark orange, blue or green. They were passing these wands around, throwing them from person to person. A little game they were playing.

Well, this cute little girl pitched one and it went flying down the rink. Danny picked it up and brought it back to the girl, who giggled and skated off. Little did Danny know, that was supposed to mean something. Because the girl's brat of a boyfriend came over to Danny and took a swing at him. Danny just pushed the punk down. I mean he was just a teenager, and Danny was a grown man.

Being the polite chap he was, Danny reached down to help the chap up. Now, when you are balancing on roller skates, in order to help someone up off the floor, you must straddle that individual to keep from falling. You get the picture? Well, the jealous little punk balled up his fist and drove it straight up into Danny's left nut. OUCH!

He had an operation called a varicocele and when last seen, Danny's nuts were still Rolling.

CHAPTER 4
THE LIFE OF AN OUTLAW

Criminal Equations

Curiosity + Puberty + Opportunity — Guidance = Voyeurism

Rejection + Depression x Rage x Lust — Counseling — Support = B&E + Rape

Outcast + Need x Excitement — Means of Support = Robbery

Dementia + Possession x Revenge = Murder

Virgin Outlaw

I hung around Shreveport for a spell... lost my job... did a couple of B&E's... got punched in the nuts at the skating rink... stole my dad's .38 cal. Smith & Wesson service revolver... robbed Charlie's Lounge and a liquor store... then I packed the .38 and hit the road hitchhiking through Mississippi and Alabama... robbed a Winn-Dixie... continued on my way to Georgia... robbed another Winn-Dixie... got busted... and wound up in the Muscogee County Jail.

May 12, 1979. Danny Rolling was named as the prime suspect in the attempted armed robbery of a Shreveport 7-11 store. When the clerk handed him the $11.00 in the cash register, he handed it back, saying, "Forget it, that ain't worth taking." No charges were filed.

May 13, 1979. His first real robbery was crazy and almost got him killed. Charlie's Lounge was a small neighborhood bar where rednecks, bikers and ruffians bellied up to their mugs of beer and listened to shit-kickin' country music.

It was 11:00 P.M. on a Saturday night, so the place was packed. The front door stood open and drunken laughter spilled out into the deserted street with the jukebox music.

The robber stood in the shadows across the street, watching the flow of traffic. He tried to talk himself out of it. He was 25 years old and no criminal. But that soon would change.

Looking at the .38 he had stolen from his father, he remembered how upset his dad had been as he tore up the house looking for it. Alone there in the dark, he was talking to himself.

"Well, I guess it's true what they say about policemen and preacher's sons. Dad, you're a cop — and I'm a misfit. Oh well, I've come this far. There's no turning back now. Look out, Charlie, here I come!"

And with his words dying in the darkness, he walked casually across the dimly-lit street like he was walking on the clouds of a dream. Standing in front of the lounge, he paused to put on the brown cotton gloves and the navy blue ski mask, then threw himself inside the door with his heart racing, not knowing what to expect. What he found was more than he bargained for.

The young robber pointed the cool black .38 in all directions from left to right and yelled, "This is a holdup! Everybody on the floor!"

Nobody paid him any attention. So he screamed at the top of his lungs. "I said on the floor! Everybody! Move it! NOW!"

Somebody turned off the jukebox and it became very quiet. All eyes were now fixed on the lone gunman.

"Get on the floor before I start shootin' this place up!"

The women were the first to obey, but some of the men became a problem. A big heavy-set man playing pool picked up a cue-ball and started for the masked man standing in the middle of the room.

"Hey! You!" the robber yelled, pointing the pistol at the drunken man coming for him. "What? You want to be a hero, mister? Do you?"

With the gun leveled at him, the man dropped the pool ball and just stood there staring defiantly at the robber.

"Get on the floor now! DO IT!" And he did.

Everyone was lying on the dirty floor except the bartender, who reached for a shotgun he kept hidden under the bar. The robber caught this out of the corner of his eye, and snapped around taking a bead on the man crouching there.

"HEY! Whatcha think you're doing, fella? Get your hands up! Do it or I'll drill ya!" He did.

A man began crawling towards the back room. "YOU! Where are you going? Get back here!" But he got away.

Finally everyone was lying quietly on the floor. Quickly now the bandit pounced to the bar and demanded all the money from the register. The tender complied, opened the cash box, and handed over the money.

The bandit, watching everyone and everything, backed slowly out of the scene of his first robbery.

Once outside, he turned and ran back across the street the way he came, bullets zinging inches by him as someone from inside Charlie's Lounge opened fire. It had been that close. He vaulted a 9-foot fence and disappeared into the night.

And thus began the virgin outlaw's road to crime, punishment, insanity, and violence beyond his wildest nightmare.

May 15, 1979. Danny Rolling, wearing a brown sack over his head, entered the L&R Liquor Store in Shreveport and demanded "all the money," fleeing on foot with about $200.00.

"Well, he had moved back in with us," said Claudia, "and like always, his dad struck a sour note with him from day one. I think it just built up until he couldn't stand it any more, so he left early one morning before I got up. The next thing I hear he's in jail in Columbus, Georgia, charged with armed robbery."

May 25, 1979. Jeanette Caughey of Phenix City, Alabama saw her nephew Danny for the last time. He came to her house and asked to spend the night. She agreed, but when he asked her to go bar-hopping with him, she declined. He asked if he could borrow her car, and she refused; after that, he went out. The next time she saw her brother's son was on TV in a story relating his latest misadventures.

Wearing a brown ski mask, blue jeans and a blue jean jacket, Danny Rolling had entered a Winn Dixie Grocery Store in Montgomery, Alabama, at 8:35 P.M. He pointed his father's gun at the two cashiers and ordered them to put the contents of their registers in a dark blue hat he used as a bag. He fled on foot to a nearby Baptist Church.

He entered the church through an open window, and once inside, counted out eight hundred dollars. Flushing the food stamps down the toilet, he left the church and hitched a ride to Columbus, Georgia. Intending to visit his grandparents, he wound up in jail instead.

May 31, 1979. Danny robbed a Winn-Dixie at the Peachtree Mall in Columbus, Georgia, bursting into the store at about 9:00 P.M. wearing a brown ski mask and flashing a revolver. He stashed the contents of the registers in a brown paper sack, and ran off into the woods.

About a half-hour later, three uniformed officers checking the woods behind the store found Danny Rolling hiding in some bushes. He surrendered without a struggle, and readily confessed to the armed robberies in Alabama, Georgia and Louisiana.

"He thought somebody would blow him away," remembered Claudia Rolling. "It was another way of getting rid of that no-count Danny. I had money lying around the house all the time. He never took a penny. He or Kevin either one. They never stole anything that I know of. And by the way, his daddy's .38 was empty, there were no bullets in it. Of course the people he robbed didn't know that."

So began my criminal education in joints across the Southeast. I've been in and out of every flea bitten, rat and roach infested jail and prison the good ol' South can offer a rebel gone mad.

House of Steel and Stone

It's hard... so very hard for me to understand.
What made this man put a gun in his hand?
Well, I guess I came to the end of my rope,
'Cause when I lost my love, I lost my hope,
Now I'm livin' in a house of steel and stone.

Prisons in America have changed immensely over the past fifteen years. Many are run as humanely as possible. Still, when you lock up dangerous men in close quarters, there is bound to be trouble.

You can judge a society by the way it runs its prisons. Even though this country tries to treat its prisoners with dignity, there is still much that needs to be done. We treat the symptom but not the cause. Give a prisoner basic human necessities and a way to improve himself. Reward good behavior and punish bad. At least give a guy a chance to overcome his mistakes.

You take a dog, cage it up, feed it slop, torment it, abuse it, and over a period of time the animal will either become uncontrollable and wild, or depressed with no will to live.

Everyone needs a reason to be. Take away that reason — and what's left? Nothing but mischief.

July 31, 1979. Danny entered a guilty plea to two counts of armed robbery for the Columbus, Georgia Winn-Dixie stickup, and received two concurrent 6-year sentences. He spent the next six years imprisoned, starting out as a trustee in the Muscogee County Jail in Alabama.

After three weeks, on August 20 he was processed into the Georgia Prison System at the Medical Classification Center in Jackson, Georgia.

He had no girlfriends at this time. The only people he had contact with in the free world were his mom, dad, brother and family. They came to see him about once a year.

Claudia Rolling remembered one miserable visit. "He looked like he had shrunk back to a little boy. I really don't think that Danny ever got much past 15. I know that right now whenever he's allowed to call me, his conversation is more mature, but every once in a while, he'll revert back to that little 15 year-old that I know so well. I don't think he ever really got much older than that.

"I had gotten a letter from him from prison, and it said, 'Dear Mommy and Daddy,' and there was two pages of 'I love you.' That's all. Just 'I love you.' I didn't know if James was going to let me go see him or not. He made me wait like a week before he said let's go.

"When we first went to the jail, the jailer made me talk to Danny through a little bitty hole. And you'd have to put your ear and listen, and then put your mouth up there and talk and let him listen, and I couldn't stand that, so Danny's lawyer got a room, one of the interrogation rooms I imagine, and he had them bring Danny in. He was wearing just shorts. No shoes, nothing. And he come in the room like a little kid.

"He went straight past me, which kind of shocked me, and he went straight to his dad, and he begged him, he said, 'Say you love me. Tell me you love me. Please tell me you love me.' And his lawyer, I looked over and his lawyer had tears coming down. And his daddy was just standing there looking at him. And Danny said again, 'Please,' he said, 'please tell me you love me.' And so James Harold finally said, 'I love you,' sort of offhand, like OK, I'll say it and maybe that will shut you up. I went over to Danny and took him in my arms to let him know that someone did love him."

October 8, 1979. Danny escaped from a road gang while chopping down trees with a dull axe, but immediately surrendered about 100 yards from the prison boundaries after an officer fired a warning shot with a 12-gauge shotgun.

May 13, 1980. After a 16-day stay in the Jackson Medical Classification Center, Danny was sent to Reidsville for about six months.

Whatsa Madda Witchew, Whiteboy?

The closest I ever came to being raped was when I first pulled up to Reidsville Prison. The racial tension was so thick you could cut it with a knife. And sometimes you would have to.

Since I was the new kid on the block, so to speak, some black prisoners thought I was an easy target. They found out different.

My new home consisted of a 120-man dormitory-style wing. I stowed away what gear I had and went into the latrine to piss. Once that was taken care of, I stepped behind the long shower curtain into the shower stall to look out the window. I wasn't in there 30 seconds when this real ugly black guy stepped behind the curtain with me and asked, "Whatsa madda witchew, whiteboy?"

Immediately, I sized up the situation and snarled, "Nothing! What's wrong with you?"

That's when he reached for me. I picked that dog up and executed a fireman's carry, slamming him to the floor. I jumped on top of his chest and grabbed him by the throat, but before I could do him in, the black guy's buddies (who put him up to it) came rushing in, thinking it was party time. There must have been 8 or 9 of the monkeys. I looked at all those staring dark eyes and knew this was trouble.

I looked down at the stinking rug-head I was choking, and said, "All right! I'm gonna let you up, but stay clear of me!" I let go my grip, rose to my feet, and got the hell out of there.

Nothing like that ever happened again, because they all thought I was crazy. Well, I guess I was, but it was a crazy environment.

Everything He Detested

Reidsville was Danny's first taste of prison life, and it was one hell of a taste. While he was there, two riots broke out. A friend of his had his kidneys punched out with a rattail file. Then three blacks caught this white guy on the third tier. Two of them held each arm, while the third butchered him. His only fault was being at the wrong place at the wrong time... and being white. He was in his twenties, and only had 90 days before his sentence was completed. Two months later, the brother of the slain man caught two of the blacks that killed his brother in the showers and stabbed them both to death.

One man working in the sawmill was thrown into a woodchipper and left for dead, but somehow he managed to hold on with one hand. He lost both legs and one arm — but he survived.

There is no place safe in prison. Even chow-time can be your end. Twice fights broke out in the Reidsville mess-hall. Danny watched in horror as one man's brains were bashed out with an industrial can opener. At the time they still had guards armed with shotguns in the mess-hall towers, and whenever there was a fight they would pump buckshot into the room.

At Reidsville, many wildcats took up housekeeping under the buildings. One black cat that Danny recalls vividly would slink from under the building parallel to the mess-hall, step up on a flat rock, and get himself a drink of cool water that dripped from a spigot there. How Danny grew to hate that cat! He became the symbol of everything he detested about being locked up. While he was imprisoned there against his will, this cat chose to make it his home.

Danny wanted to remove that green-eyed black cat that taunted him from his sight forever. But a nine-foot chainlink fence restrained him. One day he purposed to kill it. From his lair, the dark shadow crept into the light. Ignoring Danny, he stepped onto the flat slab and began to drink.

"Today's your day, bucko," Danny said and picked up a large round stone. All in one motion, he leaped on the fence and pulled himself up with his left hand. With the right hand he threw the stone as hard as he could over the top of the fence at the despised cat.

The noise startled the cat and he turned about quickly, just as the stone struck him dead center on his forehead and knocked him out cold. His feet went right out from under him.

Danny looked on, fascinated. He could hardly believe his eyes. It was an impossible shot, a one in a million chance he could hit that cat at that angle and that distance, while holding himself up on a nine-foot fence.

The cat did not move. Danny thought for sure it was dead, and went about his business with a satisfied mind. An hour later he passed back by the same spot on his way to chow. Lo and behold, the cat had crawled off. He thought, "Hmmm. Maybe cats do have nine lives — but this one now has EIGHT."

After six months at Reidsville, Alabama nabbed me up and extradited me to Montgomery to stand trial for the stickup that happened there a year earlier. While I was doing a stretch in their Hotel Royal, my lawyer had me sent to Bryce Mental Institution. I was still doing time on the Georgia rap, but I spent two or three months in Bryce. They concluded I was sane and sent me back to the Montgomery County Jail.

House of the Insane

In the fall of '79, a lone white van made its way up and down the picturesque hills of Alabama. Destination, Bryce Mental Institution, better known as the insane asylum, home of troubled souls lost in their own puzzling world beyond reason.

It is rather ironic that the clammy gray walls of Bryce stand a mere bow-shot from Alabama State College in Tuscaloosa. Both deal with the element of thought and how the mind operates — one to teach and learn the building blocks of our world, the other to rummage through the dirty cluttered rooms of insanity.

And so, as the white van pulled up the long driveway and parked before the unwelcoming doors of Bryce, we began this venture into the precarious minds of the mentally off.

"Whelp! Here we are, boys! Now let me make this crystal clear. If any of you whackos decide to bolt on me, I'll shoot your ass full of holes. Is that understood?" the deputy announced in an acute tone.

Now, you can't fully appreciate the implications of hardened indifference until you've been bounced around the countryside for hours on end shackled hand and foot in the back of a stuffy old van, only to face a tobacco-chewing good-ol'-boy pointing a fully-loaded riot shotgun at you.

"Get out," Deputy Do-Right commanded, his appearance conveying pure repugnance.

First to emerge from the cage was a thin black man named Jonesy, who argued constantly with the ghosts of his forefathers, which in turn tormented him on a regular basis. He never seemed to eat or sleep, so barely did he acknowledge his presence in this world. He reeked of days, possibly weeks of neglected personal hygiene.

Next to exit was a pale, almost translucent-looking white male who couldn't resist eating things — anything. Metal staples, ink pens, straight pins, thumbtacks, broken glass — if he could wolf it down, it ended up in his digestive tract, only to be cut out by some insensitive surgeon who felt he had better things to do than remove the broken bits of a drinking glass Carl had happily chewed up and swallowed to the horror of those witnessing the spectacle. Carl had so many scars from operations to remove those odd objects that his abdomen resembled a road map etched across his scalpel-violated flesh.

Last to emerge was a troubled young man known as Cowboy, who was seeking answers to questions only God knows, and had very little to say.

The ragtag bunch of misfits were herded into the vestibule to be admitted. "Well, Larry, I've got another batch for ya. You three sit down over there," the good-ol'-boy ordered, pointing to a long wooden bench in the corner. Jonesy never stopped mumbling to himself, but the other two sat quietly. Carl bowed his head, resting it on his handcuffs, while his cuffed hands covered his ears. Cowboy stared past the admitting desk, his thoughts on what awaited him.

"Would you look at that? See-no-evil, Hear-no-evil, Speak-no-evil! Hey! You three monkeys behave and we'll throw y'all a banana every now and then!" shouted the irritable orderly.

Jonesy continued his one-sided conversation.

"You! Shut up!" the man at the desk snarled, baring yellow teeth.

Jonesy was oblivious to the world.

"Hey! I said shut up!"

"You're wasting your time on that one, Larry," Deputy Do-Right stated flatly. "He's way out beyond left field, know what I mean? Out there in the twilight zone."

"Well, we'll see about these three right away." And the orderly got on the phone. Two men dressed in white arrived and mercy! Were they big boys! The two stood an impressive 6'3" or 6'4" and each weighed in at well over 250. Monstrous mean-looking goons.

Deputy Do-Right removed the cuffs and ankle chains from See-no-evil, Hear-no-evil, and Speak-no-evil, and left the three in care of the two giants. Cowboy saw the venom in their eyes and knew compassion would not be found there.

Within the walls of Bryce, if you obeyed the rules, you went along with the other mental defectives. But God help you if you stepped over the boundaries set by the institution's sovereignty. Punishment was swift and harsh, often brutal.

The giants separated Jonesy from the trio and took him away, then returned to lead the two other monkeys into the human zoo that housed the state's most violent and disturbed criminals.

The Thorazine Shuffle

Twisted and turned
Crimson lamplight burned
Sweet misery supreme
The night scream
Dementia… Dementia… Dementia

The word humanity somehow loses meaning when applied to the confused, babbling, shit-eating, piss-drinking corruptibles society has removed from our sight. Cowboy was suddenly surrounded by sights nobody wants to see, smells anyone would turn from, and sounds emanating from crawling, scratching, wild-eyed men turning expressions that only ostracized maniacs could project on the new monkeys.

In the middle of the recreational area, a black man danced and hopped about, his dick flopping out of his soiled, unzipped pants. Over in the corner knelt a broken man talking to the bare wall with a blank expression on his face.

A pitiful chap seated at one of the long dining tables was playing an imaginary game with no working parts. Only the motion of his trembling hands clawing at the still air gave shape to its composition. Two repulsive blacks leered at the new monkeys with such obvious expressions that even a moron could see what was on their minds.

After this unnerving introduction to his new domicile, Cowboy realized no answers would materialize in this place.

Later, he was given a change of clothes. Off came the prison garb, and he was suited up with old blue jeans, a cotton plaid shirt and tennis shoes, all donated by the concerned public. He was assigned a room with a hospital bed and a view from the fourth floor penthouse, panning out to the exercise yard below.

The rules were quite simple. Lights out at ten, reveille at six. You rose before dawn, made your bed, then meandered to the dining hall for breakfast. Afterwards, you lined up for your mind-numbing drugs. You stayed out of other people's rooms. No fighting, no stealing, no sex of any kind, and absolutely no defiance of authority.

All in all, if you didn't strike out at anyone, you were pretty much left alone to exhibit whatever behavior your fancy chose to perform for the zoo keepers to log in their metal clipboards. For instance, it was perfectly acceptable to dance about the room, drop your pants, piss in a cup and drink every drop. But if you cast the acidic liquid on the floor or threw it into someone's face, retribution was swift and ugly, bringing either raining blows of batons and floods of mace, or days locked away in the aperture to solitude known to every prisoner as The Hole.

Every morning it was the same. Dawn painted the horizon with pastel blues and pinks, and after breakfast the Thorazine Shuffle began. "Line up, boys, and take your medicine. Open wide now. Let me see you swallow all of it. That's a good monkey. Eat your peanuts and go bananas! Ha-ha!"

What was that?
Rat-tee-tat-tat
In the corner it sat
Staring matter of fact
Dementia… Dementia… Dementia

Ruined for Life

One afternoon, Cowboy singled out Carl and drew him aside. "How ya doin', Carl?"

"OK. I was supposed to get an operation today to remove a couple of paper clips and staples, but they said I've already had too many operations. So they want to just wait and see if I pass it."

"Why do you eat that stuff, Carl?"

"I don't know, I just get the urge to swallow

something."

"I see. Well, listen, Carl. You seem like you can be trusted. So I'm gonna level with you. I'm planning on leaving this dump. You interested?"

Carl just looked bewildered as he slowly turned over Cowboy's proposition. Then as if the sun broke free of the clouds, a big smile spread over his pimply pale face and his eyes twinkled. "Yeah! Sure, I'm interested! How ya gonna do it?"

Cowboy had never seen Carl smile before and it added a significant air of enthusiasm to the whole idea.

"All right, hear me out. On weekends there's only two orderlies on duty after eleven o'clock at night. You know this, because they make you sleep in the day room so they can make sure you don't chew up a light bulb or something, right?"

Carl nodded his agreement.

"Well, one is an old white man that looks real spooky to me, real shaky. The other one's a slender black guy. Neither one looks like they'd be much of a problem. If we could get one more person involved, he could fake like he was choking or something. I'd rouse the orderlies. The two of them would open the gate to the wing, and you could follow behind. Once they enter the guy's room, I can take care of the black guy, and you and the other guy could easily handle the old man. We'll tie 'em up with torn bedsheets, gag 'em, take their keys, lock 'em in the room, open the door to the nurse's station, run down the stairs into the exercise yard, climb the fence… and be gone! You game?"

"Hell, yeah! You can count on me!"

Later Carl proved to be no help at all.

That day after supper, this big black lunatic called Jerry lost it and started his own little war. Cursing, he flung plastic chairs at anything that moved.

CODE BLUE! The goon squad exploded on the scene in a determined onslaught. The crazed man fought off wave after wave of swinging batons and flying mace. He slung chairs and turned over tables. But like a grasshopper who landed on a mound of fire ants, eventually he was overpowered by them. The human fire ants pounded the captured orthoptera until he screamed his submission under blow after blow inflicted on his person. The goons dragged Jerry off by his bloody feet.

Cowboy decided then and there the wild black man would be ideal for their cause. Three weeks passed slowly, and Jerry was finally let out of The Hole. Cowboy approached him with the plan.

"Are you game or not?"

"Whatcha want me to do?"

So Cowboy ran it down to him, and he agreed to play.

The plan was to go into effect that weekend. The fateful night arrived and the players were on stage to perform their roles. But when it came time to read their lines, two of them acquired stage fright.

Cowboy tiptoed to Jerry's room and woke him up. "Damn, Jerry! Get up, man! It's time now. Come on, fake like you're choking!"

Jerry looked less than enthused, but began a half-hearted imitation of a man in trouble.

"Come on, man! You're going to have to do better than that! Choke, dammit!"

Jerry wanted to back out of the whole deal.

"Oh, no you don't! We need you! Now you start choking, hear? That's it! Yeah! Now, you're talking, bro!"

Jerry gagged and coughed and would have turned blue if he wasn't already black. Very convincing indeed.

Cowboy answered his cue with perfect timing and raced down the long corridor to the locked gate that separated the day room from the sleeping weirdos curled up in their hospital beds.

"Orderly! Orderly! You've got one choking! Better come see!"

"Get back in your room!" the black orderly demanded.

"But I'm telling you, I think he's dying! You better come quick!"

With that they jumped up and opened the gate, dashing down the hall with their keys rattling and Cowboy close behind. The old man ran straight to the room that emanated choking sounds. He knelt by the man's bed and began to check him over. The young black remained just outside the door, looking on cautiously and regarding the situation with suspicion.

"Look at him!" Cowboy blurted with a grandstand wave of his hand. The black orderly followed the motion towards the accomplices acting out the play before him. Instantly Cowboy reacted with catlike speed, took one step behind the orderly and swept his right arm around his neck. He locked his wrist with the left hand in a cobra hold, a vise grip that stops the flow of blood to the brain and knocks a man out in less than 15 seconds. It can also become a death hold.

"You move, and I'll break your fucking neck!" Cowboy shouted, applying as much pressure as he could while glaring at the fiasco unfolding before his eyes.

Jerry had stopped choking and remained glued to his bed, refusing to play his part. Cowboy stared directly into his fearful eyes, unable to believe the cowardice of this wild man who just weeks ago had taken on the whole Bryce goon squad.

Cowboy turned his eyes from that disgusting scene and looked hopefully down the hall for Carl to take up the slack, only to spot him standing lamely at the gate with obviously no intention of lending a hand.

The old white orderly raced by Cowboy, who was still holding the black man, who had now gone limp. Hope sank to the bottom of Cowboy's stomach and turned over in his guts as he heard the white orderly calling for the night watchman on the next wing.

Not wanting to risk busting the black orderly's head open by letting him just drop to the hard floor, Cowboy gently let him go. But much to his surprise, he found out the orderly had just been playing possum. The black man moved with speed and purpose, as swift as the strike of a diamondback rattler and just as effective. He grabbed his attacker's right wrist with his left hand, and held it with a strength far surpassing his slight appearance.

With his right hand came the blow that would leave its painful thorn embedded forever in Cowboy's most intimate being. Reaching behind him, the orderly grabbed Cowboy by the balls, clamped down, then yanked upward, tossing him over his hip, in a maneuver known as the hip toss. It turned out he held a third degree black belt in Tae Kwon Do, which he'd acquired in Korea.

"Ahhh! You've ruined me! You bastard!" Cowboy screamed, holding his crotch. He was to bear the pain of a torn epididymis in his right testicle for the rest of his life.

Cowboy was unceremoniously thrown into The Hole for several weeks.

Ah yes, The Hole. Complete seclusion. It sucks away your spirit like a black hole in space that draws planets, stars, even whole galaxies down into its dark funnel.

The Hole. A place without the slightest means of comfort. No chair, no bed, no toilet, no window. Just a tiny square that shows nothing but the occasional scornful face. When you need to defecate or urinate, you have to do it in the corner and cover it with newspaper pages apparently left there with that purpose in mind. Your thoughts become so loud you can literally hear yourself think.

In the End

As each day in the mental menagerie unfolded, it revealed displays of human behavior that were both pitiful and entertaining. There was the black guy who enacted a daily drama of prancing around the day room talking to the spirits dancing in his head. After some deliberation he would honor the spirits by raising a toast of urine to his lips and drinking it as if it were fine wine.

Then there was the Vietnam vet who was brain-damaged with shell-shock. He would sit in utter reclusive silence in a corner of the day room. Then suddenly! Up he would jump, mimicking the gunfire and explosions, screaming as if he were still in the steamy jungles fighting the Cong.

Late one night Cowboy woke up needing to relieve himself. He stumbled groggily down the hall to the latrine, expecting just to piss and go back to bed. But what he encountered there was to be forever lodged into his memory.

There... perched atop the white porcelain toilet squatted a naked young white man. With one hand against the wall to steady himself, he was working the other up his rectum. His whole hand was stuck up his ass... and he was pulling his guts out!

Red blood spilled over the white porcelain, splattered on the wall behind him, and mixed with the water in the toilet, turning it crimson. And on his face... THAT LOOK! It was one of determined reconciliation — penance for his sins. Whatever atonement he was digging for, I don't believe he would find it up his ass.

Cowboy just stood there at the door, rooted in shock. The young man didn't even acknowledge his presence, but continued to dig out his swollen intestines, grunting like some wounded animal caught in a hunter's trap and gnawing off his trapped appendage.

Finally Cowboy ran down the hall to get the attention of the dozing orderlies. "Hey! You guys gotta see this! There's a dude in the shitter with this much of his hand stuck up his ass."

The orderlies chuckled, and one of them drawled, "Oh, that's just ol' Gerard. He does that all the time."

"No! You don't understand! He's pulling his insides out! There's blood everywhere!"

With that they jumped up and opened the grilled gate, dashed down the hall, and took poor Gerard to the outside hospital in a straitjacket. He was laughing as they toted him off.

Gerard was a real piece of work. Late one summer night, he woke up and decided to burn down the family home, along with his mother, his father, his brothers and his sisters. Nobody ever knew why. He just walked into the garage and found the gallon gas can used to fill the lawn mower. He opened the cap, spilled it throughout the house, struck a match… and WHOOSH!

"Look at the pretty flames!" Gerard stood outside on the front lawn in his underwear watching the flames leap and listening to the screams of his family pleading for help as the fire burned away their lives. When the fire trucks arrived, he was staring into the flames in a trance… smiling. When asked what happened, he didn't reply. In fact, he never spoke again… ever. He just smiled, as if he knew a secret he wasn't going to tell.

Perhaps Gerard eventually found what he was digging for, but surely he was bitterly disappointed with his discovery… IN THE END.

A shattered mirror dream
A fragile glistening sheen
Bloody rainbows only seen
By the mindless fiend
Dementia… Dementia… Dementia

Bugger Bear

Have you ever had the displeasure of locking horns with someone you find completely repugnant? You turn from the unsavory individual with an air of impertinence, hoping they will get the hint and stay clear. But some people live in a world unto themselves.

"Knock-knock."
"Who's there?"
"Bugger Bear."
"Bugger Bear who?"
"Bugger Bear's gone eat yo breakfast!"

The eroded minds of Bryce gathered every morning for powdered eggs, lumpy grits, burnt toast, milk, butter, and jelly. One crisp red-orange morning over their feast, Cowboy met the Bugger Bear. This huge black man looked like a silverback gorilla and reeked like a skunk. He ignominiously plopped down beside Cowboy, turned his colossal hideous head, and growled, "Gimme yo jelly."

Well, now. Cowboy suddenly found himself in an indignation situation.

"Did you hear me, white boy? I said gimme yo jelly, or I'm fixin' to bust yo face!"

Cowboy continued to eat, ignoring the beast spitting in his ear. Then the gorilla reached his paw out towards the grape jelly on his tray — and Cowboy snapped. Grabbing the animal's hand, his eyes blazed with pure hatred as he whispered between clenched teeth, "Beat it, monkey, before I rip your tail off and hang you with it!"

The black man looked genuinely surprised at Cowboy's sudden aggressive response, but gathered himself quickly and snarled, "After chow, I'm gone beat yo brains out, whiteboy!"

Nice way to start the morning, with a big ugly smelly ape threatening to beat your brains out over a two-inch square of Welch's Grape Jelly. Breakfast ended abruptly and those who had enough sense to dump their trays did. The rest just did the Thorazine Shuffle back to their rooms to wait for their next dose.

Cowboy proceeded carefully along the hall, aware that he was being closely stalked by King Kong. Turning instinctively, he faced the challenge just as the ugly head filled with malice emerged from the dark. Cowboy struck out at it as though it was everything he had ever loathed.

POW! POW! POW! Three heavy blows found their mark before the orderlies broke it up and ran both men promptly to The Hole.

The next day was Thanksgiving, so Cowboy spent the holiday sitting Indian-style in the middle of a bare cell with only his own animosity to keep him company.

Warehouses of insanity
Filled with inhumanity
The ugly… the creepy…
The crawly… underhanded folly
Dementia… Dementia… Dementia

Empty Answers

Eventually all mental patients get the privilege of being examined by the shrink.

"Oh, please sit down, Mister Rolling. Relax, now tell me all about it, will you?"

(I don't think so.)

"Draw me a picture of a woman… hmmm, that's interesting… now draw me a man… OK, now tell me, why are they both crying?"

(Because they're sad, you idiot.)

"OK, then, let's play with some building blocks. Put the round one in the right hole. That's it. Now the square one…"

(What an astonishing revelation! The square one won't fit in the round hole! Damn! Ain't that something!)

"Tell me, Mister Rolling, do you hear voices?"

"Oh, yes."

"Really? Tell me about it."

"You're talking, aren't you, Doc?"

"What do you mean?"

"Well, I hear your voice…"

"Tell you what, Mister Rolling, we're gonna give you a clean bill of health and send you back to jail — unless you cooperate. Do we understand each other?"

"You know something, Doc? You guys are as nutty as your patients. I thought I could find some answers here, but I can see now, the only answers you have are empty ones."

The psychiatrist's eyes were full of years of trying to put together puzzles that wouldn't — couldn't fit. "I'm afraid we don't have time for this, Mister Rolling. You can go now."

So once again the House of the Insane yielded up yet another misfit to the waiting world. Cowboy Rolling was shackled, placed into the white van, and the doors were slammed in his face.

As the van made its way up the long winding driveway now covered with dead brown leaves, the sun peeked out from behind the gray clouds, cast a single beam of blue-white light like a razor drawn across the moody sky, and stabbed Bryce in the heart.

Ghostly dead leaves scatter
On foggy banks gather
Asks the Mad Hatter
"What does it matter?"
Dementia… Dementia… Dementia

Chaingang Livin'

Since Alabama had decided Cowboy Rolling was sane, he went to court and got his time. The judge gave him a break and let it run concurrent with the Georgia time. After sentencing, Georgia extradited him to Reidsville to finish his time there. He did another year and after his sentence was up, Alabama extradited him back to their classification center.

While he was at the Alabama classification center, they had a prisoner exchange, and he was packed up and sent to the St. Clair County Jail, a small 60-man jail up in the hills of Alabama. They made him a trustee, and he ran off after dumping the trash one afternoon. He beat their prize tracking dogs by running figure eights.

He made it out of Alabama, but got caught three days later just outside Natchitoches, Louisiana, the sleepy little town where they filmed Steel Magnolia. They sent him back to the Alabama classification center. He stayed for three months and then was sent to Staten Correctional Facility, where he worked in the fields picking crops and digging ditches for 6 months, then got a job in the kitchen as a baker. Boy, could he ever bake! Sometimes the only thing the fellows looked forward to was Cowboy Rolling's yeast rolls!

Cowboy was transported to Staten at about 3:00 A.M. The prison lights could be seen miles away, surrounded by empty darkness, like a beacon warning careless sailors away.

Staten Pen was not so bad as far as prisons go. Anyone who has done hard time would consider it a Boy Scout camp. Still, it was a prison, and it held its own dangers and distress. You see, you can't paint a pretty picture of cold stone, barbed-wire fences, and guard towers.

When he first got to Staten, he was put on the road-gang, a squad of 39 hardened black convicts. He made the count 40, and he was the only white guy.

Early every morning, except Saturday and Sunday, the men marched miles out into the fields. They dug ditches, planted crops, harvested, and when the sun hung low in the western sky, they marched back to the compound dirty and tired, under the constant eye of a lawman astride a magnificent horse with a shotgun in his saddle and a .357 in his holster.

Marching back down dusty roads in the evening, the cons would say, "Cowboy, sing that song." It never failed. He got so tired of singing it, but he'd sing it anyway.

I remember that a-cold and a-lonely night
Sireens and a-flashin' lights
Well, they took me from underneath the stars
Placed me behind cold stone
And a-steel bars

Chaingang livin'
Of your life you're given
A-many years and a-many tears
Before you see your home again.
Ooooh, I wanna go home.

They loved it.

Cowboy had a good rep as a boxer. They didn't have a boxing ring at Staten. Instead, about 300 or so convicts would make a human circle and throw the two to fight in the midst. The only rule was you had to wear boxing gloves. They had several fights. The dust would fly... and he loved it! He never lost a match.

Eclipse

Cowboy saw his first and only total eclipse of the sun at Staten. He will never forget it. They were at the center of the path of the eclipse. A friend of his had purchased a piece of dark welder's shield that one of the fellows had broken into chips and sold for a dollar a chip.

They stood there on the sandy yard and gazed skyward. Just before the eclipse, time seemed to slow, as if the whole universe stood still. The birds began to act crazy, flying about singing weird songs. They were frightened. As soon as the moon passed in front of the sun, the birds fell on the ground, and there was a dead silence. The sky changed colors, from deep blue to a dark orange. Everything appeared like a double exposure.

Cowboy grabbed the welder's piece of glass from his friend's hand and caught the eclipse at its peak. It was magnificent! As though God had stuck his mighty finger in the spokes of the universe, and everything went still.

Once the sun began to move from behind the moon, the birds began to fly again. The double exposure look came together crystal clear, the sky became blue again, and Cowboy felt small under the face of the Heavens.

The experience left a longing in his already lonely heart.

Rottin' in a smoky jailhouse cell
When I heard a rebel yell
From a man who called himself Cowboy
He had this look in his eye
Like he wanted to die
And he said to me...
Chaingang livin'
Of your life you're given

A-many years and a-many tears
Before you see your home again.
Ooooh, I wanna go home.

No Shit

Boy howdy! I'll be horn-swoggled and hung at sundown!

Cowboy Rolling's earliest role model was James Cagney in Public Enemy No. 1. But his all-time favorite movie is "The Outlaw Josey Wales," starring Clint Eastwood.

Why? Mercy sakes and a bag of rattlesnakes! You've got to be joking! Have you seen it in living color on the big screen? It's got everything any true horse-lovin', gun-slingin', dust-eatin' son-of-a-coyote could possibly want! Indians... Confederate and Union soldiers... smoking cannons... cavalry charges... blazing guns... whiskey and wimmen — and then there's the episodical presence of Clint Eastwood.

He don't take no shit. You spit on his boots, he drills you nice and proper between the peepers. A man of action and few words. Discussing the theory of relativity won't cut the dust down Clint's parched throat. Hell no! A fifth of Redeye wets his whistle and enlightens his mind.

Welcome to the close of the 21st Century. The year 2000 approaches on the dark clouds of forebode. Who knows what it will bring? Perhaps it won't arrive like a Space Odyssey, with mankind reaching for the outer stretches of space to find himself — but rather on the dusty wagon wheels of the Wild West.

I Need a Job

On June 7, 1984, I was released from Alabama prison. Mom and Pop were waiting for me outside the gates and we went back to Shreveport as one big happy family.

My Mom is the best cook in the whole wide world! She was so glad to see me, she would cook me all kinds of goodies. Homemade candies, cookies, cakes, pies and puddings, soups, fried chicken southern style, mashed potatoes with mustard and butter, mulligan stew, chicken and dumplings, shrimp gumbo — the list just goes on and on. I really miss my mom's cooking. Man! I'm getting hungry just thinking about it!

Things went all right at home for a spell, then Dad and I started in on each other as usual — and I left.

I need a job today...
and I ain't going to go away
Until I hear you say...
you're hired.
I'll work till I drop...
ain't never gonna stop
And I don't ever want to hear you say...
you're fired.

I need a job...
I need to work today
So please,don't send me away...
I need a job in a bad way...
Yes I do.

"I gave him a bed and he rented an apartment," said Danny's Aunt Agnes. "I gave him some pieces of furniture and he got a job. He got two or three jobs at different times, but he would visit me. I had a craft shop, and he come and worked for me at odd times when he wouldn't be on his jobs. So I didn't keep up with where he was working or anything like that. All I knew was that his dad did not want him there when he got out of the pen the first time. He said he could not come home. I don't know if James Harold came around and said he could, or whether Claudia insisted that he come home until he could get a job. Well then, James let Danny move in, but sure enough he did move out. I don't know whether he was forced out or what. I do know that after three or four months, Danny began to say things to me and I knew there were problems there with his dad. He knew his dad didn't want him, and he said, 'Auntie, I'm trying to find a job.' He said, 'You know, since I've been incarcerated, people don't want to hire me. They don't trust me.' And I said, 'Maybe a whole lot of that's in your mind,' but he finally moved out anyway, and got an apartment. When he moved out I said, 'Danny, don't move back in, now. Hold onto that.' But he lost his regular job and he couldn't pay his rent. He said as soon as they would find out that he had been incarcerated, they would let him go."

Claudia explained another reason why her son had a hard time holding onto a job. "For one thing he had no transportation. We live in a residential area, so to go to any kind of job, you've got to get out of the neighborhood to do it. There were two cars at our house, but Danny had to walk. There were times when James would let me take him, but very rarely."

Been to so many different places
They all had the same look on their faces
Fill out this application... now
But we don't have any jobs... anyhow
I need a job...
I need to work today
So please don't send me away...
I need a job in a bad way.

Sanctum

I have done so many B&E's I can't remember them all. I can recall breaking into at least three different homes and one apartment to steal money from a purse or wallet while the people were home. I've broken into places for many reasons: sex, thrills, power, need, desperation, or shelter from the storm. Sometimes I did it just for the hell of it.

But the prime element was always the violation of sanctum.

Danny recalls breaking into one woman's home on Christmas Eve, 1989. He didn't know her personally, but he had watched her on several occasions at night. As usual, he and his dad weren't getting along, and he found himself wanting to be any place other than 6314 West Canal. He forced a window with a screwdriver and climbed in.

While inside, he watched TV, listened to the stereo, and sampled the woman's vast collection of booze. He stayed there for hours waiting for her to come home, but she didn't show. He went through her stuff and stole about thirty dollars worth of dimes from a vase, a fifth of Chivas Regal, and the .38 cal. revolver he later used to shoot his dad. He never went back.

Several years prior to that, one night about 3:00 A.M. he wiggled open a window to a home occupied by a man, woman and infant. The woman and child slept at one end of a long hall, while the male rested in the guest bedroom adjacent to the living room.

Danny was looking for money. As the man snored away like a hibernating bear, Danny opened his Buck lockblade knife, crept into the man's room, and lifted his wallet from the pants he had dropped across a chair only a few feet away. Then he slipped down the hall, gently opened the woman's bedroom door, and watched her as she slept. That episode only netted him about $75.00, but he remembers the feeling it gave him. It was one of exhilaration — not unlike the adrenaline high a cop feels during a high-speed chase, or a soldier feels in the heat of battle.

These were not isolated incidents. He has broken

into many places — sometimes just because he wanted to experience the presence of others through the touch, taste, or feel of their belongings.

Once in Daytona Beach, he climbed a tree, inched across a limb to a telephone pole, and climbed it to an open third-story window. After removing some perfume bottles from the window sill, he wormed through the narrow space into a bedroom belonging to one of the three young female coeds living there. Once inside, he eased onto the stairwell and watched two girls below studying on a couch in the den. He lingered for nearly an hour, then left the way he had come — out the window, down the pole, across the limb, and down the tree. He took nothing with him.

Danny had always been The Watcher — on the outside of life looking in — but breaking and entering was how he found himself on the inside.

RAPE!

What does it mean? Power... control... sexual ecstasy... shame... regret... and loss.

POWER! To have complete control over a beautiful woman is every man's secret fantasy. Few will openly admit it, much less cross the line — but it is there.

RAPE! Everybody gets off on hearing about beautiful women getting raped. It's the apex of male sexual fantasy. Just look at the studies taken on that very subject. A hundred college men were polled and asked, "If you could get away with raping a beautiful woman, would you do it?" A surprising amount said "yes."

SEX! You see, to a healthy male a beautiful woman means pure sexual pleasure.

EXPLOSIVE ORGASMS! Reaching deep down into your soul, emptying out the well of lust. Yes, there is a hell of a lot of excitement, in fact it goes way off the scale of 1 to 10.

THE HUNT! The Viking's war cry that pierces the night fog. An adventure as old as the mountains that stand in the distance. Seek... possess... ravage.

EXCITEMENT! Over the top thrills! Battles for the hand of a Lady Fair have been fought for centuries. The victor takes the prize. The violent take it by force.

VIOLENCE! Even in nursery rhymes violence against women is revealed. Man's animal nature still exists — even in fairy tales. Take a look at "Little Red Riding Hood." I mean, if the woodsman with the axe had not come along, what do you think the wolf would have done with Little Red? "My, what sharp teeth you have!" "All the better to EAT you with, my dear! Oooh... GRRRR!"

POWERFUL EMOTIONS RUNNING WILD! As wild as the wolf that howls on a star-studded night. The screams... the sound of tearing clothing... the struggle... the prize... the submission... sweet submission.

But afterwards, what is left? Regrets... shame... loss. When the blood is thumping in your veins, and you are King of the Hill for a moment, the light really shines on you. But once you step down, the darkness closes in around you and you find yourself alone.

RAPE — the fantasy so sweet to taste that sours once the lust is satisfied.

You Don't Have to Do This

Crunching sounds of heavy footfalls made way over the frozen ground of Savannah, Georgia, that crisp November's night in 1984.

There in the shadows, the voyeur sought his window to fantasy, the portal to his dreams. It had always seemed so with him. Night would fall and the gentle voices of the air come calling.

Come out to us, Danneeeee...
Come and seeeee...
Pleasures hidden behind the veil
Of fantasy...

In the distance the searching eye of a beam of light pierced the darkness and drew his mind to the window of a beautiful young blonde. Closing the distance, Danny jumped a couple of picket fences, stealthy not to disturb any sleeping dogs. Now the dark figure stood watching... longing... lusting... only feet away from the damsel.

Lisa was busy cleaning her new home. She and a roommate had just rented the two-bedroom house and moved in the day before. She was alone, her roommate at work on the night shift at the same plant where Lisa worked.

The stranger outside her window observed the young beauty on her knees scrubbing the baseboard along the hallway wall. She had a toothbrush, a rag and a bucket of soapy water to work with.

2:30 A.M.: Lisa had been cleaning for hours, unaware that she was being watched. Finally, she got up off her knees and put away the cleaning materials.

"Good. Now it's showtime," the man in the shadows whispered as he moved from window to window watching.

The blonde entered her bedroom and undressed, oblivious to the Eyes of Lust peering at her through the blinds.

"Yeah, that's it," the peeper groaned as his button-fly 501 jeans became unable to contain the passion swelling within him. When the senses taste forbidden desires, reality becomes intensified.

He fell into a hypnotic trance as he undid the jeans and withdrew his throbbing rod. Then with the magic that brings unreachable worlds into reach, outside became inside. Both environments melted into one dimension, as fantasy came to life. The movie began to turn over in his mind. The focus zoomed in on the gorgeous young blonde as she lifted her t-shirt over her head and let it tumble onto the floor.

"Yeah! Oh yeah... do it, baby."

Then she reached around her back with one hand and unlatched her brassiere. It fell the floor. She examined her breasts in the bedroom mirror. And at the window the stranger examined them too. They were beautiful, shapely, milky-white mounds of womanhood. The Eyes grew more intent.

"Ahhhh!" His dick throbbed in the frigid night air, pulsing with his rapid heartbeat. Lisa peeled out of the little red shorts she wore, freeing her sweet, firm virgin bottom, and she scampered out of the room to take a warm bath. The Eyes followed.

She knelt to adjust the temperature of the water. Then she stepped in, sat down, and washed herself.

The Voices grew louder, reaching for Lisa's world. Danny disappeared in the mist of his tormented thoughts... and a different person surfaced. It was the outlaw, still unnamed, who would one day emerge as Ennad. All his instincts signaled GO!

He quietly tried the back door. It was locked. He moved on to the carport and tried the second doorknob. It turned easily, the door opened slowly, and the movie began to run in slow motion.

The intruder entered the bathing woman's dark kitchen and closed the door gently, locking it behind him. For a moment he stood in the darkness, motionless, listening. The only sounds were the splashing of water emanating from the bathroom.

The Eyes hadn't seen anyone else through the windows, but they searched the dwelling for any unwelcome presence.

Silence... then the droning sound of water draining from the tub. The day's toil swirled down the grated hole, disappearing below where sewer rats gnaw on dead cat carcasses in the dark.

Lisa rose, grabbed a clean towel from the rack, and dried herself off.

He opened the big, sharp lockblade Buck knife. Its chrome finish mirrored the dim light as he waited.

The damsel opened the door and exited with the towel wrapped around her. As she stepped into the hallway, danger greeted her.

"Oh! Ahhhhh! Get away from me!" she screamed, stumbling into the sanctuary of her bedroom.

The masked man pounced on her like a tiger springing from the bush and grabbed her arm with his leather-gloved hand. But she was still wet and she slipped away.

"Do what I tell you and I won't harm you," the intruder commanded, brandishing the menacing knife.

"I'm scared! Oh! Please don't hurt me," she begged, and began to heave salty tears down her reddened face.

Her tears brought a shift in the intruder's mind as one personality struggled with the other, and Danny emerged through the conflicting emotions surging within him.

"OK, OK, lady. Look. Hey, look! See? I'm putting the knife away. Now, you be a good little girl and I won't hurt you." Danny closed the lockblade with a click and safely pocketed it.

During the struggle, Lisa had lost her towel. Naked, shivering and shaking, she stood there with her arms crossed over her breasts. With the threat of stabbing removed, tears of relief soon turned into a cautious curiosity.

"Come over here," he ordered, as again the outlaw personality he later called Ennad took the stage.

Lisa obeyed with a look of utter bewilderment, as if it was just a bad dream and she would soon wake up alone in the safety of her home.

The rapist unbuttoned his 501 jeans and drew out the writhing snake that grew restless between his legs, shaking it at the dumbstruck lass.

"Kiss it! Go ahead, it won't bite. Kiss it!"

Much to his surprise, the naked beauty did just that. She smiled, bent over with her hands clasped together just under her chin, like a child who just discovered her present under the evergreen tree, and gave the swollen head of his sex a quick peck! Then she withdrew and giggled.

Well, now. There was something about the shy, innocent way she acted that caused another shift. Danny cut in on the dance.

"Oh, lady! I'm sorry... I don't know why I'm doing this. I'm gonna let you see my face. And if you wanna call the cops? So be it."

"No! No! I don't want to see!"

Danny removed the mask.

"Oh! Hey... you're good looking. Why would you try to rape somebody?"

"I don't know. I guess I'm lonely."

"Are you hungry?"

"Yeah... I guess so."

"Would you like some breakfast?"

"Sounds good. Tell me, what's your name?

"Lisa." And she put on her robe.

"A pretty name for a pretty girl."

They moved into the kitchen, where she prepared a breakfast of scrambled eggs, pink salmon and orange juice for both of them.

Danny peeled off the thin black gloves and crammed them into the pockets of his Levi jacket. They ate in silence, each aware of the other, each submerged in thought.

"Say," said the pretty girl finally. "I've told you my name. What's yours?"

"Danny... Danny Rolling. Like the Stones. I'm a singer and a songwriter."

"Really? I'm a singer too! Wanna hear me?"

"Sure."

"I've got a cassette around here someplace," she said and bounded out of the room. She dug around in some unpacked boxes in the living room until she found what she sought, then returned with it and proudly placed it on the bar before her unusual visitor.

"It's only a cheap cassette player, but you can tell if it's any good or not."

"Cool! I bet you have a beautiful voice."

"Damn!"

"What's wrong?"

"Nothing, I've just got to rewind it."

She pressed REWIND — whirrrr — PLAY — click — and turned up the volume. The song was "Time in a Bottle," but the voice was clearly Lisa's. Danny listened intently.

"Well? What do you think?" she asked, beaming proudly as the song ended.

"I'm impressed! You are obviously very talented. Tell me something. Does that thing record?"

"Uh-huh, sure does."

"How's about I sing you a song I wrote and you can record it?"

"OK, tell me when you're ready."

"Do it!" She pressed RECORD and Danny sang a capella.

Through misty clouds, gray morning breaks
'Cross callused hands, crusty eyes awake

In dreams, she clings like rosepetal dew
Like some ghost haunting
The cold damp wind blew
And it's a gray way, without you.

A princess, an angel, a devil from hell
With perfume and a gentle touch
She cast the spell
Crystal-blue pools in cameo glare
Transfixed by the moment
And captured by her stare
And it's a gray way, without you.

Didn't I make you my only lady?
And I was your mystical prince
But you wanted to change me
Into a raving beast
So you took away your love,
And put it on a leash
And it's a gray way, without you.

The magic moment passed and the spell was cast.

"Lisa... you wanna try it again?"

"What — what do you mean?"

"You know." He looked deeply into her eyes with the gaze all the world recognizes as the expression of desire.

"Well... you've already seen me naked."

Danny took her by the hand and led her back to the bedroom. Off came her robe, exposing her smooth, supple flesh.

"Oh! I don't know about this —"

"It's OK. It'll be all right. Just relax. I'm not going to hurt you."

"Will anyone be able to tell?"

"What?"

"I've never done this before."

"You're a virgin?"

"Yeah... I am."

That turned Danny on to the MAX! He ignored her protests and laid her on the bed.

"No! Don't! I don't feel right about this."

Danny grabbed both of her dainty ankles and spread her legs wide. The moment of surrender had arrived. His blood burned for her as his swollen cock assaulted Lisa's virginity. A little force... and POP! Ahhhh... her cherry burst, opening the gate to wet, hot pleasure.

"Don't cum in me — I don't want to get pregnant."

"Ooooooh... ahhhhh... uh... OK. I'll pull out before I do."

"Promise?"

"Yeah, I promise," he soothed, as he fondled one pointed breast and took the nipple of the other into his thirsty mouth.

She moaned as he stroked her with his pulsing shaft. They moved in unison to the beat of the symphony their bodies created. The pleasure of trembling flesh!

"Ahhh... ahhh... AHHHH!" Danny went rigid and came powerfully in Lisa's blood-wet pussy.

"You promised!" She slapped Danny on the shoulder twice.

"I'm sorry. I couldn't help it. You're just so hot and sweet. I had to go all the way, baby."

Lisa got up quickly, cleaned up, and dressed for work. It was time to bring the evening to a close.

"Do you need a ride someplace?"

"Well... you could take me home."

Danny gave her directions as they got in her gray-blue sportscar. The sun came up to begin the day as they arrived.

"Come on in for a while."

"No, I can't. I'm late for work already."

"Ah, come on, I'll make you a cup of coffee."

"No, I really can't. I'm sorry."

"Will I see you again?"

"Well... you know where I live."

Danny got out of the car and watched the pretty girl back out of the driveway and speed away. She never looked back.

Paranoid that she would go to the cops, the rapist left a hurried note to his landlord and booked out of town like Satan himself was hot on his soul.

Dead Man's Hand

Danny was a drifter, but he was not a hobo. There's a difference. A hobo is just a tramp, one of the dirty people who live by railroad tracks or in abandoned land fills. They have little or no ambition. You can see it in their eyes. They gave up on life or the pursuit of happiness ages ago. Hobos are like winos. They move slow and the life ran out of them long before the sun came up this morning.

A drifter is driven, like the wind. You hear the sound it makes, then as suddenly as it comes... it's gone. A drifter can't stay put in one place long enough to set roots, because something keeps tugging at him, pulling him over the next hill into the next town or city. Like a tumbleweed, when the wind blows, a drifter's gotta go!

So much of my life has been tortured and confused, blurred by drugs and driven by the winds of fate. How difficult it is to put a face on the wind. It blows where it will. You know where it has been, but where does it go?

January 15, 1985. Danny traveled to Camarillo, California, to visit his uncle Joe Rolling, his aunt Mira Rolling, and his cousin Donald Rolling.

I hitchhiked all over the place for about six months, maybe seven. I visited my Aunt Nadine and Uncle Eric outside Tallahassee, Florida, then went on down to Key West, where I stayed in an abandoned 3-story house by the Gulf. From Key West to Daytona, then I snagged a ride from Daytona all the way to L.A. That's when I took up with my Aunt Mira and Uncle Joe.

Joe Rolling had never had much to do with his brother James or his family, and wants nothing to do with his notorious nephew now.

Danny's cousin Donald attributed his own lack of closeness to his infamous cousin to an age difference, and laconically characterized him as "a loner with a drinking problem."

The way Mira Rolling recalled it, one day Danny just showed up without notice, calling her from the bus station and asking if he could stay with them for awhile. She agreed. He did stay about three months, and then abruptly left, saying that he missed his daughter and wanted to go back to Shreveport to see her.

Mira told investigators she was angered by the suddenness and the lack of a real reason for leaving. And then there was the money Danny owed her. She had loaned him $800 to buy a motorcycle.

It was a candy-apple red Suzuki 380 GT Cafe Racer. Danny crashed it during his lunch break while employed with Silverado Builders. The entire crew witnessed the accident. He took the bike for a quick spin around the block. Speeding down the street in front of the construction site, he went through first,

second, and third gears, but before he could shift into fourth, he rushed up on the tight curve at the end of the block.

There was fine white sand blown across the surface of the road, and when Danny saw that sand, he knew he was in trouble, because by now he was going 50 plus m.p.h. No way to negotiate a tight curve at that speed. No time to power down.

So the bike slid out from under him, but he hung on and managed to bulldog the handlebars, aiming the front tire towards the approaching curb. That move probably saved his life, because just before the front tire struck the curb, it gripped clean road and the bike righted itself, T-boning the curb, flipping end over end, and catapulting Danny some 30 feet through the air, barely missing a newly-planted tree, and plowing face-first into a soft mound of dirt.

Danny was treated for a concussion at the hospital and suffered nerve damage to his neck, but due to the sandy ground, damage to the bike was fairly minor. The handlebars, the brake pedal and the clutch lever were bent, and one turn light was busted out. All this was easily repaired, except for the busted fairing, which Danny just removed.

He drove the bike around for several weeks after the crash, then sold it to a Navy man for $500. He gave his Aunt Mira $400, but left without repaying the rest of the loan.

I've had five iron horses in my life. Prior to owning the Suzuki, I had owned a Honda 350, a BSA 650 White Lightning, a 850 Norton Commando, and a Harley Davidson XL 1000.

I love the freedom a motorcycle brings. The wind in your hair, the sun shining on the road, ahhhh, yeah... freedom! Put it in the wind, baby! But I didn't get into clubs or wear patches or piss on my leather jacket. I always have been a lone wolf. The only bikers I've known have been in prisons across the South.

I hitched a ride from Camarillo to Boulder, Colorado and stayed there for about two weeks, then rambled on down the road. I got a ride with a blind man and his chick. They were going to Deadwood, South Dakota. I stayed up in the Black Hills for about two weeks and almost froze my ass off.

Did you know they still have Wild Bill Hickock's pistol and gunbelt draped across the chair he was sitting in and the famous hand he was playing (the dead-man's hand, aces and eights) encased in a glass airtight showcase over the door to the saloon where he was shot dead? Yep! I was there. They still have a sawdust floor in the place.

As Danny was hitchhiking through Jackson, Mississippi, the man he was riding with was pulled over by police and arrested for D.U.I. He had a .45 semiautomatic handgun. After the man was arrested, Danny took the car to the police station, but he kept the gun.

He asked me to take care of it for him, so I did — from his glove-box into my backpack. I continued on to Columbus, Georgia, where I stayed with my Aunt Dot and her family for about a month, maybe two. Things didn't work out there either... so I split.

"Welcome, stranger, to the Silver Dollar Bar.
What's your pleasure?" asked the tender
with the big cigar.
Give me a whiskey, cause I'm a-feelin' a little risky.
And if that tin star's in town, tell 'em I'm around.
Mystery rider... nobody knows your name.
Gunfighter... who plays a deadly game.
Mystery rider... a rebel no one can tame.
Plains drifter... on the road to fame.

I'm the One

July 22, 1986. Shortly after dark, Danny Rolling entered a Kroger next to I-10 in Clinton, Mississippi to case the joint, then left the store and ducked into a dark alley beside a liquor store at the far end of the shopping center. Around 10:00 p.m. he donned a ski mask and gloves, and brandishing a pistol, busted into the Kroger through the cartport. He was a man on a mission, and the mission was, "This is a holdup! Nobody move!" He got what he came for.

Taking everything in the register, he exited as he entered, and melted into the night with $290. Clinton Detective Jerry Blankenship stated that police trailed him to a stand of woods across the interstate, then lost his trail.

Sleeping in the woods for a few hours, after midnight he awoke and went on the prowl. He found a house with a broken-out pane in the kitchen back door. The entire family was home at the time. He watched them until they went to sleep around 2:00 A.M. before letting himself in.

Taking his cue from a set of car keys he found on the kitchen table by the back door, he stole the baby-blue LTD Ford and drove off.

At 9:00 p.m. the next night, lost and driving the stolen car erratically in a residential neighborhood, Danny was arrested. When apprehended by officers John Lee Hust and Robert Watras, he got out of the stolen car and walked over to the cruiser. They asked him a few questions. He didn't have the right answers. He knew where it was going, so he fessed up. "Look, I'm the one that did it," he said. "I'll tell you what you want to know."

They searched the stolen Ford and found the gloves. Danny took the officers to his campsite, and along the way he critiqued Hust's novice police work, advising him that he'd made a dangerous procedural error. He should be more careful, the robber told the cop. In retrospect, Hust had to admit that the observations of the policeman's son had been well-founded.

At the campsite they found the Colt .45 used in the robbery, along with Danny's backpack, pup tent, and a small bag of pot.

On March 20, 1986 Danny plead guilty to the Kroger robbery in Clinton, Mississippi. He was imprisoned for a 4-year sentence, of which he served 3 years with good behavior, starting in Jackson County Jail.

At one point, he shaved off all his hair, including his eyebrows. Attorney Arthur Carlisle said, "When they brought him out, I didn't recognize him. He looked like one of those war prisoners. I asked him why he did it, and he said he wanted to change, that he was cleaning up."

Carlisle visited him often, bringing him Snickers bars. Danny offered to let the state cut off his arms instead of going to prison. Said Carlisle, "He was as serious as a heart attack."

I did cry out for help. No one took the time to listen. Even when I shaved my head, eyebrows, and facial hair and beat my forehead against the concrete wall until I busted it open, all I got was a swift kick in the ass from a big ugly deputy sheriff. He was upset because I bloodied his newly-painted cell wall. Later, another cop came to check on me. I asked him for a cigarette. He gave me one and said, "Know what? You're gonna end up killing someone one day." What he said troubled me, and I asked, "Yeah? You really think so?" But he just shook his head and walked away. Whatever that cop saw in my eyes, I couldn't see for myself. It would be years before the pools of blood were spilled that proved that cop right.

Said Blankenship, "He was kind of weird. I thought at the time he might have some kind of mental impairment."

Claudia took her sisters Agnes and Artie Mae along to visit her son in Mississippi. "He had gotten very thin and he didn't look good at all, but that was due to stress, I'm sure, because when Danny gets under a lot of stress it's hard for him to eat. But we visited him more than once in Mississippi, and the second time we went he looked so much better, he had gained a lot of weight. It seemed that he was doing real good in that area. He had learned to cope with whatever went on."

CHAPTER 5
A REAL KILLER

Running from the Gun

April 15, 1986. Danny escaped the Jackson County Jail by simply walking off and swimming the Snake River, surprising two fishermen casting their Zebco rods into the slow-moving river that flowed through Jackson, Mississippi.

"Look at that!" one of the men shouted, pointing his finger at the swimmer. "Hey! Are you nuts? There's snakes as big as your arm in there!"

Danny didn't stop to answer. He fought his way through the tangled, murky water, climbed the opposite bank, and disappeared into the swamp beyond.

Run, Danny, run
From the Lawman's gun

That night he heard the lonely wail of a train off in the distance. He found the tracks just as the locomotive thundered around the bend. He ran with all his might, reached up, grabbed the swing-bar, and hoisted himself between the boxcars.

The big Santa Fe train swayed, bucked and rumbled through the night. Like an angry volcano erupting on wheels of steel, it screeched and groaned its way down endless miles of pounded rail.

Moan, train, moan
Dragon of the twilight
Cast your shadow
By shimmering moonlight
Groan, train, groan

Two days later, Danny found himself walking down Interstate 20, the highway that shot straight through the heart of the parched brown Texas desert. Wandering again, he stuck out his thumb, reaching for a ride.

Off in the distance, boiling black clouds crept over the hills displaying heavenly pyrotechnics. What a light show! Few wonders can compete with the explosive power of a good thunder-booming electrical storm. Although the show was grand, he hoped someone would give him a ride before the bottom fell out of the sky.

Who knows what was going through the wanderer's mind? Hell, he didn't understand it himself. He was running again, just as he had been running from something or other all his life. He hated what he had become, but his fate just kept pushing him deeper into its threatening storms. The dark clouds grew ever larger, ever more demanding.

Moan, train, moan
And if some poor soul
Should fall into your path
Woe be the misery
Of your cruising wrath
Groan, train, groan

Smack Dab Into It

Finally an old bearded man in a green Ford camper-truck pulled over. He opened the passenger side door and they exchanged greetings common with hitchhikers and their rides.

"Where you headed?"

"Wherever."

"It's about to rain pitchforks and nigger babies… get in."

Danny did, and slammed the old rusty door behind him.

"Thanks, old man."

"Old man? Let me tell you something, boy. I can still out-drink, out-fuck, and out-fight a bar-full of whippersnappers like you any day of the week," the old-timer declared with a certain air, then grinned real big, showing off his coffee-stained teeth.

The wanderer took a closer look at this wonder and decided he probably could. The old man had long snow-white hair and a full white beard. He was tall and lean, his muscles still sinewy from hard work. His steel gray eyes peered out from under the brim of a dusty black Stetson.

"OK, pops, don't get your bowels in an uproar. So… what do I call you?"

"Just call me Tall Hat, everybody else does. And you?"

"Danny's my name. Say, where we going?"

"El Paso."

There was a moment of silence as the beat-up green camper plunged into a wall of precipitation dumped out on the road with a vengeance. It became dark as night and lightning struck everywhere at once on either side of the road.

"Looks bad. We better pull over for a spell," said Tall Hat, easing the green monster over to the shoulder of the road. He reached into a brown grocery sack sitting between the two. Shuffling the contents around some, he produced a clear baggie filled with trail mix. "You hungry, boy?" He offered the baggie with sincere concern for his new passenger.

"Thanks, old-timer."

Crack-POW! A bolt of blue-white death blasted the earth no more than twenty yards from the parked odd couple.

"Damn!" the wanderer spurted out, spewing the mulch of fruits and nuts in his mouth throughout the cab. "That was close enough to scorch the quills off a porcupine's ass!"

"Boy, you act like you never seen an honest-to-God Texas thunderstorm before," drawled Tall Hat, and with that he began to unfold his life's story.

"Now, when I was your age, that was before all this-here Texas was civilized. I remember the time… let me see… hmm… 1920, I believe it was. Folks didn't get around these parts in no mechanical contraptions. Nope. We had horse-&-buggies in those days. Nowadays folks don't give a mule's fart whether you're coming or going." He studied his passenger with knowing eyes cast under the shadow of his Stetson. "Take you for instance. You're running from something. You got law trouble?"

The wanderer suddenly got real uncomfortable. "How can you tell?"

"It's in your eyes. Restless, they are. You been running from something all your life. And if you don't find a place to take root, one day, you're gonna run right smack dab into whatever it is you're running from."

Spoken like a true prophet, Danny thought, fascinated with this old man who seemed to know everything about him. He looked out the window, not wanting to hear what he already half-believed himself.

"It don't matter to me none. I've had my run-ins with the law, but I learned from my mistakes. They hanged my oldest brother Russ for stealing cattle back in 1901. And my youngest brother Lucas was killed in a Texas knife fight over an Indian squaw in a bar in El Paso. I'm the only one of the Wilcocks left breathin'."

"Does your radio work?"

"Yep, but all it plays is country."

"That's fine with me, pops." Anything to shut him up, I've got enough on my mind, he thought as he turned on the music.

"Like I said," continued Tall Hat over the music, "I had a run-in with the law myself. Did six months in the Waco County Jail for running moonshine," he grinned.

The storm finally blew over and once again they were on their way. Danny fell asleep listening to tales of cattle rustling and gunfights in the streets of El Paso mixed with country music.

Next thing he knew, they were at a truck stop ten miles from El Paso.

"Gotta let you out here, boy. My ranch is up the road a piece, and mama don't take to no strangers. Good luck, and remember what I said: stop running!" And with that, Tall Hat drove off in a cloud of red dust.

Danny never saw him again, but his prophetic words would haunt him for the rest of his life.

The Witching Hour

The truck stop was out in the middle of the desert and the sun had gone down. During the day, the desert can bake a man to death in a few hours. But when that ball of red fire takes its leave, the desert goes through a metamorphosis.

From burning flame… with no shame
To icy cold… and windy bold
All night long… fair or foul
The lonely wind howls

So here he was, an escaped prisoner with no money on the run from Mississippi, at a truck stop a mile from the Mexican border. State troopers everywhere. Not a good sign.

The wind blew shivers through Danny's light-gray jean jacket. For miles there was nothing but the darkened desert. The only thing he could do was spend the night out there in no-man's-land.

In the gathering gloom …
the grinning full moon
Up in the windy sky…
looked down with a cold eye

Danny stuffed his hands into the pockets of his jeans and went looking for shelter. But it was like looking for shelter on the moon. For hours, he kept moving just to keep from freezing to death.

"This is insane!" he said to himself. "What the hell am I doing out in the middle of nowhere at" — he stopped and looked at his watch — "midnight! Damn! The witching hour!"

Suddenly, off in the distance, he beheld a strange sight — a flickering light. He was drawn to it, moth-to-flame. He could hear the old-timer's voice saying, "One day, you're gonna run right smack dab into it," but he was not about to stop running. Not yet. The voices were still singing the same old song.

Run, Danny, run
Till your running's done

Deeper Into the Night

The light turned out to be a small campfire tended by a humble illegal Mexican immigrant. He jumped up, yanked from his thoughts by the intruder that stumbled upon his modest camp.

Danny held up his hands and said, "Friend!" He drew up by the fire, and the two men just stood there staring at each other, each one not knowing what to make of the other, as the desert wind howled around them. To break the ice, the wanderer took out the baggie of trail mix and offered it to his companion. The silent Hispanic man with eyes that held no light hesitated at first, but took the gift and nodded in appreciation.

The wanderer stood next to him, warming himself by the fire which was soon dwindling in the breeze. Once it no longer gave its warmth, the night closed in to bite at the two standing there silent in the dark.

Suddenly the Mexican started running around haphazardly. His actions seemed like those of a deranged lunatic, but then the wanderer realized the Mexican was gathering something out there. What was it?

The Mexican scampered back to the campsite in the sand and tossed a couple of dried tumbleweeds onto the dying embers, got down on his knees, took off his cowboy hat, and fanned the glowing weeds. They leaped at his command and soon became a brilliant flame.

The wanderer started salvaging the precious fruit of the night that gave purpose to the two beings there. After enough fuel was gathered for several minutes of fire, the wanderer spoke.

"What's your name, hombre?"

"No spick ingles."

"Danny," he said, pointing at himself. "My name is Danny."

"Ahhh, Danny! Desert Rat," he proclaimed, pointing at himself and smiling to reveal his broken and rotting teeth. "Me llamo Desert Rat."

Neither one could express himself in the other's language, but there was really no need. They trusted each other enough to stand by the same fire, and for the moment, that was enough.

The wanderer produced a Hohner harmonica he had bought with the last of his cash in Dallas. To the astonishment of Desert Rat, he began to play. In between bars of harmonics that filled the star-sparked night with eerie melodic tones, the wanderer sang a few stanzas of a song he called "Mystery Rider."

Jinglin' spurs, rollin' into town.
Ridin' the dust after the sun goes down.
Black stallion, you bring a grim reaper.
Dressed in snakehide, woe, and black leather.
Mystery rider... what's your game?
You're a rebel ... no one can tame.

After the last notes of the song died out, Desert Rat bounded over to Danny with a wild expression on his face. He took him by the hand and pulled him away from the now-dying tumbleweed fire that hissed into the desolate night.

Danny was apprehensive as to what this short, dirty peasant had in mind. Whatever it was, he wanted him to follow. And so the two made their way deeper into the black desert night.

They came upon a ravine with jagged pieces of metal sticking up from its bed, along with all kinds of junk and barbed wire strung everywhere. Desert Rat pointed beyond the debris and said, "Mexico!" He crawled through and motioned for the wanderer to do the same. Danny shrugged and accepted the invitation.

No One's Friend

So now they were in Mexico. Soon they came upon a ranch house with a Mexican family sitting in chairs by a large wood fire.

The señorita sat quietly suckling her child wrapped in a blanket. The husband stood up and grabbed a rifle leaning against a nearby woodpile .

Desert Rat said something in Spanish and the surprised man put down the rifle, but remained standing. Desert Rat exchanged a few words with him. Apparently they knew each other.

The young woman just sat silently studying the strange white man the night had brought. The child continued to suck his mother's breast, wide-eyed gazing at the twinkling stars of the Milky Way.

Desert Rat approached the wanderer and said something, but Danny couldn't understand. He shrugged his shoulders and shook his head. "No speak Spanish."

Desert Rat looked at him curiously, then made like he was playing the harmonica, pointed at Danny, then at the family sitting by the popping fire.

"Oh! You want me to play! Sure!"

The wanderer drew his musical sword, walked over close to the fire, and began to wail slices out of the diamond-studded sky. Mercy, how that boy could make his blues harp cry! The wood fire danced, its wiggling fingers reaching for the stars that blushed and winked back at the souls gathered there.

He played "Dixie" and "Sweet Chariot" and "Silent Night." The sweet sounds reached far into the desert night, falling upon the ears of a stray coyote and a small community of prairie dogs beyond the scope of the fire.

The child fell asleep and his mother put away her tit and excused herself. Her husband followed her up to the house, but soon returned with three warm Mexican beers that spewed foam when they popped the tabs. The three men sat there in silence until the beers were gone.

The husband got up first, said something to Desert Rat and left. Danny sensed the end of the visit and got up to leave as well. Desert Rat stepped in front of him and spoke softly looking directly into the wanderer's eyes. Danny knew he was wishing him well, and he smiled his thanks.

So he wandered off into the desert alone to spend the rest of the night chasing tumbleweeds and fighting off the cold wind that was a friend to no one — except the scorpion, the coyote, and the sand that cooled under its breath.

The desert sun has a way of just appearing. One minute the moon shyly surrenders its light behind the earth's mantle. The next, the red sun blasts over the dunes like a flame-thrower. And the man behind the trigger has blood in his eye.

All night long, the wanderer had been too cold to sleep, and now the sun blistered his skin and parched his throat. He had to find shade. He crawled under a leafless bush and drifted off to sleep, thinking he must have invaded a sidewinder's home.

The Road to Nowhere

At midday, he awoke. It was time to be on his way. Climbing from the dunes, a pasture stretched out before him. Two beautiful women on horseback galloped past him smiling, their long hair bouncing about their shoulders.

How Danny longed to ride with them! Free of trouble — free in mind, body and spirit, in touch with nature — but he had other matters to attend. Like survival. Food and water.

He came upon a new baby-blue Chevy pickup truck parked in front of a small stable. He looked inside and saw two purses. Hmmm, he thought. These must belong to the ladies on horseback that passed me down the road.

The wanderer grabbed a softball-sized rock and flung it at the driver's-side window. SMACK! It bounced clean off. What? He inspected its surface. Not a scratch. Must be impact-resistant.

OK, Bucko, he said with the desperation only a thirsty man on the run knows. Looking by the creek that ran under the dirt road, he found what he was looking for: a rock the size of a football. Yeah! This oughta do the trick! He took a running lunge and... BOINK! It jumped right back in his face. Damn! Must be bulletproof too!

Well, what's a poor boy to do? He picked up a softball-sized rock and climbed into the back of the truck. He gave the rear window a whack and... SMASH! It shattered into millions of little glass crystals.

He searched the contents of the purses for cash. Wouldn't you know it? Credit cards. "Story of my life," he muttered to himself, disgusted.

Someone came running from the stables shouting Spanish obscenities and brandishing a pistol. Wham-bam-thank-you-ma'm, I'm outta here! And off ran the wanderer, down that long, lonesome road that leads to nowhere.

Three Strikes

Out on a windy, lonely, lonely street,
Two slingin' .44's, they finally meet.
Mystery rider... what's your name?
You're a killer... a drifter gone insane.

Two days later Danny was asleep under the shadow of an overpass, when two state troopers sped past.

"Think we should check him out?"

"If he's still there after we make the turnaround, we'll pick him up on our way back."

"Yeah, it doesn't look like he's going anywhere."

Next thing he knew there were two pistol-packin' state troopers towering over him asking for his I.D.

"But officer, three Mexicans in a white Ford station-wagon robbed me last night at the bus stop in El Paso, and that's why I'm hitchhiking. I've got to get out to Los Angeles by yesterday to help my aunt. She fell and broke her hip..."

The two officers laughed. "Sounds like the best damn story I ever heard. Whatcha think, Dick?"

"Yeah, right. Now how's about that I.D.?"

"I told you, officer, I got robbed last night. They took my wallet with all my I.D., credit cards and all."

"Well, we're gonna hafta take you in to run a check."

Danny could see where all this was leading, so he just spilled it right then and there. "OK, officers. I'm gonna make it easy on ya. My name's Danny Rolling, and I'm an escaped prisoner from Mississippi."

WHOOOAH! They took three steps back and looked at each other in disbelief. They turned to the man they had just questioned with different intent in their eyes.

"Don't bullshit us, boy."

"I'm not lying."

"Turn around and put your hands behind your back."

Danny felt the all-too-familiar slap of cold polished steel clamp down around his wrists.

The troopers led their prisoner to the cruiser and carefully deposited him in the cramped and narrow back seat. The distance between the overpass and the county jail was covered in minutes. They had caught a big fish this time, and that would mean a pat on the

back, maybe even a promotion.

"Hmmm… Danny Harold Rolling," intoned the booking sergeant. "Escaped from Jackson County Jail six days ago. Incarcerated for armed robbery, burglary of an occupied dwelling, auto theft…" He studied the fish flopping on the floor in front of him. Yeah, being arrested is exactly like being a fish out of water. And they do love to watch you squirm.

"Oh, but there's more goodies here. Did time in Alabama for armed robbery… escaped from there too… did a stretch in Georgia for armed robbery… another escape…" He shook his head. "Well, boy, that's it — three strikes and you're out. Good work, Officer Bradley. This is gonna look good on your record, come promotion time."

And so Danny's wandering days were put on hold, but only momentarily.

Texas Tank

Overflowing with violence and treachery, the El Paso County Jail was no place for a gringo. Towering over the surrounding buildings like Godzilla over Japan, it was filled with the Mexican wetbacks that sought their fortunes by braving the polluted Rio Grande, and a dangerous lot of criminals they were.

Danny Rolling was once again a prisoner. He found himself in a pod with 20 Chicanos. One bitter young man with jet black hair and dark hateful eyes was in for stabbing his own father to death over a bottle of tequila. He spent his time running from one wall to the next, kicking out at the walls with all his might.

The head honcho was a Mexican Indian called Flaco because he was tall and lean. He had tattoos covering 90% of his body. His face, etched with Aztec designs, never showed any expression. The inked patterns seemed chiseled into cold stone. He rarely spoke, but when he did, all the Chicanos listened.

Every day Flaco would sit at his table drawing ancient Aztec Indian art. One day the prisoner sat down and drew a portrait of him at work on one of his creations. After an afternoon of working silently, he handed it to the Indian. Flaco was a difficult man to read. Still, he appeared taken by the prisoner's gift of the portrait, and for the first time, the Indian spoke to him, blessedly in English.

Flaco told the prisoner that his father was a direct descendent of the original Aztec Indians, and his mother was a blonde-haired blue-eyed American, which accounted for his pale blue eyes that never seemed to blink.

The next morning there was a face-off. The crazy kid who stabbed his father, the fat slob who brushed his teeth constantly, and four other Chicanos encircled the prisoner. "Gringo! Hey, gringo! We no like gringos here. We kill," said the crazy kid, brandishing a knife with murder in his eyes.

The prisoner jumped up and backed into a corner. "Let's see," he observed. "1-2-3-4-5-6 — and one of 'em with a shank. Not good." It looked like curtains for sure. Suddenly Flaco yelled something in Spanish and the mob backed off. Whew-WEE! We're talking a mighty close call, y'all!

The prisoner thanked the Indian, who didn't bother to acknowledge his thanks, and after that there were no more problems.

Finally the dreaded day came. The marshals showed up to extradite their prisoner back to Mississippi. They shackled him hand and foot and threw him into a van along with twenty other prisoners. The van was only supposed to carry eleven, and there was no ventilation.

Prisoners were picked up and dropped off at every hell-hole this side of the Pecos. When they got to Waco, they dropped off their human cargo at the Waco County Jail while they made a side trip to go get a prisoner somewhere up north.

For those of you who haven't had the pleasure of Waco's finest hospitality, let it be known the accommodations are less than a dog kennel. The nights are cold, the days hot as hell, and the food smells like swill.

For five days, they slept on the cold bare concrete floor without mattresses, pillows, or blankets.

There on the inhospitable floor, unable to sleep, the prisoner listened to the wind howling across the desert like a bonafide demon seeking a soul to possess.

Once again he could hear Tall Hat's gravely voice, "One day you'll run right smack dab into whatever it is you're running from." Words of wisdom are never sweet when you have to eat them with your own bitter broken luck. He fell asleep with the emptiness of the desert wind vacating his heart.

The next day the marshals came back for the prisoners. They were road-weary and in no mood to be pleasant. "Awright, girls, we don't want no bullshit on this run. If you gotta piss, better do it now. Cause we ain't stopping for shit till we get to where we're going."

And so it was. Eight straight hours of highway passed by while their bladders were screaming. One by one, the men were dropped off. Finally it was the prisoner's turn.

Home of the Slaves

May 4, 1986. Mississippi Delta land stretched out in all directions — its major crop: KING COTTON. As far as the eye could see, rows and rows of puffy white cotton and brown soybeans. And in the middle of it all loomed Parchman Prison, the largest penitentiary in the world, standing like a giant tombstone reading "Home of the Slaves."

It was a blistering hot summer day when the prisoner arrived at its gates. The marshals dumped him off with a nice little farewell. "Hey, Cowboy, enjoy yourself now, ya hear? Hope ya like pickin' cotton and diggin' shit ditches! Cause that's what you're gonna be doin' for a long month of Sundays." And they sped off laughing like it was some kind of hilarious private joke they never grew tired of repeating. They really cracked up over their punch line: "a long month of Sundays." Yeah, sure. Ha! ha!

The prisoner didn't even get a trial. The first thing they did was bring him before an internal kangaroo court and give him a choice: eight more years added to his sentence or solitary confinement for 240 days.

The Only Voice

The light of life once danced in your eyes. The hopes and dreams of all that seemed good and beautiful became your soul. Then one dreadful day, the hand of fate lay heavy on you. Naked, stripped of pride and dignity, you were bound and cast into solitary confinement.

SOLITARY: A state of being alone. Lonely. Not much frequented. Single. Sole.

CONFINEMENT: Imprisonment. Seclusion.

So you see what you get when you combine these two words. You get nothing — nothing at all.

You can't imagine the effects until you have experienced total absence of the visual and physical stimuli our brains need to function properly. Solitary confinement is a subtle beast that feeds on your thought process, exhausting and consuming the very essence of your inner self.

Take away the sun that burns by day, hide the moon that shines by night. Remove the green of wind-ruffled fields, and replace all that you see under the blue heavens with miserable, colorless, lifeless walls of stone. And there you sit — ALONE.

You learn to cheat at solitary. You talk to yourself, you stare at a blank wall for hours... and hours... and hours... until you can't see it any more.

As you take a journey down the long corridor to the basement of your own soul, along the way are pitfalls, and you inevitably stumble into them as you descend to great depths. There at the bottom of all things, you cry out for deliverance — but in solitude, 'tis your own voice you hear.

A face painted bland tan appears beyond the bars of iron. Friendly! Or is it one of scorn? 'Tis at least a face, a reflection of your own humanity staring back at you. (Animal in a cage!)

Face, what is that in your hand? Is it a morsel of bread? A bit of porridge perhaps to feed the beast?

"Ah thank you, kind sir." And in silence the creature gratefully consumes the substance placed before him, to keep his sorrows still.

Oh, the sound of heavy chains clanking and rattling day and night — it draws your heart away, bruising your soul. There in the tiny closed box, your heart is filled with nothing and your mind is filled with rocks. And with each beat of your empty heart, with each cry for relief, the only voice that answers is your own.

So it was with Danny Rolling, the prisoner of extremes. Solitary... blasted nothingness! It's a foe without substance. To fight against it is to battle with yourself. You lose every time.

One can strike at the face of adversity, but the silhouette of solitary confinement is composed of solid stone, unmovable and unforgiving. Little by little it draws the precious essence from the captured misfortunate found in its dull embrace.

When denied diversity and starved of creativity, need gives way to release, and the mind folds within itself. Dreams become reality and reality becomes dreams.

The Hot Box

The prisoner's home for the first four months was called the "hot box," because it was a closed cube literally designed to simmer a man in his own juices. No air ventilated it. While he was enjoying his new surroundings, his mother and her two sisters came to visit him. They were even given the opportunity to visit his cell block and step into his cell. What should have been a treat for his concerned family turned out more like a nightmare.

"Oh my..." said one aunt to the other. "This is just... awful!" His mother fanned her face and asked him, "Son, how do you get any air in here?"

"You don't."

Two weeks after the visit, he was moved to an obscure compound way off by itself, miles away from the first one. Ninety days passed, with nothing to occupy the prisoner's mind except watching the blackbirds that flocked outside his window.

During his stay in the hot box, the guards beat a prisoner so bad he almost died. Blood was everywhere, but they just kept on beating and beating and beating the man while his screams shattered the silence.

Notes from the Hole

I'm going to try and write a little, but my insides are so knotted up it's a wonder I can think at all. They've stripped me of my privileges and stuck me in solitary confinement. The empty nothingness grips my thoughts like a concrete vise. Perhaps the strength of my soul will return. But for now, I die daily... a little bit at a time... by inches and degrees.

I won't be allowed outside any more and I will quickly lose my healthy look. After a few weeks of being cooped up like this, I will begin to appear pale and drawn. Over the days ahead, either I will become resigned to this drudgery or it will get the best of me. Whichever way it goes, the battle for my sanity has begun. Will I fall down the deep dark shaft of despair? I pray not.

I breathe... but there is no joy. I close my eyes... but there is no peace. I pray... but there is no answer. I am as lonely as I have ever been in my whole life.

Tomorrow will be the same as today, and on and on — bitter, harsh emptiness. Oh surely the grave is better than this?

On this wing there is little air. And what there is of it ain't even close to fresh. There are moments when I can hardly breathe. There's no way to heat water. So I must drink my coffee cold. No music, no nothing.

There is so much wrong with my life right now. I think they are pressuring me to end it in some way. I am so very tired of all this. I do want to put an end to the misery. I can't go on and on like this. Everyone needs a reason to be.

Yesterday evening I walked the long hall to the very end of the line in a daze. I didn't even realize the shackles around my ankles cut into my flesh.

If I am to be forgiven, I must forgive. I can't allow this to turn my heart bitter against my fellow man. A man should keep his pain to himself and share his joy. But when one's pain becomes agony… they shoot horses, don't they?

I am a Christian man. Therefore I cannot take my hand to my own life. So I must bear this suffering. Even when it is unbearable, even when I cry out to my Maker, "End this misery, Oh Lord! Let not your fallen servant continue this way! Take my life back to you!" I must wait upon the Lord, for he is wiser than I.

It's all very strange. I feel isolated and vulnerable. I'm worried, and I haven't a clue as to what this is all about. I want to write, but I'm too confused and upset. God help me.

From my cage I look 14 feet beyond to the barred and screened window on the hallway wall. You can't see very well from where I stand, but I caught a glimpse of the most beautiful rainbow! Thank the Lord for allowing me to see it!

There they are — the tears of my soul. I am thankful. See? I do have something to be thankful for. At least my heart can still be moved. In tears we find our true self, the bare essence of soul and spirit.

I'm too disturbed to sort out my feelings right now. It's hard, so very hard to exist like this. How long before this misery feeds on my mind, heart and soul, until there is nothing left of Danny?

I am so lonely. This paper tablet where I place my words begins to stare back at me. A cold, hard face it has. I touch it, but it does not respond. To give it life, I must pour myself out onto it, and still it remains unmoving.

Sitting here wondering what I'd be doing if I wasn't here. One of my favorite things to do in the cool of the day was to put on a pair of stereo headphones, plug 'em into the Walkman and go for a 5- to 7-mile run. How I loved to do that! The wind in my face and good jams thumpin' in my ears. Those were the good times — no worries, no problems, no pressures — they all melted away in the sweat that poured from my body.

The sun just went down. God only knows how I hate it when the sun goes down on this graveyard for misfits. How I need to be held, to be loved. That's gotta be the hardest thing about all this. Well, at least I haven't had any real nightmares lately. I'm thankful for that.

In some ways DEATH has always held a certain fascination for me, because I believe in a hereafter in paradise. If one believes and trusts in Jesus Christ as Lord and Savior — but I no longer wish to end my life. I have a reason to be — to live — as long as the good Lord above grants me life in this world.

I have not given up the fight for DANNY. Oh! I have moments when I feel like ENNAD and there are times I feel GEMINI reaching for me. But I resist. Enough is enough. GEMINI has to go. ENNAD and DANNY have to make a pact and merge in order for both to survive, the yin and yang, a complete man.

The rain came beating upon the window pane of my lonely cell. Rain, sweet-smelling rain, dancing in the puddles outside my prison… where I am hidden away from the holy tears of heaven that wash the earth below.

Oh, how I long. How I hurt! So deep in the well of my heart there beats a hunger that threatens to consume me with loneliness so profound I dare say it is much heavier than I can tote. I am filled with regrets.

Last night I had a lulu of a demonic visit. I was tossing and turning in my lumpy bunk when I felt that presence. I opened my eyes, but there was nothing there. Still, the hair was standing up on my neck and arms as though I was in an electrical field. Then... it happened! This slimy thing leapt from the shadows and jumped right up on my chest like a jackal on a rabbit! It pinned my arms to the bunk. With this hideous grin and glowing red evil eyes, it shoved its scaly claws into my mouth and pulled it open. Then it stuck its tongue down my throat and tried to choke me to death! I couldn't breathe. Struggling, I managed to get it off me. I screamed, punching at it. It slithered away snickering, and pointing at me said, "How does it feel to kiss a snail?" And then it vanished. Mercy, mercy me! I've never kissed a snail before. Hell! It grossed me out! I've heard this place is haunted, and I'm inclined to agree.

Here we go round the Mulberry Bush...
the Mulberry Bush... the Mulberry Bush...

From my cage of steel and stone I can see it is a glorious Sunday afternoon. When I was free as a wild stallion, about this time of day I would dress-out in jogging shorts, running shoes and bandanna, hook up my pocket stereo and headphones... and put it in the wind! Good Golly Miss Molly! How I loved to run across country this time of day! The sky turns a richer, deeper blue and the air is so cool and fresh. I could run for miles and miles and miles. On an average run, I'd put seven to ten miles behind me, sprinting two or three miles of that along the way. God only knows how much I miss running long distance, listening to some jamming sounds.

Oh! Howdy, Four Walls, and how are you today? I'm just hunky-dory! What? Cat got your tongue? Oh, I know. Concrete walls can't talk. Well, I disagree! They just speak real soft. You have to be confined in a stone box for a spell, but after awhile, these ol' blank walls takes on a personality all their own. One minute they're just standing over me like granite tombstones, mute as a butte... the next thing you know, all kinds of voices and noises are bouncing off them. Of course, those sounds may originate down the hall or from the next cell, but you never see the faces that speak the words, the phone that rings, the TV chattering away downstairs. So you see, after a couple of weeks these lifeless, tan walls take on a whole new perspective.

Lah de dah de dah... Jack and Jill... went up the hill... to fetch a pail of water— Wait a minute! Jack didn't go up that hill to bob for apples, you know! That's bullshit! Jack dragged Jill's squirming ass up that grassy knoll to DROWN THE BITCH! Because she had been running around and painting the town... and he couldn't stand it any longer!

It's a Friday! Boy howdy, it might as well be a Monday. Dahhh... what's up, Doc? Just a jolt or two from the land beyond the norm.

I can hear the melodic drumming of crickets singing in the shadows of the night. Their song drifts through the distant window into my lonely prison cell. Ahhh... my heart is so heavy. My soul is so hungry for human touch, the touch of love.

My heart breaks. I feel as though I might as well be stranded on the dark side of the moon. My mind, my mind, where is my mind? The computer in my head has been in neutral for the longest time. I reach for thought and it flies away like a strange bird of prey, taking within its tightly clenched talons myself and all my hopes and dreams.

I hurt inside, deep within my center self. What have I done? Dear God have mercy on my soul! How could my life have ended up so? Last night I couldn't sleep. I tossed and turned staring at silhouettes — shadowy bars like reaching fingers shading the walls a grim and lonely gray.

Here we go round the Mulberry Bush... the Mulberry Bush... the Mulberry Bush...

Images of the deep emerge from the wellspring of expression. Branching tributaries flowing into one, drawing creativity from the darkest eclipse, the blackest abyss, lifting, flowing to the surface and basking under the blazing sunshine.

I feel MADNESS in the air. It's as if some slow-moving ancient shadow has stretched its dark wings over Mother Earth and threatens us all. I don't know, but even though I am cut off from the outside world, I sense something of a malignant nature stirring out there amongst the inhabitants of this planet Earth.

Mary had a little lamb, little lamb, little lamb... Mary had a little lamb, whose fleas were white as snow— Ho now! You hold that pachydermatus by the horns and I'll give it a swift kick in the ass. You mean to tell me Mary's lamb only took on albino fleas? Ah, picky picky picky! I suppose Mary only played doctor with Martians too?

Hey! Have you heard the one about why a bird's life is so rough? Well, he's the only critter in nature who has to eat with his pecker. Ha-ha! Sneakers and tee-hees!

Little Miss Muffet sat on a tuffet, eating her curds and whey. Along came a spider and sat down beside her... and gave her a big fat slobbery kiss! And Miss Muffet promptly died of fright!

Tomorrow... tomorrow... will it bring joy or sorrow? We laugh... we weep... as another tomorrow becomes yesterday.

Oh! The night before last, after the lights winked out and the floodlights standing watch two hundred yards yonder cast their beams searching the darkness of the cave dwellers, I was sitting here on the iron bunk staring at the small bundle of a linen sheet piled on top of the iron footlocker against the wall, the eerie light accenting the shadows. Lo and behold! A mushroom-man appeared there in my pile of linen. I was going to sketch it — ah, but alas. I fell asleep and lost the image. I guess art is like fishing. When it's hot, they bite a lot... ol' dit and jot-tee-tot... but every now and then you hook a Moby Dick out of the sea of thought... then as you are reeling it in... sometimes you LOSE IT. Damn! The big one that got away! Shit fire and save matches! HAW-HAW-HEE-HEE-HA-HA...

Despair is a foe I know well. If I stand at the bars and look out across the hall beyond the window there, I can see it's a beautiful day — but not for me. No, ol' emotion despair is fighting for my sanity. Some days the foe wins, some days I win. But here lately, I've lost a lot more than I've won, as the dark clouds of depression close in.

There is another Danny — worried, depressed, angry and afraid. That part of myself I keep hidden. He sits alone in a dark cell crying his heart and soul out.

Tomorrow is Thanksgiving! What have I to give thanks for? Should I thank my Lord for continuing my miserable life? Perhaps it pleases him to see me suffer? I don't know. God forgive me for feeling this way. I must express myself. I need someone to counsel me. I need help in making the right decisions. But it's the holidays and my lawyers will be with their families enjoying Thanksgiving. So I'm stuck with trying to sort out my feelings alone. The guards are rattling chains and laughing on the quarterdeck. They seem happy. I'm sure they will be with their loved ones too this Thanksgiving. I must try and get through this holiday. They brought my festive turkey and dressing dinner tray by at noon. I refused it. Food does not even comfort me any more.

I am immersed in an ocean of emotion. At moments like this, I feel like a man drowning in a dark sea of loneliness. I need to know something good. Anything, anything at all. I desperately need a visit. No one visits me any more. Here I sit surrounded by hostiles without a sympathetic soul in sight.

I spoke with my new counselor the other day. Nice fellow (he wants me dead). Oh, he didn't come right out and say it, but I saw it in his eyes. So I don't think I will get any assistance whatsoever from him. That's just the impression I got. Maybe I'm wrong, but I don't think so.

What's the most pitiful creature you can imagine? A bird in a cage. I can't imagine a sadder creature (except myself). If I had my way I'd set free every captive bird in existence. Just think of all those wings beating the wind to clear blue skies!

Right now, I've reached an all-time low. My heart skips like this blasted pen. It's raining outside and it's dismal indeed inside. It's very difficult for me to write. I'm very, very low emotionally. I can't even begin to tell you, but I'm pretty close to rock bottom. That's just the way it is — a GRAY WAY.

I finally got to go outside and get some exercise and beautiful warm life-giving sunshine! You really can't appreciate the outdoors until you've been cooped up in a concrete box for several months without blue sky overhead. Physically, I'm still holding up rather well. I looked in the mirror today and liked what I saw. I can't always say that, because more times than not, I don't like what I see in my eyes (the loneliness) or my face (the depression of 24-hour confinement).

The further I have plunged from the mainstream, the lonelier I have become. It started long ago as a child, with that deep-down feeling of being the Outsider, the odd man out in the game of life. The pain, the anger and the violence still haunt me. They hide in the dark corners of my broken self. The light! It must beam down on these demons that hold influence over me. Oh God, help me overcome the darkness that surrounds me, so my angels can lift me up from the depths of demise where I am cast!

Pain for pain… suffering for suffering… terror for terror… I look in the mirror and peer into my wounded soul and ask myself how? How can this be?

Forgive me, Precious Jesus. Pour your cleansing blood spilled from Calvary's cruel cross over me and hide my sins from your ever-watchful face on Judgment Day, that this fallen angel might worship and serve you forever on your holy mountain. In Jesus' Name I pray. Amen.

The Frozen Sparrow

His next cell was even worse. A place of torment, it was a crumbling capsule, stinking of ageless neglect. It had become fall, and the first night there was cold and horrible. Someone down the long hall screamed all night long, and sleep came fitfully.

The next dismal day, the prisoner awoke with his stuff — such as it was — floating in three inches of water. This phenomenon occurred every single night. Finally one day the major came by, and the prisoner pleaded to be moved to a cell that didn't flood out. The major agreed and moved him that very day to a nice clean cell on the third tier.

Unfortunately, his new cell had been occupied by a black prisoner who was the favorite of the black sergeant in charge of the cellblock, and the hapless white prisoner became the object of his scorn.

In two shakes of a cat's tail, the Sarge had him moved again — to the worst cell in Parchman Prison — a rat-infested roach hotel that flooded out two or three times a week. But this time, it wasn't just water, it was the raw human excrement that fermented in the blocked-up sewer under the prison.

The hallway was at a grade, and his cell was at the bottom. At least three times a week raw gray-brown sewage seeped in through the floor and belched from the drain up the hall. The sludge would creep down the hall and bubble through the floor, filling the cell with filth. It was the most horrid smell imaginable.

It was winter, and one day as the snow was falling from a gray sky and covering the hard brown ground, a lone sparrow flew down. The prisoner watched from the cell window as it landed in the snow, and during the night, it froze to death. The image of that little frozen sparrow left a cold spot in his heart.

Then there was the time he pulled back the covers on the bunk to go to bed, and a rat jumped out from underneath. He escaped under the narrow space between the cold steel door, and scampered gleefully away down the hall.

Filled with the will for revenge for the way he had been treated, for years all the prisoner had to live on was his hatred for the system and the society that put him there.

Gemini

The moan, the groan...
The silver moon shown...
The whisper... the cry...
Dead leaves fly...
Through the haze
It smells your fears...
Then... it appears...
Your nightmare
come to life...
A maniac with a knife.

As the days and nights ran into each other like madmen in an insane asylum, the isolation and filth sent the prisoner over the edge of sanity into the land beyond reason. He snapped. And now when he talked to himself, new and striking voices talked back. He didn't call them. They came into being because he was incomplete. Pushed beyond his endurance to cope, Ennad or Jesse became real to him, and then Gemini exploded in his mind. And a plan, or a scheme if you will, began to form.

Come on, Danny...
I'm the one... let me come...
Inside your mind... I'll help you find...
Revenge for what they've done!

For many months, the late hours of the freezing cold cell were filled by Gemini's screams as the sewage gurgled up through the floor.

Ahhhh! Ahhhh! One soul for every year!
They'd better not ever let me out of here!

Sometimes the Dark One would come creeping outside the cell window, peering in from the dark cold night, laughing out loud and calling to Danny.

Ha-haaaa! Here comes Gemini!
And tonight... little butterfly...
Dead leaves will fly...
Tonight... someone will DIE!

Then the howling wind would sweep Gemini into the dark corners of the prisoner's own broken mind. And the whispers and screams would go on and on.

Tonight... in the arms of Gemini...
A captured butterfly will die...
Burned red with fever...
Then turned cold forever...
Forever, my dear...
No more pain... no more fear..
Close your eyes, my dear...
And sleep.
Into the night... comes Gemini...
And tonight... You DIE!

I realize my mind is confusing, but the Danny-Ennad-Gemini personalities are real parts of my psyche. I didn't make them up to spice up the Danny Rolling saga. Ha! I wish it was that simple. The truth of the matter is easily seen. All you have to do is look at the complete opposites everyone has noticed in my life.

DANNY: Good natured... sensitive... impressionable... kind... loving... easygoing... religious... caring... intelligent... talented... troubled... tormented.

ENNAD: Strong... self-willed... courageous... bold... daring. He can be as dangerous as a tiger, but he does have a conscience. Even though he has an explosive temper, he does not enjoy hurting people. He is an outlaw for sure. And if you get in his way, look out! It's payday. Ennad might rape you... but he would not want your blood.

GEMINI: Darkest night... evil... destructive... powerful... your wildest nightmare... come to haunt your dreams with screams... demon... grim reaper... murderer... bloodthirsty... psychotic... terrible. Gemini came from all the hatred, all the pain, everything sick and insane that had happened.

I've had some very serious mental problems, phasing in and out of these personalities. Nothing that goes on in my head is easily explained. I guess that's why I've had a ton of headshrinkers picking through my brain. Notwithstanding, I am not using that as an excuse to cop-out.

As a child, my tender consciousness was wounded. I became damaged by a type of mind control at the hands of my father. I learned to hate from him, and as a result, my personality split. I had good qualities. I was a handsome lad with a loving heart and a bright mind.

Ah, but alas. If you live in a tempest, you are bound to exhibit foul weather somewhere down the line. At a tender age, the door to my mind was opened to the forces that roam this earth and the Evil crept in. I became a tool for Satan to work his vengeance on Mother Earth's children.

When I was a child, my dad would not let me just be Danny. I was never good enough for him. But I don't place the blame on Pop. He was just one of the wheels that ran over my personality.

The outlaw Ennad developed as a rebellious soul against the harsh realities of my childhood. He loves the thrill of it all — like walking along the edge in high places, for the pure adrenal excitement of it; Danny doesn't. Ennad might take Danny places that Danny doesn't want to go, but he never leaves him alone to handle a tough situation without support of some sort. When Danny can't make the scene, Ennad's the one that comes through.

The alias is Jesse, but the mind behind the mask is not Danny. Jesse is the nickname Ennad uses. I mean, can you imagine coming up to someone at a bar or a bus stop, and saying, "Hi, I'm Ennad"?

Jesse is really Ennad, and he is in the proper character when he robs a store and has it out with the cops. But I also see Danny there in the middle of it all, and it's rather confusing to me.

Ennad is not completely without conscience, so I would not classify him as a psychopath. Gemini, now, that's a horse of a different color for sure. He is a psycho from the word GO. I mean you can't get any badder than that dude. He is PURE EVIL.

I Peter 5:8 says: "Be sober, be vigilant, because your adversary the devil, as a roaring lion, walketh about, seeking whom he may devour." He has many faces and he goes by many names: The Dark One... The Devil... Lucifer... Beelzebub... Satan... Covering Cherubim... but I just call him GEMINI.

Gemini is really a spirit — a demon, if you will. He is our mortal enemy and he is constantly seeking a soul to consume. If we open the door to our minds to him, he will possess our thoughts and influence us to do terrible things — ungodly things.

I had seen the Evil One face to face before, although I never heard its name until it became real to me at Parchman as Gemini. The shadows of the night that dance on the wings of darkness had been there all along, lurking within my troubled mind. I just did not see its identity clearly until then. Nonetheless, Gemini is a real being from another dimension that coexists with our own — the nether world, where the fallen angels dwell.

You see, I wanted revenge. I wanted someone else to suffer the way I suffered. That's why Gemini became real to me. Gemini lusts for revenge against God Almighty's righteous judgments against him, and since he can't touch the Creator God, he goes after the next best thing — the creation of God, mankind.

Gemini called... and I answered. At the same time, I beckoned... and Gemini promised me revenge — if I would open my mind to pure Evil. Sure enough, I was led to the revenge I demanded — one innocent soul for every year of imprisonment. But there is no peace in revenge. It only leaves one empty and troubled. Oh, God forgive me!

A Real Killer

Besides the spirits of the night, the prisoner had other companions in solitary confinement — the spiders spinning their webs in the corners. He gave them proper names — Ned, Ted, and Fred — and he fed them. He was quick enough to snatch a fly out of the air, then he would pull its wings off and toss it into the sticky web. The insect would struggle desperately to free itself, but to no avail. The spider always got its prey. He'd feel the vibrations of the wiggling victim in his web of death, and the legs that brought the end would stealthily approach.

The spider would stretch strand after silky strand from its abdomen and wrap the victim with its spindly legs until it was encased in a neat little package of webbery. Then, once its prey was completely immobilized, the spider would pounce on it with ravenous lust, and inject the poison with its deadly fangs.

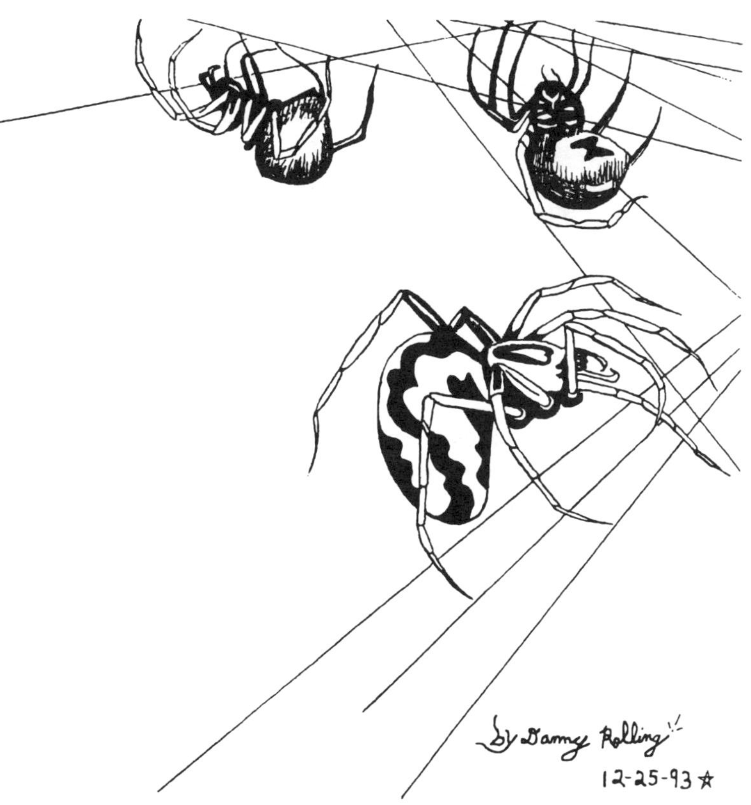

Though he has no teeth, nor jaws with which to chew his food, the spider is equipped with an ingenious method of consuming the nourishment he needs. The poison acts as an acid that turns the insides of the victim into a liquid. Thus, all the web-slinger has to do is wait patiently until the work is done, sort of like waiting on a bartender to mix up your favorite concoction for you to eagerly shove a straw into and suck it dry. The spider sticks its fangs into the expired critter embedded in its web and has a drink. Slurp! Ahhhh…

And so life in The Hole went on, with its spiders, its roaches, its rats — and its creeping crud. The flooding filth that invaded the prisoner's cell became a constant battle. But the enemy had no human form the prisoner could defeat with blows and kicks. The only weapons that would work were the broom and the mop. The trouble was that good ol' Sarge would leave the prisoner locked up for hours with the floating shit before opening his cell so he could clean it out.

Ned and Ted had begun to reject the daily offerings place in their webs, and it was getting on the crazed man's nerves. "Now Ned, you see that big fat roachie-bug I caught for you? Come on now, eat your roach like a good little boy, hear? What's the matter with you? Ted? You're not hungry either? Damn! You good-for-nothing spiders! I go to all his trouble to catch you guys bugs — and you don't even eat them!"

One day as the prisoner sat observing his spider pals, he just couldn't take it any longer. "Ned and Ted? You guys are so finicky. Well, boys, it looks like Judgment Day has finally arrived!" And with that he jumped up, grabbed his brown brogan, and smashed Ned and Ted with the heel. SPLAT! And that was that.

Now it was down to just Fred. He was the biggest of the three, and he never turned up his nose at a fly or a moth. Attacking any living thing in his path, he would pounce on it with a vengeance, bite it, wrap it up in his silky bonds, and save it for a rainy day.

Fred was Danny Rolling's kind of guy. A real killer.

CHAPTER 6

THEY CALLED HIM PSYCHO

Blood and Bumper Jack

It's hard, so very hard to understand
What made this man put a gun in his hand?
Well, I guess I came to the end of my rope,
'Cause when I lost my love,
I lost my hope,
Now I'm livin' in a house
of steel and stone.

Thus he watched summer turn to fall, and when the gloom of winter settled in, the prisoner shivered under a thin blanket, blasted by the cold draft from his open window. Except for an hour a day in the yard, the only time he saw a human face was when a guard would shove the food through the slot in the door.

Over the winter months, the prisoner came to know the other convicts by yelling through the food slots. There was Blood, a fierce black man who walked as tough as he talked.

There was Rambo, a young white guy who had OD'd on acid and took two M-16's he had stolen from an armory, hit the street, and fired on anything that moved. When the cops showed up, it was a war. Two cops were left dead and several were wounded. Rambo wound up with several life sentences.

Then there was Bumper Jack, who got his nickname from the weapon he'd used to bash a man's brains out. That big black nigger had no morals, no scruples, nothing but hard time bedeviling his mind.

One day on the yard, Blood and Bumper Jack got into it. Blood produced an ice pick and plunged it to the hilt into Bumper Jack's upper right chest. Then he stabbed him on the top of the head, the left shoulder, and the left hand, before Bumper Jack could scramble away and pick up an empty milk crate to defend himself.

Suddenly, the prisoner stepped in between the two fighting men yelling, "You got him good, Blood!" Blood's eyes had glazed over with murder, but the prisoner tried to reason with him.

"The guards are coming. Come on, man. Give me the pick before you get into some serious shit." The two men continued to struggle, but the prisoner kept trying to break it up. "Come on, Blood, don't do this! You got him good. He ain't worth killing. Give me the pick, man. Look! The goon squad's coming!"

Finally Blood's eyes cleared. He looked around and pitched the weapon up on the roof. When it was all over, Bumper Jack survived, and Blood became the prisoner's friend.

Rambo

Now, Rambo was as crazy as a sack full of rattlesnakes. He cared no more about living than he did about dying. He had been locked up in solitary for three years since his battle with the forces of oppression, and he was insanely dangerous. He would yell out from his cell, "You black muthafuckas ain't worth a shit! You worse than dogshit! Yo mama's a monkey, yo daddy's a coon!" On and on he would rave.

The prisoner tried to tell him, "Hey man, you need to cut that shit out. One day them blacks are gonna jump on you, Rambo or no Rambo. You ain't got no M-16's in here!" But Rambo wasn't listening.

One day Sergeant Black got tired of Rambo's mouth. He was the color of the ace of spades, and he hated whites with a passion. So good ol' Sarge handcuffed Rambo behind his back, as they always did, and pulled him out of his cell. But this time, he let a couple of the blacks that Rambo had been calling dogshit out with him — except they weren't cuffed. Rambo was kicked senseless, and after that they never heard a peep out of that bad boy. He just sat in his cell and stared at the walls.

When they took me,
I was so tender and full of life,
But now this prison cuts my heart
Like a sharp and deadly knife.

When the nights cast shadows
It's a gray picture at best.
You close your eyes but you never seem to rest,
Livin' in a house of steel and stone.

BLAM!

The prisoner was looking out beyond the bars in his cell window, his thoughts dancing on the horizon, longing for freedom. A flood of emotions erupted through the dam of his troubled heart, and this time there was no turning back. It was the creeping crud again. He had pleaded to be moved to another cell, but kindhearted Sarge was playing games. He'd promise to move him but he never did. Well, by God, today was going to be different! Like Popeye says, "I can't stands it no more!"

The prisoner grabbed hold of the solid steel desk that crowded his tiny cell and slung it into the iron door. BLAM! It crashed into the immovable iron keeper of his person that was blocking his way to freedom.

BLAM! BLAM! BLAM! The heavy metal desk slammed into the door. "You damn well better let me out of here this time!" BLAM! BLAM!

"Cause one way or another..." BLAM! BLAM! BLAM!

"...I'm coming up out of this shit!" BLAM! BLAM! BLAM! BLAM! *BLAM!*

This went on nonstop for an hour and the iron began bending away from its hinges. Finally, Sergeant Black came running down the stairs screaming over the racket, "What the hell are you doing?"

"This is it..." BLAM! BLAM! "...do or die..." BLAM! "...you bastard!" BLAM! BLAM! *BLAM!*

"You promised me months ago..." BLAM! BLAM! "...you would move me out of this shit-hole!" BLAM! "All you've done is laugh at me!" BLAM! BLAM! BLAM! "Now I'm coming out!" BLAM! BLAM! "...one way or another..." BLAM! "...I'm coming up out of this sewer!" BLAM! BLAM! *BLAM!*

"Well, you can just rot in hell for all I care," said the big ape as he stormed back upstairs. He didn't want to get his nice polished boots soiled.

Like an animal pushed too far, the crazed man went wild, assaulting the iron door — BLAM! BLAM! *BLAM!* — until it jumped away from its frame. "Ahhhh!"

Sarge came running back down the steps, this time with a worried look on his face. "You — you quit that, you hear? Or I'll charge you with escape!"

"Ha! Ha! Ha-a-a-ah! That's what I'm in here for, you asshole!" BLAM! "You're not gonna move me?" BLAM! "I'm busting down this god-damned door!" BLAM! BLAM! BLAM! BLAM! *BLAM!*

"OK, OK... pack your shit, you got it."

And so the next day the prisoner was let out of solitary confinement, only to discover they had kept him in the Happy Hotel from Hell six months longer than they were supposed to. Thanks a lot, Sarge.

Believe I heard a rebel yell
From a man called Cowboy
Singin' Chaingang livin'...
of your life you're given
A-many years and a-many tears
Before you see your home again.
Ooooh, I wanna go home.

They Called Him Psycho

When the prisoner they called Cowboy was taken out of his solitary cell, he was put on the chaingang. The first day out, he was loaded onto a modified trailer that had been cut in half lengthwise. They herded 400 convicts onto it like cattle. Front to back, crammed in like sardines. If someone farted, there was no place to go. You just held your breath. It was freezing cold, and he was not issued a jacket.

In the early morning frost, the trailers drawn by old John Deere tractors rumbled off down dusty, bumpy roads, into the angry red eye of the rising sun.

The turnkey's eyes said to me,
"Look a-here, son, don't you run
Or I'll bring ya down with my gun."
Chaingang livin'... of your life you're given
A-many years and a-many tears
Before you see your home again.

When the prisoners reached their destination, they were unloaded and given wooden-handled hoes. Cowboy overheard some of the boys making bets as to whether or not he would last the day long. He pondered this, and decided he would endure, no matter what. And what a trial it proved to be!

They were set to work against a square mile of cane-grass. Their hoes cut the cane and beat the hard ground all day, except for a 30-minute lunch break and two 15-minute breaks.

At the end of the day, the prisoner literally crawled back to the trailer. They had to send him to the hospital. When he finally got to see the doctor, he took one look at him and laughed, "There's nothing wrong with you! Get out of my sight!" Ha! That was Parchman. It's just the nature of the beast: kindness was preyed upon, the weak abused, and the ruthless respected.

Cowboy was forced to pick cotton and dig ditches until he was exhausted and sick. You had to get no less than sixty pounds of cotton a day or you were punished. Rows upon rows of white cotton gleaming in the blistering sun. Eighty pounds of cotton dragging in a sack behind you.

Off in the distance dust devils whirled about like demoniac sentinels, keeping watch over the slaves. The guards on horseback would shout, "Awright girls! All I wanna see is assholes and elbows! Get that cotton!" And that's what they would do.

One day picking cotton, they brought the water tractor around as they did every day. The men were filling their water jugs. But Cowboy never used a jug. Instead, he would kneel and drink from the spigot.

As he knelt to drink, someone threw water in his face. He stood up and looked about, but nobody said a word. So he knelt down again — he was thirsty — and again, someone threw water in his face. This time he jumped up and punched the man nearest him.

Someone in the gang yelled, "It ain't him! He didn't do it!" Cowboy stopped fighting the man and asked him if he did it. "No," he said, so Cowboy left him alone, and turning toward the gang he demanded, "Whoever threw water in my face ought to be man enough to own up to it!"

The biggest, meanest, ugliest, blackest man he had ever seen before in his entire life stepped forward snarling, "I done it, Whitey. Whatcha gone do about it?"

Cowboy took one look and charged him, feet and fists flying! They ended up rolling in the dust like mad dogs. After that day, they no longer called him Cowboy. They called him *PSYCHO.*

Bunnie

July 29, 1988. Danny was paroled from the Mississippi pen under the conditions that he return to Shreveport. He moved back into his parents' home. James Harold had met Bunnie Mills, a 58-year old country singer, and introduced her to Danny. She became his lover, paying for their dinners and movies, taking him on trips, buying him clothing and gifts, and taking care of his vehicle repairs with her credit cards.

As Bunnie described it, "I had given his dad one of my country and western tapes, and he called me on the phone and invited me over for dinner. He had put his wife on the phone, and she invited me too. They were very friendly. I didn't know Danny was there. So I go bouncing through the back door and say, 'Hi everybody, how you doing,' and all of a sudden this good-looking guy comes out of the living room, and he says, 'Oh my goodness,' he says, 'She's a beautiful woman,' and he says, 'I think I'm going to lose my heart.' I went over to him and patted him on his heart, and I says, 'That's okay, honey, I'll take care of your heart.' It was just friendly.

"We had dinner, and after we ate, they asked me to play my guitar and sing. I did, and Danny says, 'Oh, I love your guitar.' He says, 'Let me play it.' And of course I didn't know that he could play. So he played, and he sang a couple of songs that he had written, and right away I recognized that he had talent, he could write well and he could sing well. I'm always looking for songs, and I was interested in perhaps producing him one day and publishing his songs, and helping him in the music all that I could. So I called him back that night, and told him I would like to get with him so we

DEMENTIA
Fuck you
by Danny Rolling 10-13-93

could talk about our music. And that's how it started.

"Danny came to me every time he got depressed. He would come to my house constantly and confide in me, though the relationship was back and forth. I never knew when Danny was coming to my house and when he wasn't.

"Danny was a very humble person, and he would tell me that he couldn't get along with his dad, but he wished that he could. When he would talk about his father, he would cry. He would get so upset, he would tell me how his heart would hurt. It was almost like you could crawl inside of him yourself and feel the pain that he was feeling.

"Sometimes he would get on his knees like a little child and tell me that things were so bad at home he couldn't live there, and I would say 'But Danny, you can't break your parole, you have to live there. So if you go see a psychiatrist, maybe this will end some of your anxieties or whatever this thing is with you. And you'll get well.'

"I begged Danny to go for mental health counseling. I don't remember who made the appointment, myself or Claudia, but he said, 'I'm not going, if I go and my dad finds out what I've said, he'll kill me.' And I said, 'But Danny, the psychiatrist is not supposed to reveal what you say to them,' and I said, 'It may come to where you have to have the family there with you.' I said, 'If you can get that far along with your therapy, that would be great.' And he said, 'No.' He said, 'My dad would never go.' And I said, 'Well, we'll just go to your dad and find out.' And we went through this several times. He'd say 'Oh, God, I don't want to say nothing else about my dad,' and I would say, 'Danny, I've made the appointment, we're going to go over to your house and talk to your mother and daddy.'

"We went to his house and talked to his mother and daddy. I said to them, 'I have talked Danny into going to see the psychiatrist, and so I said to James, I said, 'If it comes to the point where Danny does go into this therapy, will you support him?' I said, 'If you have to go, would you go?' And he said, 'Yes, I would.' He said, 'Maybe it's me that needs to go.' And I said, 'Yeah well, I don't know about that,' but I said, 'I'm going to take Danny,' and Claudia said that she would support Danny all the way. So I said to Danny, 'OK, Danny, there you are, so we're going.' So then Danny — he said yes, and then he said no. And then he started to run. I chased him all the way around the apartment building about four times — him just a-running and me right behind him. I'm screaming, 'Danny, you have to go to the psychiatrist! You have to get well!' And he'd say that he was afraid of what his dad would do to him if he found out he talked about him in therapy."

I met Bunnie Mills when I first got out of Parchman Pen. My dad introduced us. She is a great woman, with a real taste for traditional country music. She is a wonderful songwriter with many records decorating her wall to prove it. We had a lot in common, especially our love for music. That was the glue that held us together. She did spend a good deal of money on me. That kept my interest in her, but eventually the relationship was destined for the rocks.

Bunnie was very, very good to me. Once the bear finds a honeycomb in old tree, he doesn't look at the tree. No, he is more interested in the honey, and he keeps coming back for more until it's all gone. Then it's just another old tree.

She was the first woman I had even been close to in over 3 years. I did not notice the age difference then. As time went on, it became more difficult to overlook the difference, and that finally resulted in our breakup.

Our union lasted just over a year, and during that time, Bunnie bought me four brand-new white-letter racing tires, four brand-new Mag wheels, a new 4-barrel carburetor, new battery, new water pump, and $500 worth of clothes, jewelry and shoes. We ate at all the best restaurants, her treat. We'd go to the officer's club she belonged to at Barksdale AFB and play Bingo. She'd buy me all the margaritas I could stomach, take me to the movies I wanted to see, give me money to play my favorite video game at the arcade (Cabal), and take me on trips with her. She bought me a nice Walkman radio for my birthday. It went on and on.

Before I realized it, I began to use her. It didn't start that way. It's just that she would not let go of me. I tried to let her down easy, because she was completely in love with me. I didn't want to hurt her. But she wouldn't take a hint. I laid it out for her so many times. I even staged it so she would find me with another woman. Nothing worked. I just began to ignore her.

Did we have sex? Yes we did, several times. But it got to where I had to pretend she was someone else. Still, I do not have a bad opinion of her. She is a decent woman who has country fans all over the world and a wall full of records to prove it. My final thoughts about her are that she is a fine lady, one to be respected and loved.

All I Need is a Job

I went to the unemployment office today.
Oh, they said, "Sorry, son, no jobs today."
Johnny said, "Take this job and shove it."
But give it to me, oooh, I'll love it!
I need a job, yes I do, I need to work today.

"He tried to find work when he came back in 1988, but he didn't have a whole lot of success," said Claudia Rolling. "He had been trying to get a job as a forklift operator at Busch Distributing Company, that's up the street from us, and he was there almost every day talking to them, pleading with them. Then he got real discouraged because they would show a lot of interest, but then they wouldn't call him back.

"We was sitting out in the front yard one night and he wrote a song called "I Need a Job." I wish you could hear it, because it's a darling song, and he said, 'You know what I'm going to do, mom?' I said, 'What?' He said, 'I'm going to take my guitar and when they open in the morning, I'm going to walk up and down in front of that place, and I'm going to sing my song.' And I said, 'You do that, Danny, then maybe they'll hire you.' He was so depressed. He even told me, 'I'm useless, I'm not worth anything, I can't even get a job.'

Take a look at my worn-out shoes
Look me in the eye,
I've got the unemployment blues.
Come on, give me a break
All I need is a job.

"His job record is very sporadic. They always loved him, his bosses, because he would do his job well. He went to work on time. If they had a dress code, he followed it. I've had a lot of his bosses tell me, he was one of the best employees they had. But if he was going to get promoted, he was going to leave that job one way or the other, because a promotion meant that he was of value, and he could do things that some people couldn't do. And to Danny, a young man who's had all of his self-esteem destroyed, that's running words. You get out of there, because you might fail, and if you do you'd feel real bad about that.

"Now, the very last time he came home, he did get a job. My nephew had a car and he told Danny that he could have it for $500. Danny saved his money and bought the car, so he did have transportation. He had worked at Pancho's and Western Sizzlin' long enough to buy him a car and get insurance.

"He jogged around the neighborhood. He built him a workout table and he worked out in the backyard. The kids all over the neighborhood would come. They liked to watch Danny do karate, but he just did it to entertain those kids. He didn't really know anything about karate."

The only dojo I've attended was in prison, and hardened black-belts taught me. I have knowledge of Wing Chung and Tae Kwon Do. I am quick with both hands and feet, and I can most certainly handle myself in a fight, but I choose to follow peace. I only use my knowledge of the arts in self-defense.

There have been several photos of me published from that period. It's easy to see I was lean and mean, 6'3" and 180 pounds of pure hard man. I was in the best shape of my life.

I ran seven miles every other day. I worked out with weights and ran around our one-mile long block with a 90-pound 5-foot-long pine log across my shoulders. The reason for that exercise was simply to increase my upper and lower strength and stamina. I've never seen a puny logger. I was jogging around the block one fine summer day when a neighbor had cut down a couple of pine trees in his yard. I saw a nice size cut and thought,

Hmmm... so I took it home with me. It was Adopt-a-Log Day! Ha!

Little Rocky

I had a puppy my dad mistreated after I got out of Parchman. I loved that puppy. He was so cute and loving, and he was a purebred English bulldog — you know, the bulldogs that grow up tall and proud. The English bull is the most intelligent and loving of the bulldog family. They are even good with children. They are not mean like pit bulls. Well, anyway, I named him Rocky, of course, after the late great Snoopy look-alike of my childhood.

At the time I was working at Pancho's Mexican Restaurant. I came home from work one afternoon around 3:00 P.M. As I entered the house from the carport, Dad was in the back yard and I heard Rocky yelping. I opened the door and dad was kicking the little feller. I said, "Dad! What the hell are you doing?" He just smiled like a little child who got caught with his hand in the cookie jar and was playing it off like nothing ever happened.

I looked at Little Rocky huddled up, shaking and licking his wounds, and remembered watching my dad kick my first puppy to death. I immediately scooped him up and took him away. I gave him to a Mexican cook at work, who let the dog go to a friend of his, who later said the dog was stolen one night. So who knows what happened to little Rocky? I hope he found a good home, because that dog was special. His father was a champion several times over in England, and his mother was purebred.

Weapons of Choice

Gemini prefers knives and machetes; Ennad loves guns. Ennad actually likes all types of weapons. So do I.

Guns:
9mm automatic handgun
...a beautiful weapon.
45-cal. Colt auto
...extremely powerful close range.
.38-cal. revolver
...very accurate and reliable.
.22-cal. Ruger auto
...also accurate and reliable.
.308-cal rifle with Leupold variable scope...
BINGO!

Knives:
Ka-Bar Marine Fighting Knife
...deadly, sharp and huge.

Staff:
Ancient Chinese Kung-Fu weapon.

Stars:
Shuriken or throwing stars.

All these weapons I have owned at one time or another in the course of my life. I became very *relevant*, you might say. I was an expert with these weapons.

GUNS. While I was in the Air Force, I outshot the instructor at the indoor firing range and qualified as EXPERT with the .38-cal. revolver. I was given a ribbon for that. My dad taught me how to handle a .38. And when I was very young, barely a teenager, I could pick off a bluejay in the top of a tall pine swaying in the breeze.

THE BOW. I have always been fascinated with the art of bow hunting. I have owned several and I used to go to the Red River Bow Range and practice. I'm not bragging, but I was pretty good. I've killed deer, rabbits, even birds with the bow. Now if you think hitting a target as small and quick as a bird with a bow and arrow is easy, try it some time.

THE KNIFE. I have had several knives in my days, from Old Henry's to Ka-Bars. Any weapon just takes up space, until the human hand finds work for it. Then it becomes as deadly as its master's intent. I'll never forget the first knife I bought. It was a Buck lockblade. After I purchased it, I walked out of the mall, took the knife out of its sheath, and cut my finger to the bone. After that lesson, I never cut myself again. A Ka-Bar is a foot-long fighting knife, but it was comfortable hidden under a light jacket. I made an improvised

I always loved the legends
of lion-like men
And beautiful lasses
who stole their hearts away
A magical, simpler time
When one won the favor
of his Lady Fair
By how well he could wield
a two-edged sword
And stand his ground
against his enemies.

shoulder holster from a black leather belt that I threaded through the Ka-Bar's holster and carried it under my left armpit. Sometimes I carried it in a waist tote bag along with a gun, or wedged between my waist & pants, or hung from my belt, but I never carried a knife in my boot.

THE STAFF. It's an ancient Chinese weapon. I went into a cane grove once and selected a long bamboo staff, cut it down, took it home, and practiced with it every day. I am very good with a staff.

THROWING STARS. I've possessed a few in my journey through this life. They are fun to play with and they can be very dangerous in the right hands. I had a target nailed to an old oak tree, and I would throw the stars at the target. I never missed. The metal stars would embed themselves so deeply into that hardwood oak I would need a pair of pliers to pull them out.

Nothing Better

The Snow Queen boards her icy sled and takes wing, freezing everything beneath. Sunsets linger in a brilliant glow of orange and red, receding to deep purple and shades of blue. Nights grow longer, embracing winter's harsh elements.

Lovers groan and moan under patchwork blankets quilted by aging hands as the silver full moon rises, joined by billions of twinkling stars.

Ice skaters take to frozen ponds of green and blue, dancing about on steel blades, cutting figure eights across the cold hard home to the bass and turtle.

That's when the hunter takes to the woods, aiming to bag his favorite wild game: dove, turkey, rabbit, squirrel, bear or deer.

The brisk winter air bites at his bones as he tiptoes through the fallen pine cones. With the gray skies above, and the snow below, it's just the hunter and his .308 Remington bolt-action hunting rifle.

He's hiked for miles into deep forest to the place he knows that trophy buck is bound to be. He was there before dawn, to find a good vantage point downwind and wait for the sun to come up.

As dawn arrives he scans the area through his scope. So far, nothing but a few cat squirrels dancing in the trees above. They peer down at him wondering what kind of creature he is. Completely cammoed-out, he doesn't move. He looks just like a tree.

Then, suddenly! He hears it — *TAT-TAT-TAT* — the telltale sound of a buck prancing through the underbrush headed his way! His pulse quickens, his senses go on full alert. At that moment, the hunter is more alive than he has ever been.

He searches through the crosshairs in the scope. Then it appears, a rack that could be mistaken for a pair of moose antlers. The hunter holds the breath that puffs out of his open mouth because of the cold. He puts the crosshairs just below and behind his front shoulder, dead center over the deer's heart. He eases out his breath, and as he does he squeezes the trigger.

KABOOM!

Through the scope he sees the big fella fall, so he knows he has hit him. But kicking and raising hell, the deer gets back up and charges back into the thicket. The man waits patiently, listening to the animal barrel into trees, making all kinds of noise until he falls again. This time he won't get up.

The hunter eases down the blood trail in search of the fallen whitetail or mule deer. He takes his time. There's plenty of blood sprinkles to lead the way to the animal's side. The hunter knows the prey is his, even before he walks up on his carcass.

There he lies, a magnificent eleven-point muley. The man takes the muzzle of his rifle and nudges the muley just to make sure, but his tongue is hanging out of his mouth and his eyes give it away — the cold fish-eye stare of *DEATH*.

He kneels beside the animal, extracts his Ka-Bar hunting knife from its sheath, splits the deer open and cuts out his insides. He will take his carcass to the butcher for steaks and sausage.

I have also been bow-hunting, and that is a much more difficult hunt. When your instincts are good, there is nothing better — except a good piece of — can I say this? A good piece of *pussy!*

Like a Werewolf

November 4, 1989. Jay Mitchell, Danny's boss at Pancho's Mexican Buffet, claims that Danny was fired for missing work three days in a row, and that he exploded in a fit of temper and threatened to kill the manager and the cook.

That is just not the way it happened. I was the best damn worker they had. But the manager at that time had a grudge against me because I was dating all the waitresses and none of them liked him. He was married and tried to hit up on several of the girls, but they put him down. They called him a dirty old man behind his back. I guess he resented their flirting with me.

Anyway, after work one day, as I always did, I checked the shift roster twice before leaving and I was scheduled to be off for the next two days. I made double sure, because I had just moved into an apartment of my own, and didn't have a phone yet. Apparently, my boss changed the roster sometime after I left work, and didn't or couldn't contact me about the new schedule. That's why I blew my stack on being fired, because it came as a complete surprise, and without a job, I'd lose my apartment. Which I did.

I came to work thinking everything was fine — until the manager said, "You're fired."

November 6, 1989. Julie Grissom, 24, a petite brunette who modeled clothes at a Shreveport mall, was found murdered, along with her father Tom Grissom, who worked for AT&T, and her 8-year old nephew Sean Grissom. The medical examiner placed the time of death two days earlier, the same day Danny was fired.

The killer reportedly used duct tape to bind Julie, and then raped her, stabbed her to death with a Ka-Bar Marine fighting knife, left bite marks and saliva on her breasts, then carefully cleansed her vaginal area with vinegar and posed her body provocatively. The duct tape was then carefully removed, and the crime scene apparently cleansed of prints. Julie's just-washed blouse was left in the washing machine.

The killer was blood type B, and a secretor like Danny Rolling; however, later DNA testing failed to conclusively link him to the crime scenes, and to date he has not been charged with this triple slaying, although Louisiana authorities have declared the case closed.

Danny's pastor, Rev. Mike Hudspeth, stated that one night about the time of the murders, Danny showed up at church, somewhat incoherent. "He wanted to stay around the church a bit and pray. I got the impression he was really high on something." The church was just down the street from the scene of the crime.

The bodies were discovered by Bob Coyle, a neighbor who said, "It was a nightmare over there. Just a bad, bad situation. You just don't think about that happening in a neighborhood like this."

Julie went down to the creek
to fetch a pail of water.
She ain't been seen since.
Wonder where she's been?
Don't want to get lost in Boggy Bayou,
way down in the swamps.
Fishing in Boggy Bayou again,
thought I saw Julie there.
Must have been a mirage,
turned and she was gone
I don't get no sleep at night,
she haunts my dreams
Comes around at night by candlelight.
I know one night she'll come for me
We'll kiss, oh, and hold each other tight
She'll take me to where the spirits
come alive at night.

The only statement Danny has made about this case was reported by Bobby Lewis, the jailhouse snitch who testified against him at the Gainesville student murder trial. In an interview with *The Florida Alligator*, Lewis recalled what Danny allegedly told him. "The old man was outside doing some barbecuing or watering the yard or something. He went and put a knife to him, took him in the house and tied him up. Taped up the old man, the girl and the kid, then he took the old man into a utility room and killed him first. Came back into the living room and took the little kid, rolled the kid onto his stomach and killed him. Stabbed him in the back through the heart. Took the girl into the bedroom, raped her and killed her. Did all kinds of stuff to her. He was like a werewolf. He had all the power over everybody to kill them or do whatever he wanted with them."

Windows to Fantasy

You'd think even the most dedicated voyeur must have bad nights. True enough, but this one never wasted time on unattractive targets. His mission always consisted of beautiful women. He had several backups. If one objective didn't work out, the next one would. He covered a lot of ground.

Take for instance this one gorgeous babe he used to look in on. She lived a good six miles from the little house on Canal Street. He knew her routine down to the days she had her period. He would rise early (4:00 A.M.) and jog the six miles to her parents' home in near-freezing temperatures to watch her get up, go through her daily devotional, and have her bath, before she went to work. She was one *beautiful babe!* The hopeless dreamer fell in love with her.

Well, as the seasons began to change, sunrise came earlier and earlier, until one morning the Eyes were outside her bathroom window when morning broke. The cloak of darkness was yanked away, revealing the voyeur's presence. But he couldn't make himself leave. He had to see her — possess her in his mind one more time.

As she was drying off her silky skin, she saw the man in the window staring at her. Their eyes met.

She froze. She stared back at him. For a moment frozen in time, they stared deeply into each other's eyes. The voyeur came — then left, never to return.

Look, I am not so dense I don't realize that in real life, girls don't get off on strange shadowy figures peering through their bathroom windows lusting for their charms. That young damsel that caught me checking her out at dawn was so petrified that she couldn't even move! That's what I saw in those pretty baby blues — *shock!* That would be the natural response when one's privacy is invaded, especially a woman's bathroom sanctuary. I doubt very seriously that the lady was turned on by it all.

The main reason why I never went back to her window was the element of secrecy had been compromised.

This time the voyeur was cruising a new neighborhood in Bossier City searching for a window to his fantasy.

He parked his canary yellow '71 Malibu in the parking lot of a shopping center near a Kentucky Fried Chicken and set out on foot, drawing on the thin black leather gloves he kept in the glovebox of the Chevy.

Time, approximately 11:00 P.M. Moving in and out of strangers' back yards, checking out the lay of the land, he came upon a house standing by a vacant lot. Like a moth to the flame, he was drawn to it.

No rest for the wicked. Peering in one window after another, the Eyes quickly discovered it was occupied by a gorgeous young blonde. Time passed and the damsel finally retired around 12:00 midnight.

Danny had not come to harm anyone, so Ennad took control. It would be rape, not murder. He searched the carport and found an old black t-shirt. Poking holes in it, he fashioned it into a mask and pulled it over his head.

At that moment, the Dark One grew ever greater — ever stronger. Gemini had arrived, thirsting for blood. But this night, thank God, he would be denied his crimson flow of pain. Instead of a red river, it would be just a stream easily dammed.

The front door was opened and the Evil entered the sleeping woman's home. Danny had brought no blade or weapon of any kind, but Gemini searched the kitchen in darkness, and the street light pouring in the window revealing a large, sharp carving knife on the cabinet counter.

The air became very still as the intruder crept stealthily into the young woman's bedroom. The Dark Shadow stood over her bed and watched the gentle rise and fall of her chest as she slept. Suddenly, the blonde sensed a presence. She awoke to a masked Reaper hovering over her, brandishing a carving knife.

Shocked and terrified, she screamed! But only once, and briefly at that.

The intruder quickly subdued his prey. But during the struggle, the woman reached up and grabbed the blade of the knife to defend herself. *S-S-SHUCK!* It was yanked from her grasp, slicing her thumb and palm to the bone. By this point, the attacker was on top of the woman, muffling the screams with his hand over her mouth. The woman settled down after being cut.

"Let's take a look at you, lovely." And he eased up the t-shirt over her breasts. She was about to die, but a very unusual thing happened, which entered the mind of Gemini and drove him away.

The woman had an infant perhaps eight months old lying next to her. The child had been overlooked until then. She did not cry or appear frightened, but rather interested. She just sucked on her bottle and gazed wide-eyed with wonder at the strange man on top of her mother. At that moment Gemini was conquered by the innocent eyes of a tender child.

The little angel took the nipple of her bottle out of her mouth and smiled sweetly at the masked figure. It was a smile that lights the world with joy. Something in that beautiful infant's eyes drove the Evil Spirit away and Danny regained himself. He saw the blood on the terrified blonde and on himself.

"Oh, Lady! I'm sorry! I — I didn't mean to hurt you." And he got up off the traumatized woman.

She looked confused. Then slowly, carefully, like a caged wild animal whose captor just released

it from prison, she got out of bed, then dashed out of the house barefoot in her t-shirt and panties, screaming at the top of her lungs!

The child was left behind and Danny stood there alone, admiring the calm, angelic behavior the infant exhibited. She just lay there in her spot and resumed feeding on her baby bottle, completely satisfied. Realizing the child would be all right, Danny fled into the night.

That woman had looked into the eyes of *DEATH*. But that night the bewildering gaze of a wide-eyed child conquered, as Evil gave way to innocence.

Danny would never forget the eyes of that precious child. They held the same look he once saw in the eyes of his own child, Kiley — the very same look. It was as if Kiley were looking at her father, pleading with her beautiful blue eyes, "Don't do this, Daddy, please don't do this!"

The Night the Big Chevy Died

The Grim Reaper
came seeking a soul,
Swung his sickle,
but his aim was low.
In the darkness an angel
of light appeared,
Stood champion,
honored and revered,
Matched bloody sickle
with flaming sword,
And broke fate's cruel cord.
The wind screamed
and the storm cried
The night the Big Chevy died.

April 27, 1990. 'Twas a night meant for neither man nor beast, an angry storm brewing in the east. The thunder of its approach threatened Shreveport, but that didn't stop Danny Rolling from having a night on the town. He splashed on his favorite after-shave, and dressed himself in virgin white from head to toe. Gazing in the mirror, his reflection portrayed him so:

Small gold chain about his neck
White cotton Bugle Boy shirt
Gold watch on his left wrist
Black silver buckled leather belt
White cotton Bugle Boy pants
Patchwork python snakehide Acme boots

Thus he stepped out into the gathering gloom, a white spot in a pool of India ink. Pausing for a moment in the cool breeze, he dug into his pocket, pulled out his keys, and opened the door to his favorite chariot. That car! That beautiful car! All that chrome trimming a cool-black 1960 Chevy Belaire two-door hardtop, with the legendary 283 under the hood.

He ran his hand affectionately over its smooth surface. Every time he looked at it, the love affair began all over again. He had nicknamed it the Batmobile. Everywhere he went in that car, people would smile, wave, and give the thumbs-up. It was a rare sight, a vision from the past, when automobiles were put together to last, each one with its own distinct character.

"Time to spread your wings and fly, my love!" Danny said, as he sat in the driver's seat. He shut the door with an assuring thud and fired it up, and its Mag wheels chirped off.

He arrived at his favorite watering hole, the Superior Bar and Grill, a trendy hangout for Shreveport's upper class where every Thursday through Saturday evening, big spenders and beautiful women piled in. Danny had always been somewhat amused at the changes people went through after they had a couple of drinks under their belts. Doctors who only minutes prior had been looking up some poor slob's hemorrhoidal anus were now looking across salty glasses of tequila and down the low-cut blouses of cooing kittens competing for their attention. Lawyers who entered the place all starched and prim with clients on their mind soon loosened their proper ties and got starry-eyed, spilling alcoholic beverages on their expensive shoes.

"Hey, John! How's about fixin' up a couple of those frozen wonders you make? And put it on my tab, will ya?" Danny asked his favorite bartender. John was used to this, and whipped it up lickety-split, then placed two tall drinks on the bar and nodded his approval. Danny grabbed both, one in each hand, and drew one of the protruding straws into his dry mouth. "Ahhhh... good stuff!" he said gratefully.

The place was jam-packed. Music was playing, but he could hardly hear it over the laughter and loud conversation.

After four or five margaritas he was feeling tight. He plotted a course through the happy hour crowd, their faces appearing and disappearing in the smoky haze. He found the front door and exited.

The sweet night air greeted him. He stretched out on the wooden bench under the bar's pane-glass front, with the light spilling into the street. How often had he done this? There in the dark, watching the people inside, how he wanted to fit in! But somehow... he never quite did.

Lightning cast its jagged fingers earthward, striking nearby. He looked skyward and saw the wind-driven clouds racing across the heavens. "It's gonna rain bloody hell! Oh well..." he said as he continued to slurp on the frozen green margarita. Then it began to rain.

Funny, Danny thought, how every time he got into deep shit it would rain, almost as if the heavens were weeping over him. It rained the time he got busted in Columbus, Georgia for armed robbery. And it rained the time he got arrested in Mississippi for armed robbery, house burglary, and grand theft auto. It was raining now, and darker storms lay ahead. Lightning flashed again, and the wind began to wail.

Daaaanneeee... Come to meeeeee...
Daaaannneeeee... Into my cold embrace...

The night had always had a hypnotic effect on him. Like a lover, it would call to him, caressing him, soothing him. He put down the now-empty glass on the wet wooden bench, stood up, and went walking into the downpour.

"Jose Cuervo, you are a friend of mine!" he sang. "I'd like to shake old Jose's hand right now! You betcha!" Singing and muttering to himself, he danced alone in the rain, oblivious to the storm swirling around him.

Dashing across Line Avenue with the streetlights dancing on the road's surface, he reached his car and fumbled for the keys. They slipped from his dripping fingers and fell onto the parking lot. Wavering, he picked them up and unlocked the Big Chevy with some difficulty.

Inside, he found the ignition and turned the key, sitting there a minute to let the engine warm. The rain began pounding a warning on the metal roof, as the street gutters opened their gaping maws to inhale the murky waters into the depths of the earth, never to be seen again.

Danny smiled to himself as the Batmobile eased onto the swimming street. Zero to fifty he plunged down the hill.

Suddenly, the Big Chevy did a one-eighty to the right, jumped the curb, and leapt sixteen feet into the air! Striking a wooden telephone pole with the crash of busting glass and the scream of twisting metal, the car was cut halfway in two. As if in slow motion, slivers of glass flew all around, like little glittering rainbows.

The door sprung open, and Danny was thrown from the wreckage onto the gritty pavement, head-first. *Wham! Bam!* And out went the lights.

He came to with the rain splattering on his bloody face, raised himself on his skinned elbows, and surveyed the damage.

"Oh my God! My brains are bashed out!" he cried as he felt his head. Blood poured over his face, and his once-white shirt was now completely red.

Fortunately, he had landed on the thickest part of his anatomy. Eight stitches would mend the damage to Danny's head, but the Batmobile's wings had been clipped. The only sign of life was one bright headlight staring aimlessly into the stormy night.

At the hospital, the police questioned Danny about the accident as a doctor stitched up his throbbing head. Amazed and baffled, they wanted to know how on earth the Big Chevy had become airborne and struck the telephone pole sixteen feet above ground zero, snapping in two like a dry twig — while all Danny had to show for it was a 3-1/2" gash in his head and a few scrapes and bruises. It remains a mystery to this day.

There's Gonna Be Trouble

Danny worked briefly in a phone room, until he was fired for what manager Corey Minard later told investigators was low productivity.

Phone solicitation has to be one of the most emotionally stressful jobs out there. You sit in one spot for eight hours or so, and go down the telephone listings one after another, pleading, "Please contribute to the Fireman's Fund," or whatever. "Oh! so you contributed last year? Uh-huh. Well, we need your support again this year… Oh, I'm sorry to hear that. When did he pass away?" And you go on and on in that vein, surrounded by edgy and grumpy oddballs filling the room with smoke from the cigarettes they burn one after another.

It just wasn't for me. So when that tub of lard Corey Minard pulled me into his office and threatened to fire me unless I got more contributions, I almost slugged him. Instead I said, "Hey! You don't have to fire me. I quit! Take this lousy job and shove it!" He got all emotional and called for his pee-on-buddy for support.

They hemmed me up in his office. That was a mistake. I came very close to giving those pukes a taste of chaingang fury. I turned to the hotshot assistant and said, "You better get the fuck away from that door and let me out of here — or there's gonna be trouble!" I guess the look on my face and my tone of voice was enough, because he *moved.*

And I left.

Something Bad is Going to Happen

Agnes Mitchell saw the storm clouds gathering over the little white house on Canal Street.

"After the second time Danny was in prison, he came home, only with the promise that when he would get a job, he would move out. He was working extra time, and I would have to go and pick him up and take him home. And I was always greeted with James Harold yelling, "He's no good, he's not going to live here, I hate him. One of these days, he's going to cross me just a little bit, and I'm going to hurt him, I'm going to hurt him bad, I want him out of here!' That was the tune every time. He would just start talking about how he didn't want Danny. 'All his mother does is cook and wait on him, and she's not supposed to wait on him. He's a grown man,' and he would go on and on like that.

"I went by one day to pick him up, and Danny had painted his dad's house that day. And James was sitting in the front yard with his pistol across his lap, and he was just in a raving, raging disposition. And I said, 'What is the problem?' He said, 'I'm going to kill him. I run him away from here, and I don't want him back here anymore.'

"I said, 'What in the world happened?' He said, 'I told him to paint that house, this end of the house first, and I come back here, and he was painting that end there. I don't want him here anymore, I want him away from here.'

"I said, 'Well look, let me tell you something,

you could get in trouble with waving that gun around,' and he said, 'I'm telling you now you better keep him away from here, I'm going to kill him.'

"And Danny was a hard worker. Danny would do whatever job that you laid out for him to do. There's been times that I would go to East Texas, and I would help him oversee the shop, close it down and stay with the shop, and he handled the money for me. Never one penny short, my money always come up perfect. There was no way Danny could have taken a dollar and I wouldn't have known it.

"When Danny came back from the penitentiary, he was behaving very friendly, very humble at that time. He was always a humble person, a person that you really wanted to take under your wing.

"Danny would have done well. He would have come out of every bit of that and done well, if his dad had not been so abusive to him. James Harold never let him think any different, he always told him he was sorry, he was low down, and he'd never amount to anything.

"The last time I seen Danny was the Sunday afternoon that I took him to look for a truck, because Danny was moving. James Harold talked to Claudia that day and threatened Danny, he threatened to kill him. That was the day of the shooting. And Claudia called Artie before it happened, and said, 'Something bad is going to happen here, I feel it.'"

"Kevin was going to buy a house, and he was doing it strictly to get Danny out of our house," said Claudia. "Because he felt like I did, something terrible was going to happen. I knew it, I felt it. And James would say things like, 'He's getting out of here one way or the other. I'd as soon shoot him as look at him.' He had been saying things like that for two months. And not only had I heard this, but Kevin had heard it and the few neighbors that came over had heard him say it. My sister heard him say it."

Crossing the Bridge

May 18, 1990. The dark figure stood alone on the old stone bridge. As the wind whipped around him, he looked up at the thickening night sky and began to cry.

Oh my God, how can this be?
I have become a Cain driven from his kin!
I have committed the great sin!
I've sown the wind... and reaped the whirlwind!

Lightning fired its blue-white bolts from Heaven's mighty bow, and it began to rain. Only three hours past, Danny Rolling's life had had some sign of normality, if you could call anything in his tortured life normal. At least he had a home, a family, a future. Now in the wink of an eye all that had changed. He stood under an angry sky wondering... *why?*

Earlier that day he had left the Superior Bar and Grill, where he had drunk his fill, and pulled his 1971 canary-yellow Chevy Malibu into his parents' driveway.

Getting out of the yellow hot-rod, he heard thunder off in the distance. "Hmmm... a storm's coming," he said as if he were talking to the wind. He hurried towards the front door, kneeling to perform the Rolling ritual of taking off one's shoes before entering the house. And the clock of fate began to tick.

The little white house on the corner of West Canal and Grassmere held many memories for Danny. There were days when the sun had shined on the Rolling family, but now the storm clouds that had gathered so many times over this house were growing sullen and heavy.

Danny went to his room, changed into his tiger stripe combat fatigues and jungle boots, and started out again. He went into the kitchen to grab a bite to eat, and James Harold asked if he had washed his hands, as he always did. The man was scared to death of germs.

"No," said Danny, and went back into the bathroom and pretended to wash his hands to appease his dad's phobia, then returned to the kitchen.

"Hey, Dad, you going to work tonight?" Danny asked his father.

"Yes, son, your mother should be home soon," James answered matter-of-factly and walked away, leaving Danny standing alone in the kitchen.

"OK, Pop, be careful," Danny called after his

"Oh no, you're not!" said Claudia.

"What is it you want from me!?" demanded Danny, his temper flaring.

James appeared at the kitchen door and leaned against the frame, smiling innocently.

Danny turned to see his father there and blurted out, "What do you think is so funny?" The alcohol was talking now. "You've made my life a living hell!" And with that he grabbed hold of a chair and flung it across the floor, slamming it into the refrigerator.

Freeze frame. The color drained from James Harold' face. Danny knew that look all too well. It was the 1,000-yard stare of a soldier in a frozen foxhole in South Korea. James wasn't even in the kitchen any more. He was reliving a battle in which his buddies were being bayoneted to death all around him, and he was burning up the Browning Automatic Rifle, laying waste to the North Korean Rock soldiers.

James turned and stormed out of the room, with Danny shouting after him, "That's right! Go ahead and get it! Get your gun! I know that's what you're after!"

Danny sensed the situation had gotten out of control and fled. As he ran down the driveway, his father burst from the carport door, gun in hand. *POW! POW! POW!* James fired into the night.

Danny sprinted down the sidewalk and crossed the street, running a zigzag pattern, dodging bullets. Then James ran back inside the house and slammed the door.

Standing on the street corner, Danny caught his breath. "Damn! Dad has really lost it this time!" He waited a minute, then ran back to the house.

dad as he reached into the refrigerator for a quick sip of orange juice.

Then James told Danny to roll up the car windows. Tension between father and son was building, and Danny decided to leave.

Up to this point, everything was normal family stuff. Funny how the course of a life can change in a few seconds of hot temper!

As he reached for the door, his mother Claudia opened it and stepped inside. Mother and son faced each other.

"Where do you think you're going?" asked Claudia, obviously concerned about her son.

"Out," replied Danny, the smell of alcohol heavy on his breath.

He tried the door, but it was locked. He began to worry about his mom, trapped inside there *(no place to run)*. And Dad had his gun. So Danny ran to the back yard, opened the toolshed, and fumbled in the dark until his hand found the cool smooth wooden handle of his .38-caliber revolver.

"I've got something for you this time, Pop!" he yelled, bolting through the front yard. He charged the carport door, jumped into the air, and kicked the door in.

Danny took a shooting stance, pointing his weapon at this father. James was on the phone. "You ain't gonna call the cops on me again, ol' man!"

James Harold let the phone drop and grabbed his weapon off the table.

"If you want to kill somebody, kill me! But don't you dare hurt my mom!"

James Harold pointed his service revolver at his son. *POW! POW! POW!*

Two bullets zinged through the open doorway, missing Danny by inches as he ducked behind the door frame. The third bullet punched through the frame and passed between his legs only a hair from his groin, spraying wood splinters.

Danny answered his father's volley by pointing his .38 around the corner, firing blind. *POW! POW! POW!*

The first bullet went high to the right, slamming into the kitchen cabinet. The second drilled through James' stomach, and the third struck him right between the eyes. He fell like an old oak tree at Danny's feet.

Danny went wild, kicking his fallen father and screaming, "Die, motherfucker! *DIE!*"

Then... everything got real still. Thick red blood pooled under James' head. He looked up at his son, dazed, and began to cry, "Claudia, call an ambulance... call an ambulance..."

With his father's pitiful voice ringing in his ears, Danny suddenly realized what he had done — and he ran.

Run Danny run... run Danny run...
Louisiana's after you...
For the things you've done...
And she's surely gonna find you...
If you don't keep on the run

He jumped into the Chevy and peeled rubber. He couldn't believe what had just happened. Pure panic-stricken, he drove like a madman, running red lights, making hairpin turns at neckbreak speeds. He was a man on a mission. And the mission was...

Run Danny run... from the Lawman's gun
Run Danny run... until your running's done

The yellow Chevy came upon stopped traffic at a red light, and he had to wait for the light to change. Two squadcars raced by, red-blue lights flashing and sirens screaming.

Daaannnneeee...
Daaaaannnnnnneeeeeee...

And the cops disappeared off into the night.

Red to green. Danny stomped it, pushing cars out of the way. 70... 80... 90... 100... the Malibu thundered through the night. Time stood still. The only sounds he could hear were the roar of the engine and his father's broken voice pleading, "Claudia, call an ambulance... call an ambulance..."

He pulled into a local motel near the airport and left the Chevy, its engine crackling hot. "This oughta throw them off for a while," he muttered and dashed across the street. He dove into the thickets and vanished.

As Danny bulldogged his way through the thorns and thickets that ripped at his flesh, lightning stabbed an old grandfather pecan tree, slicing through its wooden heart. He could hear the sirens off in the distance. The dragnet had begun — but they would not catch their fish this night.

Meanwhile, an ambulance had arrived at the Rolling residence, and paramedics were working over James, trying to save his life.

Elsewhere, the Clausens were preparing for bed. They were a well-to-do couple who owned the Coca-Cola bottling plant in Shreveport. Soon, they too would become part of the tragic play.

Danny had met Steve and Luisa at the Superior Bar and Grill some months back, and they had become friends. Even before making their acquaintance, he could tell they were an interesting couple. They were nice and uniquely dressed. They'd had a few drinks and light conversation. As the night wore on, they had invited Danny to their mansion nestled away in the woods, and he had eagerly agreed.

With its majestic white pillars, the two-story structure resembled the beautiful plantation homes of the Civil War era. Their sprawling, pruned grounds had three beautiful fish ponds stocked with big-mouth bass, and the Clausens themselves fit in the picture perfectly. They were both elegant and stately people.

Lightning stretched its burning fingers across the heavens. In the thunder and downpour, the confused and desperate fugitive slooshed his way through the mire that surrounded the Clausen estate.

As he reached their residence, the Clausens turned out the lights downstairs and climbed the winding staircase to their luxurious bedroom.

The shadow in the night lurked outside their living room pane-glass double doors. He looked through the glass, a silhouette against the bluish strobes of lightning that revealed his presence.

He could see one of several giant chandeliers hanging from the ceiling and the solid white grand piano by the fireplace as he pushed his way in. His muddy boots trailed across the plush white carpet. The security system began to sing an alarm.

Up the winding staircase the shadow crept, leaving muddy brown footprints with every step. Once at the top, he took out one of the .38's he carried and burst into the room.

Meanwhile, James Rolling was on the operating table awaiting emergency surgery for two gunshot wounds. As the surgeons examined his x-rays, they exchanged surprised and baffled glances.

"Look at that, will you? Can you believe it?"

"He's a very lucky man."

"I'd say it was more like a miracle! Look here. See how the bullet entered the skull? And then split in two separate halves after it hit the brain? And look where they traveled!"

"Yes, completely around his brain! And then exited the back of his head! This man's brain must be as stubborn as a mule!"

Both men laughed, trying to take the edge off an already hectic day. Then their attention concentrated on the second wound.

"Well, bust my buttons! He must live mighty close to ol' Saint Pete!"

"Yep, through and through. No vitals even touched. This one will heal without any help from us."

"Well, it's gonna be a long night. Let's see if we can patch this old soldier up."

Steve was lying on the couch, and Luisa was stretched out on their massive bed like a pampered calico cat, when Danny Rolling jumped into their quiet world. He pointed the .38 at Steve.

"Don't move, Steve. I want your money. I know there's a safe around here some place. Where is it?"

"We don't have any money laying around here, and there is no safe."

Steve got up and approached Danny. With his left hand outstretched, he was pleading, "Give me the gun, Danny. Come on now, give it to me."

Surprisingly, Danny did just that. Steve took the .38 and unloaded it. As he did, the phone rang. Both men looked at the phone.

"Tell 'em it's OK, Steve." He knew it would be the security service answering the alarm.

Steve picked up the phone and gave the password. "Yes, it's Heaven. That's right, it's Heaven. Thank you." And he hung up.

Danny had a sudden change of heart and pulled the second .38, pointed it at Steve, and barked, "Give me back my gun. Come on, give it to me. And the bullets too."

Steve, obviously upset, handed Danny the guns and the bullets.

Luisa burst in, "You're upsetting him! He just got back from the doctor today. He has an ulcer." Then turning on Steve with her voice rising shrilly, "This is the last time we ever pick up anyone from a bar! The last time! You hear?"

After a tense pause, Danny said evenly, "All right. Let's all go downstairs."

They all went down into the kitchen. Luisa took one look at the muddy carpet and wailed, "Look at this carpet! We just had it cleaned!"

Danny was apologetic. "Let me clean it up for you."

Luisa stared at him. "No, just let it dry," she

said uneasily.

They all took up places in the kitchen.

In the clear light of the kitchen, Danny got a close look at Steve and Luisa and burst into a torrent of sobs. "My God! What am I doing? Why am I doing this? You guys are my friends. I wouldn't hurt you for anything in this world. I've just shot my dad. I've killed him for sure. I'm so sorry. I don't know what to do."

Luisa leaned toward him and spoke gently. "How do you know you've killed him? Have you called the hospital?"

Danny looked up at the concerned woman through his tears as if seeing her from far away. "No," he said softly, and brightening, "Do you think I should?"

"It wouldn't hurt. What hospital do you think they would take him to?"

"The Willis Knighten."

Luisa called information, got the number, dialed it, and handed the phone to Danny.

Burrr... burrr... burrr...

"Hello, Willis Knighten Hospital. May I help you?"

"Yes, I'm a friend of James Harold Rolling, who was shot earlier tonight? And I was just wondering, how's he doing?"

"I'm sorry, I'm afraid I can't give out that information."

"Look, lady. James Harold and I are old police buddies, and I just want to know if he's OK."

"Hold on a minute, sir... he's still on the operating table."

"Thank you." He hung up the phone. "Thank God above! He's still alive! I don't know why all this had to happen. I'm so sorry for disturbing you. Look, I'll go now."

Steve gestured to Luisa, "Honey, give Danny twenty dollars."

"Oh no!" Danny looked offended. "I don't want your money!"

"Look how he changes!" said Luisa.

"Go ahead and give it to him."

Luisa grabbed an apple, some cookies, and a twenty dollar bill from their bank bag lying right there on the kitchen table, and urged Danny to take it. He did, and left with tears streaming down his face.

Into the now-calmed storm he fled, weeping, "What has become of my life?" as the night embraced him. The storm threatened to pour out its wrath again. The lighting crashed, the thunder roared, and Danny stumbled on through the dark.

He came upon a stream where a beaver swam playfully, flipping its flat round tail with a smack atop the cool water. Danny sat there on the banks of the stream and watched.

"How I wish I were you, little feller. No troubles, no worries, just plenty of trees to gnaw on, and lots of nice cool water to play in."

He sat there for a while, until a big black water moccasin slithered near. He moved on. He came upon the old stone bridge and stood there alone in the cool night, listening to the wind rustle through the trees. The air was sweet, heavy with night smells. Lightning flashed across the sky and the wind began to cry.

Daaannnneeee... my wayward child...
Daaannnneeee... so dangerous and wild...
Daaannnneeee... come to me and know...
I will not judge you... oh child of woe...

Rain began to fall. A shadow amongst shadows, the cursed man bid a bitter farewell to his past and crossed the bridge, as once again the night engulfed him.

Contemplation of Mortality

To Think of Life and contemplate death
That which gives and takes breath
Vague illusions of euphoria
metaphoric visions of dementia
Down the winding staircase into The Abyss
Where shadows pulse & twist

by Danny Rolling 1-17-95 ★

CHAPTER 7
GETTING BABES

Goin' to Kansas City

The fleeing felon was next sighted at a Best Western Motel in Kansas City, Kansas. The front desk clerk, Mr. Feliz Brown, later ID'd Danny Rolling from a photo-pak, remembering that he carried a guitar, used a duffel bag and a tote bag for luggage and a taxi for transportation, and hung around the motel lobby. Brown told investigators that Danny had said he was in town to play at a local bar.

When I was on the run as an outlaw, I packed a guitar. I sang my songs in parks and wherever people gathered. I was never in a band that earned money playing gigs, but I have played in a couple of bars here and there and in a couple of talent shows. At night I might drift into a bar or sidewalk cafe and sing a song or two, then disappear into the night. I'd play for the ladies to get some filly interested and then take her back to my room for drinks and kinks. HA!

I met this hippie named Roam in Kansas City. He gave me a crystal I wore on a twisted silver chain. This sexy redhead and I took a trip with him and his girlfriend up to the Superior National Forest for the annual Rainbow Festival.

I did commit several burglaries and robberies while I was in Kansas City, including a Taco Bell and two grocery stores (one of them twice). I tried to rob a bank too, but that turned out to be a joke.

It was a cloudy day in Kansas City the year of our Lord 1990 when a masked bandit brandishing a loaded .22 caliber revolver proceeded to enter the bank in question. Inside, three men dressed in business suits had their casual conversation abruptly interrupted by a most curious sight. As they stood there with bewildered faces, a masked bandit stood outside the bank's entrance shaking the pane glass with grave intent. Ah, but alas. 'Twas not to be as he willed. Either the robber had come calling a bit too early, or tried the wrong door. At any rate, the doors were obviously locked. For one brief moment, bank attendants and discouraged robber gawked at each other, not knowing what to think of each other. Finally the moment passed, and the outlaw shrugged his shoulders, held out his hands, shook his head, then dashed off without a penny of the bank's money.

June 2, 1990. Michael Kennedy returned home from a trip to find his home on Canal St. in Kansas City burglarized. The thief had stolen two handguns and the identification papers of his deceased son, Michael Kennedy, Jr., who had been born in England in 1949. His had been a brief and troubled life. He lost both legs in Vietnam in 1969, and then became an alcoholic and a drug addict. He would have been 41 if he hadn't died in 1975 under suspicious circumstances. Now Michael Kennedy, Jr., began an equally troubled life as the new identity of a serial killer on the run from the law.

June 12, 1990. A masked bandit wearing black gloves and brandishing a large caliber handgun robbed the Westwood United Superstore in Kansas City, getting away with $1,661. He was videotaped telling witnesses, "Thank you... God bless... please pray for me... God knows I need it."

June 22, 1990. The restless outlaw was on the run again, catching a bus from Kansas City to Denver, then from there to the outskirts of Boulder, where he camped out for about a week in the foothills of the Rockies before returning to Kansas City.

June 30, 1990. The masked bandit paid a return visit to the Westwood United Superstore in Kansas City, this time getting away with $2,001.

A few days later, the same bandit made out somewhat better at the Sunfresh Grocery Store, a

by Danny Rolling 3-29-93

half-mile down the road in Westport, Missouri, where he hit them up for $8,902 and quipped, "Sorry guys, life's a bitch," upon exiting the premises.

Nothing more was heard from the elusive fugitive until July 9, when he made a couple of collect calls to Shreveport from a Kansas City pay phone, in which he described hiding in the woods and evading police. When urged to turn himself in, he said he couldn't do that, because he had violated his parole by shooting his dad, and he refused to go back to prison. He'd rather be dead.

I Want In

It was in Kansas City that he first smoked cocaine, and came close becoming either a cocaine cowboy or a bucket of fishbait as a result.

After downing several margaritas at a club one night, he was walking back to the crashpad where he was staying with a bunch of hippies, when he noticed a thin white guy talking to a black dude.

As he approached, the black guy walked away and the white guy opened the driver's door to a brown & white Lincoln Continental.

"Hey man!" the tall stranger hailed the driver. "I'll give you ten bucks if you give me a lift to Rainbow."

"Sure thing, hop in," the driver said, and introduced himself as Steve.

"I'm Mike," said Danny, "Mike Kennedy."

But instead of visiting his favorite hippie hangout, Michael Kennedy was going to take a little side trip through the world of organized crime.

Steve guided the Continental onto the highway and they ended up in a giant parking lot out in the middle of nowhere. He pulled up beside another Lincoln Continental identical to the one he was driving, except the rear bumper was bent away from the frame on the left side. That wouldn't have been so strange if it was a used car lot or dealership with many cars alike, but it wasn't. It looked like a lot where people leave their cars to go to work. But there weren't any other Lincolns in sight.

Steve got out and unlocked the trunk on the other Lincoln. While he was fiddling around, Mike noticed some fine white powder on the console. "Ah, cocaine," Mike said to himself. Steve returned with an attaché case and put it in the back seat.

"Is that cocaine?" Mike asked as they pulled back on the highway. Steve gave him a guarded look. Turns out he had been driving non-stop for three days transporting cocaine and marijuana for the mob.

Steve and Mike ended up in a room on the 52nd floor of a plush hotel. Mike ordered room service, and over steak and eggs Steve described how Mike might fit into their little family.

Mike needed some kind of gig, and it didn't matter what kind of work they could offer. He ran down the whole story of how he was already on the run from the law.

Steve said Big Louie was on the way and it would be up to him. They had a couple of hours to wait, but it looked good. Steve needed a relief driver, and if Mike checked out with Big Louie, he was all set. If not — well, you can guess the name of that tune.

After breakfast, Steve opened his black and silver attaché case and Mike saw it was filled to the brim with white powder and weed.

The fugitive rolled a couple of joints while the mobster prepared a glass pipe for freebasing. They sat there smoking killer Colombian reefer and freebasing practically pure cocaine.

Suddenly there was a knock at the door, and before either man could get up to answer, the head maid opened the door. If the chain had not been on it, she would have just waltzed right in on the party.

Mike freaked out big-time. He could just see cops crawling out of the woodwork at any minute. He jumped up and dashed to the door, slamming it in the woman's face.

"Hey!" he called through the door. "There's people in here!"

"Oh, I didn't know!" The maid looked startled as he peered at her through the peephole. "We're just cleaning. You should've hung out the Do Not Disturb sign." But she didn't go away. She just stood there in the hall, as Mike watched her through the peephole.

When she finally walked away, Mike said,

"Steve! Man, I know that broad knows something's going on here. She had to have smelt the weed. I think we oughta split.

"Yeah, man, I believe you are right," said Steve. "Tell you what — you go on down stairs and I'll gather up my stuff. Just take the elevator and I'll meet you at the car."

"OK." And Mike dashed down the stairs, all 52 floors. Buzzing away with cocaine-fed paranoia, he was afraid of being hemmed up in the elevator.

He hurried out to the Continental and stood beside it. And stood… and stood… and stood. For an hour he stood by the car waiting on that spaced-out wise guy.

Finally, he decided to go back up to the 52nd floor and find out what gives. The cops hadn't shown up, so he figured what the hell.

He banged on the door, but no answer. Peering through the peephole, he could see Steve crashed out on the bed. Man! Here he was way the hell out — he didn't even know where — and this guy was playing him for a chump!

Mike beat on the door until he woke up everyone on the floor — everyone, that is, except ol' Steverino.

Finally, someone must have complained to the manager, because he showed up, along with the head maid, the security guard, and two big ugly goons. They did not look friendly.

"What's going on here?" demanded the manager.

"Hey, I'm sorry about the ruckus, but I stepped out for a minute and my cousin locked me out. He's been driving all night, and he's crashed. Can't wake him up."

Well now, the door had a deadbolt lock on the inside, so the passkey didn't help. They had to get the maintenance man to take the door off the frame. It took about twenty minutes, and all the while, the guy inside didn't budge an inch.

Can you imagine his surprise when he was rudely awakened by the manager, the security guard, the head maid, the maintenance man, the two big ugly gorillas?

By the time the door was reattached and everyone had left, Mike had the distinct impression the hotel was a family-owned operation.

Steve was fuming. Mike looked into his bloodshot eyes to see that old familiar tombstone stare that says, "You done fucked up this time, kid, and you're one step away from the grave."

"What the hell!" Steve spat. "I've got a lot to lose here!"

"Hey man, why did you leave me standing outside?"

"You better get the fuck outta here before Big Louie shows up. Cause if he finds you here, you're dead meat."

It was exit stage right for Mike. After running back down the 52 flights of stairs again, he stepped out onto the parking lot just in time to see Big Louie himself thunder up in a black and gold Trans Am with another wiseguy on board.

He knew that's who it was because Steve had let it slip that Louie drove a souped-up Trans Am, and there was that certain something in the way the man carried himself.

He must have been coke-crazed, because he got right in Big Louie's face and said, "I want in."

"Who the hell are you?" Louie snarled, looking at the stranger like he was a mangy dog about to be pumped full of bullets.

"Steve said I could have a job."

"Listen! You better get as far away from here as you can, as fast as you can, and don't bother Steve again. Have you got that straight?"

"Yep! Clear as a bell, brother. I'm outta here!"

And so the hapless wanderer was on the move again. Walking away from one death trip, he kept right on walking towards another.

Close Call

Up the path that snaked through the foothills of the Rocky Mountains, the solitary man trudged.

Overhead, a million stars twinkled in the dark moonless sky. Climbing, he sought a place to camp for the night. Recently it had been so every night, the weary soul searching in the dark for rest, like Dracula returning to his coffin before sunrise.

He found a suitable spot and cast down the brown sleeping bag he toted on his back.

There on the rocky hilltop he could see for miles. Boulder, Colorado sprawled out below, swimming in the dark sea of night. What a magnificent sight!

The cold breeze whispered through the mountains and chilled him to the bone. Quickly! He stripped and zipped himself bare inside the inviting cotton and nylon sleeping bag, and fell asleep gazing at the stars keeping watch over him.

He awoke early the next morning to the sound of a jogger making her way around the trail. She hopped up and smiled gaily at the sleepy-eyed man stirring in the bag. He waved. She laughed and waved back, then disappeared down the path.

The man peeled off the bedding, stood up naked and stretched, letting the early sun warm him. Another jogger, a young man, raced by and disappeared where the path split like a serpent's forked tongue.

Then it came! It loved the night, but today it burst into his mind unannounced — and Danny became GEMINI. Whenever that force seduced its way into his subconscious that way, he succumbed to its will.

Naked on the hill, Gemini pulled the knife from its hiding place and slashed at the air laughing.

Danny's out, I'm in... Danny's out, I'm in...
Let's go hunting... my hopeless friend

He then reached down, picked up his pants, put them on, and gazed about the land for a victim to prey upon.

At the bottom of the trail she came. Jogging happily up the steep grade, her golden locks swishing in the mountain air, her athletic lungs and heart pumped her steadily on, towards a very close call with *DEATH.*

The only ambush spot on the barren trail was a small weeping willow standing alone by a trickling brook midway up a long hill. Gemini waited patiently there, like a tiger in a stand of bamboo ready to pounce.

He hid the roll of duct tape in the back pocket of his striped hippie pants and stuffed the hunting knife down the small of his back.

Here she comes... Oh, my pretty...
Come to me... Into my misery...

Closer and closer she ran up the foot-pounded path. Sweat poured down her beautiful porcelain face and over her perfect breasts.

Gemini was watching the blonde approach, when he became distracted by the babbling of the brook. He was drawn into the crystal clear water flowing gently down the hill. It calmed him, hypnotized him... and for a moment, Danny returned to himself.

Then he looked down at the young damsel drawing nearer, and the struggle between the forces wrestling for control within him began. Ah, but alas, Gemini was stronger and prevailed.

He stood up just as the blonde athlete rounded the willow. She stopped dead in her tracks startled for the moment. He smiled. She smiled back, relieved, and continued on by him.

Quick as a lethal hooded cobra he struck his victim! Drew the blade, and in the same motion grabbed the running girl by the arm.

She screamed and turned with fear burning in her blue eyes! He flung her to the ground like a rag-doll, and was upon her, knife poised above, blade mirrored in the hot sun's blaze of fury!

But the woman was not easily felled. The adrenaline spurting through her brain gave her blind courage and strength. She began to strike out, surprising her assailant with determined desperation.

Smack! Smack! She punched the crazed man in the face with all her might. *Pow! Right in the kisser!* But what followed was a terrible beating.

When Gemini tasted blood in his mouth he went into a rage. *Thud! Thud! Thud! Thud! Thud!* Blow after blow rained down on the once-beautiful face staring in shock at him.

"Ah... Ahhhhh..." the crazed man screamed bloody hell and brandished the knife in her face. "You're gonna *DIE!*"

He turned the paralyzed beaten lass over on her stomach and bound her hands behind her back with the gray tape. She began to weep. "Why are you doing this? You're a good-looking guy, you don't have to do this," she pleaded from her broken and bloody face as he wrapped the sticky gray tape tighter, like a spider spinning its web.

Heaving sobs, she made one last effort to gain sympathy and freedom from this web she was caught in. The scene reminds one of the old black and white version of the movie, *The Fly,* where the mutated split persona of the mad scientist with the head of a man and the body of a fly was entwined in the spider's web. As the black spider slowly, deliberately made its way to its prey, the fly-man began to plead, "Help me… help meeeee…" But in the movie the fly did not escape. This one would.

She began to plead with one spoken word: *"NO!"*

As if it were a magic word, presto! Danny came to himself. Looking down at the trembling girl in a daze, he turned her on her back. Her face was a bloody mess and the frightened young woman was weeping pathetically.

Danny's heart squeezed within his chest as he spoke. "Oh, Lady! I'm so sorry! I didn't mean to hurt you. Here, let's get this tape off you."

He released her from the bonds. She hesitated for a moment to see if her captor truly intended to set her free — or was he toying with her? She stood up slowly, then ran violently down the hill screaming at the top of her lungs, arms waving about helter-skelter!

Danny stood there shaking his head as he watched her.

Once she disappeared from his sight, he ran up and over the hill in the opposite direction. "They'll be coming for you now, boy," he whispered to himself as he poured the coals on and sprinted like a runaway freight train out of control.

He ran for two mountainous miles. Crossing the only road in the area, he climbed a thorny undergrown hillside, and fell exhausted. The brush was shallow, parched brown by the sun, and gave little concealment, but it did offer the only cover, and it gave him a good vantage point from which to witness the search he knew was approaching.

It did not take long. The flashing red lights, the wailing sirens, they came. The dragnet was underway. It was a game Danny had played many times before — the fox and the hounds. If caught, the fox would pay — and pay dearly. He lay very still, intently watching and listening.

What's that you hear?
Hound dogs a-howlin' and just as you fear
The lawdogs found you for the things you've done
Take a look around you, now where will you run?

For eight hours, every available man and woman in uniform beat the bushes and climbed over rocky peaks bird-dogging for the hiding man.

The sun rose directly overhead as noonday arrived. Its hateful rays burned into his flesh. Hour upon painful hour, he did not move — he could not. Those that sought him were everywhere. Hound dogs bellowed near, some only feet away. He could even hear their masters' conversations.

"He's out there, I can feel it. We'll get 'im."

"I don't know… there's something different about this one. It's been six hours… and nothing. Two more hours and it's shift change. We'll have to call it off by then."

The hours dragged on. A brown eagle circled. The sun dove behind the pine-covered peaks. And finally the police left empty-handed.

Later that night as he knelt by a cool mountain stream to feed his thirst, he promised himself he would never do this again. But how many times had he made that same promise? The stars came out, the wind whispered through the mountains, and the haunted desperado survived… for now.

This is the Place

July 17, 1990. Michael Kennedy, Jr., checked into Room 124 at the Travel Lodge in Tallahassee, Florida. The next day the same man went to a Tallahassee Army-Navy store near the bus station and bought the Ka-bar Marine fighting knife that Danny Rolling would later characterize as "deadly, sharp and huge."

At the Gainesville student murder trial, inmate Rusty Binstead testified that Danny had told him he had selected that particular weapon because it was exceptionally well-designed for killing, featuring a blood groove along the blade that allows it to "go in like butter and come out like butter."

July 22, 1990. The dangerous drifter packed his new killing blade and took a Greyhound Bus to Sarasota, Florida.

As I passed through Gainesville headed for Sarasota, I heard the voice of Gemini again.

This is the place, Danny.
It will happen here.

I knew then I would be back and something terrible would happen there, but I just didn't want to believe it. I was having too good a time with the thousands of dollars I had stolen during the robberies in Kansas to entertain a blood bath in Gainesville. My destination was to be Key West, then the Virgin Islands, then Jamaica — but I ended up in Sarasota, and I liked it there so much I stayed and spent several thousand dollars doing the town. When I ran out of cash, I robbed a grocery store. I spent that as well, then sold my guitar for cash to go north again to do another robbery so I could acquire the dough to continue my quest to find a Jamaican maryjane farm and make the place home. Ah but alas, I never made it to the jungles of Jamaica. My cash got me as far as Gainesville — and the rest is history.

Getting Babes

July 22, 1990. In his first two weeks in Sarasota at the Cabana Inn, Danny had his hair styled and started sporting fashionable jewelry, eyewear and clothes, easing the transition into his new identity as Michael Kennedy. During his stay in this resort community, he bought marijuana and a gun, dated several girls, and committed several crimes, including a rape and an armed robbery.

Investigators later interviewed James R. Ford, who told them that he had first met Mike Kennedy in mid-August, when he entered the young men's clothing department at Burdines, an upscale department store in the Southgate Plaza Mall. He described Kennedy as having fair skin, a thin face, well-sunned brown hair, huge hands, expensive Ralph Lauren gold-rim glasses, and an extremely firm handshake. Wearing Reebok high-tops and jeans, he bought a white Francis Girbaud polo-type shirt and multicolored beach pants, paying about $100 in cash.

The next time Ford saw him was near the front entrance of the mall, as Ford was getting off work the same day. Kennedy greeted him in an "extremely friendly" manner, and suggested they have dinner together. They ate at Beasley's in the mall, and Kennedy paid for everything, as he always did. During dinner, Kennedy told him he was a trucker who had sold a country song for $10,000. Ford observed that his new friend was a big tipper, that he did not seem preoccupied with sex, that he did not ask about local prostitutes, and he never displayed any homosexual tendencies.

However, when he saw him again two days later, Kennedy inquired about local bars and "getting babes." Ford agreed to show him some of the local night life, and they went out together twice, along with Ford's roommate Derek Kabobel.

Kennedy was wearing a bandanna tied around his head when he pulled up at Ford's house in a taxi. He came inside, and while there, spotted Ford's 9mm Taurus semiautomatic pistol. He immediately offered to buy it for $500, and later Ford did sell him the weapon.

They started out at the Cabana Bar, then walked to the Five-O Club. Later, Kennedy asked the Yellow Cab driver to take them to Club Mary, a nude bar, but when they got there, it was closed.

Their second night out, they went to dinner at the Chop House Restaurant on the Sarasota Quay. After dinner they went to the Club Bandstand, where Ford observed Kennedy "acting goofy."

Ford and Kabobel left him at the club after they allegedly saw Kennedy with a heavily made-up plump brunette woman. Investigators later reported Ford's statement that Kennedy had been thrown out of the bar after an altercation.

I do not recall meeting any plump woman with heavy makeup. I do remember being kicked out of the place though. I was drunk and made a pass at some broad. I grabbed her by the hand and asked her if she wanted to dance. Apparently she complained and I was thrown out. The police security came and got me and threatened to throw me in jail. That sobered me up quick. There was no fight, I just went peaceably. If the bouncers had tried to rough me up, well then, there would have been one *hell* of a fight!

Ford stated that he believed Kennedy had given the woman a gold chain which she later returned with a letter. When he later visited Kennedy in his motel room, he noticed the letter, and since it had no postmark, he assumed it had been hand-delivered.

Misconception. Ford & I did go to the Quay,

but the thing with my putting a gold chain in some dame's neck is *bullshit!* I did give one of the gold chains I wore to a girl, but she was a blonde I met at the Cabana Inn. I gave it to her in my room. She kept it a couple of days, then hand-returned it in an envelope.

Kennedy played an Ovation guitar and sang some of his original songs for Ford, who thought he was an excellent rhythm and blues guitarist. He suggested they go out to a club where Kennedy could play, but Kennedy declined. While Kennedy played guitar, Ford noticed that his ring finger was amputated right below the first joint.

Later, Ford sold Kennedy a quarter-ounce of marijuana for $100, and at that time he noticed the Ovation guitar was gone. When he asked Kennedy what happened to it, he replied that he had pawned it. Ford told investigators that he also noticed numerous stuffed animals from the Cabana crane machine, and a large amount of currency in a box under the bed.

Ford has got his wires crossed. I never kept a large amount of money in a box under my bed. I kept it in the motel dresser. During Ford's brief visit to deliver the marijuana, for some strange reason he just pulled one of the dresser drawers open and bingo! There lay stacks and stacks of folding green. I don't know where he got this box under the bed thing.

When the investigators told Ford that Mike Kennedy was really Danny Rolling, the suspect in the Gainesville murders, Ford replied that he thought he had recognized his face in the paper, and had even drawn glasses on the picture to make it look more recognizable.

A Cold Anger

In 1991, Florida State Department of Law Enforcement investigators met with LoLaLe Seamans at her Sarasota home for two interviews about the man she knew as Mike Kennedy. Throughout the first interview, she denied any intimacy, but when pressed by the investigators in second interview, she finally gave explicit details of several sexual encounters with him. She characterized him as harmless and nice, and said he never forced himself upon her in any way.

She met Mike at the Cabana Inn. She lived nearby, and while her car was in the shop, she would ride her bike to the bar for happy hour. She enjoyed meeting new people, but she protected her privacy by never giving out her home address or phone number.

The handsome stranger drinking screwdrivers and bloody marys made a good first impression. Tall and trim, muscular and athletic, he was wearing baggy jeans with high-top athletic shoes. He was neat and clean, with freshly-trimmed light brown hair combed straight back. His expensive eyewear contributed to the distinguished young professional look, and when he took his glasses off, she was drawn by the searching gaze in his soulful hazel eyes. As she moved in for a closer look, she noticed the receding hairline, the missing fingertips, and the small gold earring.

The Cabana Bar had one of those toy crane machines. When she told her new friend she couldn't make the crane work, he went straight to the machine and pumped it full of quarters, returning directly with an armful of stuffed animals and a big smile for her. It was a good ice-breaker.

He bought her round after round of drinks. When questioned about the evening a year later, she described her condition as quite drunk, and added that she couldn't remember whether she'd had sex with the attractive stranger that first night or not.

The man who introduced himself as Michael Kennedy spun an intricate web of half-convincing lies to cover up his criminal lifestyle. He described himself as a trucker on vacation. He started out saying he had a girlfriend in Kansas City who was living in his house, but then added that he was actually breaking up with her, and she was supposed to move out by the time he came back from vacation. He said he had been married once before, but he had nothing to say about his ex-wife.

He told her he was a veteran, and had gone to Vietnam as a specialist in the Army. Warming to her company and testing her responsiveness, he told her he liked Sarasota, and was thinking about starting a business and relocating there. He mentioned in passing that he had come to Sarasota from Texas on a bus, then demurred that he rode the bus because he didn't like to fly or ride a train. LoLaLe thought that was a bit peculiar for someone in the trucking business.

The second time she saw him, she knew they were going to have sex when they left the Cabana Inn that morning. He took her out to eat, but she can't remember where. She remembered the dinner conversation was boring. It seemed all Mike wanted to talk about was his money.

After dinner they came back to the Cabana and had a few drinks. This time she is sure she went back to his room and took a shower with him. The way she recalls it, their second date was the first time they had sex. Investigators reported LoLaLe's version of sex with Mike Kennedy.

Mike asked her to have anal sex with him, she said, but when she declined he accepted her refusal without pressing the issue. She admitted that Mike went down on her, but denied returning the favor. He had two orgasms, she said, once depositing his sperm on her abdomen and once on the sheets.

She remembers being sexually intimate with him three times, but denies that there was ever any penile penetration — although they did come close several times. She describes herself as the more aggressive one, always taking the lead sexually and sometimes even being pushy with him. He never forced himself on her and he was always reserved with her sexually. He never did anything she didn't want him to, and she saw no sexual idiosyncrasies she would describe as bizarre, although she noticed that he did like to stroke himself to heighten his excitement. When she reached down to touch his balls she noticed that he flinched painfully, explaining he'd been injured in a fight.

On their third date, they went to the movies at the Sarasota Square Mall. Mike wanted to see *Young Guns* but deferred to her wishes, and took her to a Bill Murray movie instead. Even though Mike got on her nerves by complaining like a kid and making sarcastic remarks throughout the movie, nevertheless after several rounds of drinks back at the Cabana, once again she accompanied him to his room to enjoy him sexually. This time, she says she brought along a vibrator, and Mike was open-minded about using it to satisfy her.

In the ten days she knew him, she spent several evenings with him in his room, where he was often dressed in a brand-new freshly-pressed black karate gi. They would have sex, and afterwards she might read a book while he watched TV. Though he treated her well, she refrained from "snooping around his room," because underneath the smooth surface she sensed a potential for violence.

He showed her a little black bag containing a great deal of money, and told her he had brought ten to fifteen thousand dollars with him on vacation. Every time she saw him, he would tell her, "We've got *x* amount of money left."

He liked to play his black round-backed Ovation acoustic guitar and sing what she called "message songs." Once she interrupted him while he was recording a song, and she told investigators she thought that a comment she had made about the keys being in the door had been taped.

When he took her out, they took taxis everywhere. She asked him why he didn't rent a car, but he never replied. One evening in the Cabana, he came back from the john to find her talking to another man, and made a scene, which struck Ms. Seamans as juvenile.

He behaved like a teenager with her. Whenever they went to the mall, she would practically have to drag him away from the video arcade. He lost his temper over little things, and was preoccupied with what he could do to people with his karate skills.

One evening Mike started crying and complaining that he was depressed about life. He mentioned the breakup with his girlfriend and the Vietnam war, saying that Vietnam vets weren't treated fairly. She didn't want to hear it.

He would go off on tangents. One minute he'd be talking about the Army and getting all upset because Vietnam veterans were disrespected, then he'd start going on about his black belt and demonstrating his karate moves, or he'd pull out the guitar and start singing. It was weird.

When he offered to buy her some expensive jewelry, she refused, explaining that she just wanted a casual relationship. Here he was talking about moving to Sarasota to be with her after only a few days acquaintance. He was taking the whole thing too seriously. Finally, one night at the Cabana, she ignored him. She could tell Mike was upset, but instead of making a scene as she had feared, he just started talking with some other people, and the evening passed uneventfully.

Later, LoLaLe felt guilty for how she had treated him, and gave him a call. They had a cordial telephone conversation, and then she came to his room to pick up her bike, leaving him a card thanking him for how nice he had been. Although he was friendly, somehow she sensed "a cold anger" under the surface. He told her he was down to his last $200 and he was going back to Kansas City. He had come to town on a Greyhound, he said, and that's how he was going to leave .

The next day, when she called the Cabana Inn, Mike Kennedy had checked out.

I have never — repeat, *never* — asked her or anyone else for anal sex, period. I don't even believe in it. I don't know why on earth she would say that about me. She knows it's a lie. Perhaps she is trying to save face because she had to admit she had sex with a serial killer.

I may have jacked off after sex with her, because she said she wasn't on the pill and I didn't want to get her pregnant. We did have intercourse and oral sex though. She said there was no penetration. Bull! We went the distance. There was penile penetration on at least three separate occasions, and it was great! We both had a good time.

And yes! I did go down on that beautiful girl, and she loved it. She can say she didn't go down on me — but she did.

She said I was a reserved lover: NEVER! I've never been a passive or reserved lover. There have been few women who could keep up with me.

I doubt if the women I had the brief affairs with in Sarasota will ever tell it like it was — sexually, that is. I don't know. Maybe they will. Still, I feel they must have their guard up.

I don't want to cause them any embarrassment that can be avoided. But since they have been called upon to speak on the matter, and have placed their versions of sex with me in the public record, I'm gonna have to tell it like it *really* was.

I have nothing bad to say about those girls. Each one came back a second time, and that's a fact. So it couldn't have been *that* bad. Each one was treated by me as though she were *royalty*, and she knows it.

The Rolling Tape

While staying at the Cabana Inn, Danny used a portable stereo tape recorder to record the first half of an audiocassette which was later played in court.

The tape consists of two sessions. The first session, recorded in Danny's room at the Cabana Inn, is a tearful farewell to his family followed by several original songs. The Sarasota session ends abruptly when LoLaLe Seamans interrupts the taping by knocking on the door.

The second session was recorded in Gainesville, immediately before the murders. It concludes with what have been called the most ominous words ever intoned in Gainesville, "I got something I gotta do." Testimony later revealed that Danny Rolling had murder in mind when he spoke those words.

I don't know what people think any more. All I know is I'm just one man alone facing the whole world by himself. But I'm making this tape for the three people I love the most, and I'll always love the most. I love my mother, I love my father, and I love my brother. And no matter what anybody thinks about this man Danny Harold Rolling, I want these three people that I'm talking to right now to know that this is not the road I wanted. But it is the road that is before me now, and I will walk it like a man.

You know I love you, Pop. And I'm sorry, Dad. It rips my heart out by the roots to think what happened between you and I. I'm sorry, Pop. If it means anything, I'm so very sorry. And I suffer a lot behind this. I hurt in my heart. And it never goes away, Pop. I wish it had happened to me instead of you. This isn't easy. Nothing's ever been easy for me. I always wanted to make you proud of me, Dad, but somehow or other, I always fell short. But I promise you this much. No matter what happens on the road ahead of me, at least I'll walk it as a man. I will do that.

Mom, you're a precious, precious soul. There ain't a woman on the face of this earth that can cook like you can, sugar. You hear me? You've got to be the best cook in the whole wide world. And believe you me, I miss it. I love you, Mom. I want you to know your boy's OK. I'm gonna be all right. There's something I want you to understand. The last time I saw you, I saw how much it hurt you to say goodbye to me. And you know something, Mom? I'm not gonna put you through that again. I love you too much for that. But I want you to purpose it in your heart that I'm a man now. And even God himself said that being a man wasn't easy. And oh, how well I know it isn't easy. Especially a man like myself. Can't trust anyone, can't be totally true, I have to always live this lie that I'm living.

And Mom, don't blame yourself for anything in the past. None of it's your fault. I don't really believe it's anybody's fault. It's just the way things happen sometimes. Sometimes we want so much for things to be right, especially with the ones we love. But it doesn't always happen that way, does it, Mom? But we have to go on, as long as there's breath in our bodies. We've gotta go on, Mom. You've gotta go on. You're a very special woman. And oh, how well I know that I was raised by one of the sweetest women on the face of this earth. And I know Dad is so glad to have you. He picked him a gem all right. Yeah, Pop. You got you a good one. And she got her a good one too. You're a good man, Pop.

Mom, I want you to go on. What I'm trying to say is, after this tape, you're not going to hear anything else from me. Just — just forget about me. Well, I won't say that. Because you can't forget your own. I want you to go on and live your life. I don't want you to have sleepless nights because of me. Do this for me, Mom. You deserved a hell of a lot more than the pain that I've brought you. And I regret it with all my heart. But if you want to make things easier for me, Mom, please, I'm asking you, go on. I love you. Go on and live your life, and enjoy your life, for your life is your own. And no one can take that from you. I love you, Mom.

Pop, you probably hate me now. And I don't blame you for that. But maybe in the hereafter, when it's all said and done and everything's sorted out, perhaps we'll understand it one day. I don't understand myself, half the time. But I know there was once some good in me, and perhaps there is still, a little. Because my heart can still be touched. Perhaps there's some hope in that.

Kevin, I love you. You know, you said something to me that hurt me, and that made me wonder, maybe you didn't know me as well as I thought you did, maybe I didn't know you as well as I thought I did. The last time I saw you, you said that I enjoy this. You're wrong, Kevin. I hate this. I hate what's happened. I hate the way I have to live. I'd trade it all, I'd trade both my arms, if I could go back and do it all over. Please believe me that I don't enjoy this.

I'm not going to say that you're a good man, because you can't handle that. Why, I don't know. When your loved ones tell you how much they think of you, why can't you accept that, brother? You are good, as good as men go. I know that we're all basically evil. But there is some good in you, Kevin.

You said that you didn't care any more. Don't say that, brother, please. I beg of you. As your brother speaking to you now, I know not what the future holds for me. But I know that you care, Kevin. And you care a lot. So don't bottle up your feelings, brother. I know that it's easy to get hurt when you wear your heart on your sleeve. That it's easy for people to reach up there and grab it. And squeeze it. But Kevin, you've got a lot of good in you. Mom and Dad need you right now. They need you now more than they ever have. And between the two of us, you were the strongest.

I love you, Kevin. I love you, brother, more than words can even justify. I wished it could have been different. I wanted so much for you and I to strike out together and make a dent in this world, and make something out of our lives. It doesn't always happen that way, does it? No, I guess it doesn't. But I love you, brother. I want you to go on, I want you to have a good life.

My life as it is, is not easy. But I will walk the road that is before me the best I can until the Lord decides to take me home. And I've prayed, I've asked God, I've said, Dear Lord, God of Heaven and Earth, I would rather be judged of you than judged of men, because I know the judgment of men and how it STINKS. Man does not judge rightly, or justly. No, this world is corrupt. And so is the system that runs it. And that system is the system of the Devil. Civilization is not of the Lord. It's of the Devil, brother.

I've asked God that if I'm to be judged, not to be judged of men, but let me fall into the hands of my Maker, whom I still love, and believe in. I'll always believe in my Lord and my Savior, Jesus Christ.

Seek you out a church, brother. And take Mom and Dad, because we both know the time is short. And let's not be hypocritical. We can't come to God on our terms. We can't have God the way WE want him to be. We've got to humble ourselves and come before God as HE said. Humble. And meek like a child. And does a child think how the father should be? No. The little child loves his Maker, loves his Father, and looks to him for everything. And no matter what, He loves you.

Try to get Mom and Dad to go to church with you, Kevin, and y'all pray for me. I need your prayers. You don't know how difficult it is. I haven't done without. I'm well. I'm well-fed, I'm well-clothed, and I have a place to stay.

Please look after Mom and Dad. And look after yourself, brother. And maybe with your prayers, you can touch the Throne of God, and in his mercy and his wisdom, he'll look down on me with compassion, and see a way out for me. I don't know any more. I really don't, brother. This is very hard for me. You said that I loved it. I think you only said that out of your hurt, I don't think you meant it. I think that if you ever really knew me, you knew that really all I ever wanted to do was serve God. I loved him so much. How could I have went so far astray? I don't know, I don't know. I regret it all. But I can't change it. And I am NOT going to deliver myself into the hands of men to be tormented by them — by men that are even lesser than myself. No, I'll go to my grave first.

I love you, brother. Take care.

[He sings eleven original songs, and then the tape is interrupted by knocking.]

Rolling: Somebody's knocking at my door. Who's that knocking at my door?

Seamans: Why is your key in the door?

Rolling: Is it?

Seamans: Yeah.

Rolling: Boy, that's pretty stupid. Did I leave my key in the door?

Seamans: Well, see?

Rolling: I guess I did.

Seamans: Somebody did.

Rolling: Here, let me turn this off. We're signing off for a minute. I got a visitor here. Say hello.

Seamans: It's hot in here.

Rolling: Yeah, I guess it is hot in here, isn't it? Bye!

Did It Feel BIG?

Michael Kennedy stood waist-deep in the warm clear-green waters off Sarasota's coastline hand in hand with a beautiful beach bunny. They waded out until the waves caressed their breasts. The silver moon smiled on the couple kissing passionately and holding each other close. For the man the moment was magical, exciting! A quick affair — the flash of a Roman candle rising high in the starlit sky and exploding! Sparkling down and disappearing into the dark waters.

"Ah, babes, you are so beautiful," he said softly into her ear while feeling her bottom under the water. His erection targeted her thighs like a torpedo fired from some submerged submarine.

"What's that?" the woman exhaled suddenly. Looking upset, she broke their embrace.

"What do you mean?" he asked her, puzzled. "Something, ah, rubbed up against me," she whispered, looking about, troubled.

"Ha! Ha! You mean this?" he said, pulling her to him.

"No!" she cried, pushing him away. "I mean, something in the water!"

Michael began to get concerned. They had waded a good forty yards out, and the water was dark there. Everyone had seen the movie Jaws, and the thought had crossed his mind.

"Did it feel... *BIG?"* he probed, taking in the now-forbidding waters surrounding them.

"Yes... it did," she said.

"Let's get the hell out of here!" And they made a mad dash for the shore, sure that some horrible creature swept up from the deep with jagged teeth and gaping mouth was right behind them.

They drew up on the beach and fell exhausted on the wet sand, laughing and carrying on as if there was no tomorrow. Michael kissed her and drew her delicious tongue into his hungry mouth. With his left hand, he felt her firm breast, and pulled down her bikini top. Her breasts sprung free of their confinement, and she giggled playfully.

As he twisted her nipple between his expert fingers, she moaned, "Oh yeah… that feels so good." He left her lips and trailed her soft neck to find the other nipple. He sucked on it gently. It tasted salty like the ocean swell. Her flesh held the night air like an exotic smell. She ran her hand down his shorts and began to stroke him, bringing his throbbing member to life.

Then she stood up and untied the bikini top, letting it fall onto the sand. She smiled, stepped out of her briefs, and stood there erect — naked against the ocean breeze — letting him enjoy her full beauty.

She paused, then knelt down beside her man. Michael knew what to do. Jack be nimble, Jack be quick! He yanked off his shorts and his rod sprang to attention, like a flagpole flying its colors.

Moaning, she grabbed him in one hand, opened her mouth and engulfed him, working him there until he could stand it no longer.

Straddling the fiery steed, she slipped him into her wetness to quench her need. They moved together to the rhythm of the tide. They reached for the stars… climaxed and cried… whimpered and sighed.

Sexual Healing

During the course of his life as Michael Kennedy, Danny had wild, crazy sex with a lot of girls, but his affair with the barmaid at the Brown Derby Lounge in Sarasota was really something to remember.

She pranced over to his table and asked, "Can I get you something?"

He ordered a double Margarita and watched her wiggle back to the bar to fill his order. Mercy! He got a hard-on just watching her walk. She had beautiful legs and an ass to go with it.

She brought his drink and he asked her out. She smiled and said, "Yes." He nearly flipped over backwards! This chick was Penthouse stock. She was one of the blondes that was supposed to testify at the bank robbery trial a year or so later, but she got pregnant around trial time and didn't have to be there because she was due any moment.

In a short length of time, he spent at least five to six hundred dollars on fun and games with that babe. One time he took her and her family to eat at Outback Steak House. In the cab on the way there, he gave her a gold braided bracelet that cost him $120.00. The meal cost over $100.00 and he tipped the waitress a twenty.

The next night he took her to the Quay, the finest restaurant in Sarasota. Then they went to a jazz lounge by the ocean for late evening cocktails on the patio under the stars. Later at the hotel, things got firecracker-poppin' *HOT!*

They both knew they were going to end up in bed. There in the dim table light of that small hotel room, they kissed, their tongues dancing and the juices beginning to flow.

"Oh, Mike," she cried as he fondled her firm ample breast with one hand and with the other squeezed her tight ass, kneading it like fresh dough.

His swollen cock pressed against her. She reached down and massaged it through his pants. He unbuttoned her blouse, kissing her deeply. As the wrappings fell away, he drew back to gaze upon her beauty.

"Pretty bra," he charmed, sliding a strap down one perfect milky smooth shoulder and then the other. The bra fastened in the front, making it easier for him. He unhooked it and with both hands brushed it aside.

Perfect beautiful bombshell breasts greeted him. Her pink nipples stood erect with the pulse of excitement! He kissed her on the neck and played with her breasts. Then he drew one of the inviting buds into his watering mouth, and sucked at the fountain of life as he toyed with her other rise of pleasure.

"Take off your jeans," he commanded, breathing heavily. She kicked off her shoes and peeled out of her Guess jeans. She stood there naked except for a pretty pair of skin-colored French panties.

He took off his shirt and shoes and dropped his pants. Now he was wearing nothing but a prize boner.

She sat down on the bed and he slowly took off her pretty lace panties. Now she sat there completely bare. What a peach she was — a true beauty! Her body was the kind young boys in high school dream about. An even tan ran the length of her exquisite nakedness, except for where her bikini had hid her sex shyly from the harsh rays of the Florida sun. The tan line accented her breasts and bottom to the fullest. Her beauty was a rare sight to behold, touch and taste.

She lay back on the bed and spread her silky thighs, offering herself to him. He leaned over her as she guided him with a gentle hand into her wetness.

Oh! It was good! They fucked for about thirty minutes that way — her legs reaching around his waist, their sexes working together to bring the sensual ecstasy they searched for into their bodies.

"Uh... uh... uh... oh *YEAH!* So-o-o good!" Wet and lively, she drew close to her climax, murmuring, "Yeah! Uh-huh... like that... don't stop!" and "Uh... uh... uh... oh *yeah*... ahhhh..." The girl tripped the light fantastic!

"Now it's my turn," he urged. "Turn over. Let's do it doggie-style."

She didn't utter a word, just rolled right over and raised her beautiful white bottom for his eyes to feast upon and his cock to savor.

He plunged into her cunt from behind! She gave a little grunt as he pulled her buttocks against his stomach, drilling her slick pussy.

A man loves to do it this way, from behind — doggie-style! It leaves his hands free to play with the woman's tits and gives a direct angle into her mound of joy. Plus! Big plus here! It gives a grand view of her ass as his thighs smack up against it, making it quiver like a bowl of firm jello.

"Ah... ah... ah... I'm cumming!" And he exploded into her, emptying himself in great spurts of anguished pleasure.

That night they slept together, and when the sun came up they were at it again. This time she added some spice into the fun. Mike was going at it missionary-style, when she said, "Let's take a shower."

Here he is grinding and finding, mind you, and the girl wants to take a shower!

"Well... we can have fun in the shower," she said with a twinkle in her eye.

Hey! Who was he to argue? So they disconnected and scampered into the tiny bathroom and jumped in the shower.

The water was cold at first, and she let out a yelp! Then she bent over with her hands clasped together and pressed her head against his chest, her breasts drawn up that perky way you see in *Cosmopolitan*.

Eventually the water warmed and they kissed, while rivers of soothing water drenched their bodies. What happened next would be forever etched in his memory.

She smiled and knelt down before him, taking his cock in one wet hand and palming his balls with the other. The shower was spitting jets of water down on her pretty face as she opened her mouth and went down on him.

She was good... *REAL GOOD*. The sight of her wet face and dripping hair as she was sucking his dick and looking up at him with those big blue eyes drove him *INSANE WITH PLEASURE!*

"Uh-huh... that's it... yeah... like that," he moaned as he reached down to pat her on the head giving her some encouragement.

He was close. "Oh babes! I'm... I'm... almost there," and gripping a handful of wet hair, he shoved his yearning pole down her throat.

"Ohh... ahh... let me jerk it off in your mouth, baby," and he fisted his throbbing rod into her drooling, giving mouth.

"Ah... ah... m-m-m... there!" *(Squirt! Squirt! Squirt!)* "Ah... yeah," and he pumped his hot sweet load of jizz into her luscious mouth as she closed her eyes and savored every bit of it.

When he withdrew she stood up and swallowed, then licked her fingers wickedly.

And that was some heavy-duty sexual healing.

Trouble Believing

August 5, 1990. Running low on cash, Michael Kennedy moved into less luxurious digs at the Sunnyside Inn across the street from the Cabana Inn. He sold his Ovation guitar, which was still in excellent shape, to Michael Minks, Jr., for $200, telling him he had bought it for $600 up north. Minks recalled him playing Katie Joe and thought he had a nice voice and played pretty well.

Investigators later interviewed Teresa Cousins, who had dated the man she knew as Mike Kennedy a half-dozen times over two weeks, sometimes going to his room with him. She told them that while she had noticed Mike in the Cabana Inn and the Brown Derby Restaurant, it was when she was tending bar at the Brown Derby Lounge that she first actually met him.

She described him as "nice," over six feet tall, missing one or two fingertips on one hand. She remembered that he wore jeans with Kansas patches, and occasionally wore gold-rimmed glasses.

He had come in the Brown Derby Lounge with Steve Smith, a swarthy young guitar player she knew, and the two of them left without paying for their drinks; however, they later returned and paid the tab.

Mike told her he owned Ace Trucking Company in Kansas City, and that he thought he had a buyer for it. He was considering moving to Sarasota, he said, and spoke of being in Vietnam. She had trouble believing everything he told her.

One day he came to the Brown Derby Restaurant and asked her to have dinner with him. She agreed, and he returned to meet her at the end of her shift. They walked to the Maison Blanche Department Store, where Mike bought himself a shirt and a pair of shorts, and then they went to dinner at Ripple's Restaurant. They got a ride with two friends of Teresa's, who later joined them for drinks at the Down Under. Mike picked up the tab, paying cash. After that they went to the Cabana Inn and continued drinking until the bar closed.

On their next date, he took her to the Outback Steak House along with her sister and a girlfriend, paying cash for their food and drink. Before they went to dinner, he told her he had "a surprise" for her, and later gave her a twisted gold rope chain bracelet in a Tilden Ross Jewelers box.

Mike told her his money was being wired to him from Kansas City and that he had recently sold a guitar for $400, but he wished he had kept it. He had a tape recorder, which he used to play tapes of himself playing guitar and singing for her. He liked to play with the crane in the bar, and he gave her two stuffed animals from it — a monkey and a snake.

Once Teresa went outside the bar to talk to another guy, and Mike stormed outside looking for her "like a crazy man," and when he found her, yelled, "If you need to talk to someone, you talk to *ME!*" Another time when she went to the bathroom, he reacted the same way.

Strange Fish

When his grubstake gave out, the fugitive became desperate and as usual, a robbery was the answer.

He scoped out all the prospects in town. The Sarasota banks did not look good. Their locations were obviously constructed for security, with sprawling parking lots seated on main streets.

A large grocery store on the outskirts of Sarasota became his new target. It was a big job for a lone bandit on foot, and proved quite a challenge. He cased the place well and immediately saw the flaws in this particular robbery. For one thing, he was looking at a 75 yard dash with the cash down a customer-crowded walk, then some 100 yards of parking lot to chew up until he reached The Wall — a formidable 9-foot tall obstruction of bricks — then beyond that was private housing for the retired rich.

The plan was to rob the store, scale The Wall, disappear into the housing area, hide until early morning, and then walk out. But these things seldom work out as planned.

The sun went down over the Florida coast town and danger came calling on the residents of Sarasota. With the wind at his back and cloaked by the night, the bandit sprang into the crowded store.

"This is a holdup," the masked and gloved robber shouted, pointing a fully-loaded Taurus 9mm automatic at the cashier. "Do as I say, and nobody gets hurt. Open the register and dump the money in the sack." He tossed her a cloth tote-bag. "Come on, hurry up! Move it! Or I'm gonna shoot-up the place!"

The frightened woman obeyed and quickly emptied the cash box into the bag. "That's it... all of it. Thank you."

He was in and out in less than a minute. He only held up one register because the place was so crowded he actually had to push his way through customers to get to the money.

Now the night greeted him as he sprinted the 175 yards to the wall. As he crossed the parking lot at the rear of the shopping center, two bag-boys came out the back door acting like they wanted to play hero. But as the fleeing robber pointed the 9mm cannon at them, they had a change of heart and ducked back into the store.

Then The Wall presented itself. The robber put the gun in the bag with the stolen money and heaved the lot over. After a couple of tries, he followed. He almost didn't get over, but desperation can spur one to do things that are ordinarily impossible. He made it over by mere strength of will, scooped up the money and gun, and continued on with his flight.

Running alongside a canal, he startled an elderly couple sitting on their back porch as he sped by. The woman screamed and they both scurried inside.

Bounding through back yards, around shrubs and trees, across one street after another, the outlaw fled. Another challenge arose above him like a preying mantis stalking its victim. A police helicopter was prowling the star-studded sky over the retirement homes, its searchlight probing the shadows for signs of mischief.

A cat-and-mouse game began.

Run Danny run
Till your running is done

The robber would duck behind a house as the copter flew directly overhead. While the spotlight searched one side of the home, he would dash around to the opposite side. They soon flushed him out and the chase was on! Then he lost them again and disappeared into the shadows of a thick stand of trees.

While he paused for a moment to catch his breath, the copter was spitting out warnings to the civilians below. "There is an armed and dangerous man in your vicinity. He is armed with a handgun. Do not attempt to apprehend this man. If you see him, dial 911 and give us his location."

This went on for a good hour — the copter crisscrossing through the night, poking the dark with its piercing light, while shouted warnings blared from its public address system. The wanted man knew if he stayed in that neighborhood much longer, eventually they would close the net on him.

He looked for a boat to cross the channel and shake the massing forces searching for him. He stumbled upon a leaky old wooden boat with no oars.

"Damn! No oars! I've got to find something to paddle with." Fumbling around in the dark he found a 2'x4'. It was rotten but it would have to do. He reasoned, as long as the boat did not sink, he would eventually make it across. He crawled in and pushed off with the 2'x4'. He had to work doubly hard to achieve forward momentum, and he was soon drenched in sweat.

As the boat cleared the treeline, the helicopter became visible once again. "Damn!" he thought. "If they look this way, I'm done for!" But the searchlight continued to stab the housing area behind the disappearing figure in the leaky boat.

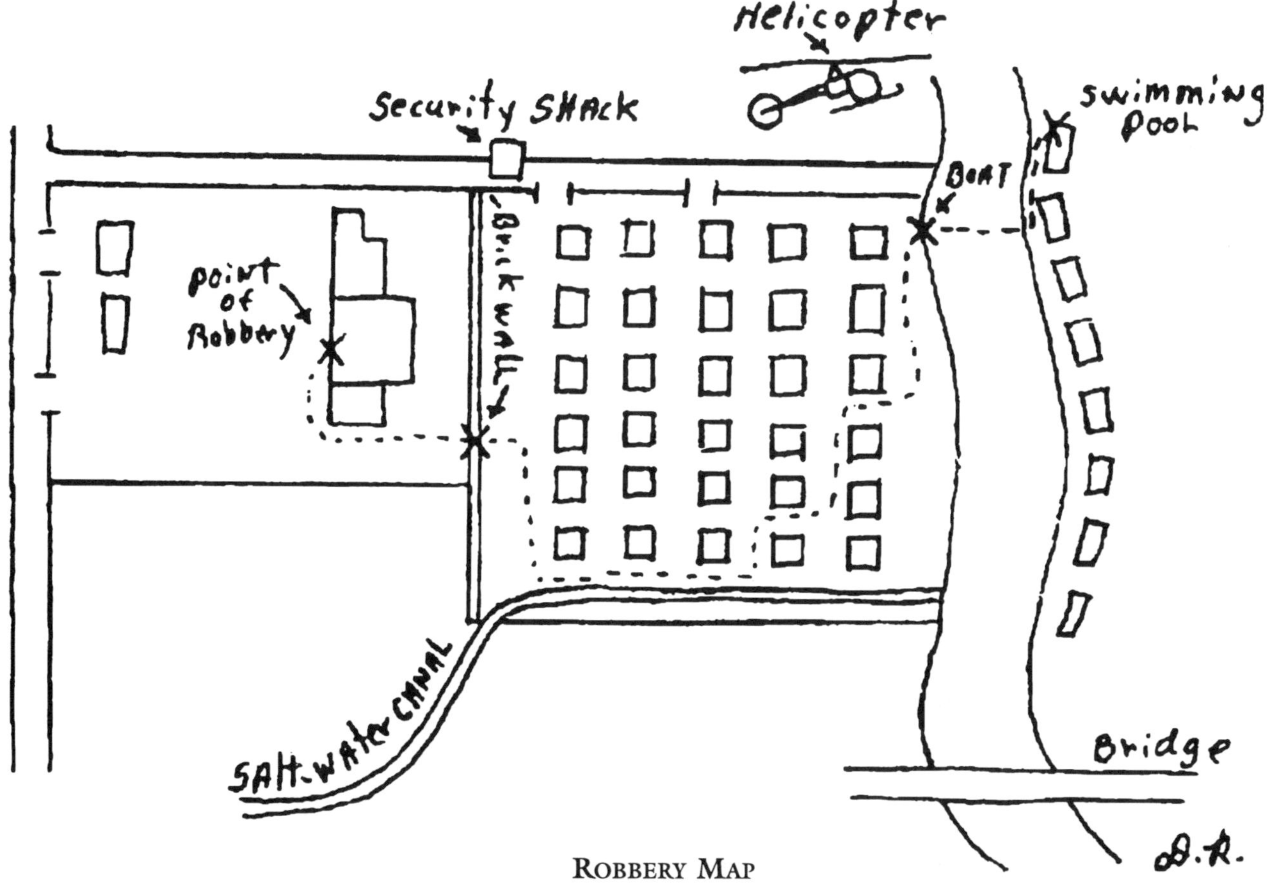

Robbery Map

Halfway across the channel, it became clear that the little boat was sinking. A fishing boat trolled by, but offered no assistance. It was just as well. Strangers only tangle things up.

As he struggled, something large in the inky black water finned its way alongside the crippled craft he nudged along. It occurred to him that the channel was filled with strange fish, and he had no intention of ending up as shark bait. He redoubled his efforts.

Finally he made it across. Snatching up the money and the gun, he stepped out of the waterlogged boat, leaving it wedged on the sand.

He was worn out and filthy. He chanced upon a nice home with a screened-in swimming pool on the back patio. The owner, a middle-aged woman with silver hair, was sitting at a desk in the living room reading a book.

Michael Kennedy let himself in and enjoyed a refreshing dip in the cool water, while the owner sat reading a few feet away, unaware that an intruder was using her pool for a bathtub. After the chlorine did its job on his person, he crawled out of the pool and left.

Later, he found a catamaran on the beach and slept there until first light. When the sun peeked over the horizon, he called a taxi and the cabby drove him back to the motel, where he showered and counted the take. It came to about $1,700. "Oh well," he thought, "not too bad for a couple of hours work."

It was time to celebrate. He bought some weed and got stoned. Ahhh... to drift away on clouds of sweet, sweet smoke! When he was high, his problems did not seem so near.

Later that night he had several drinks at the Cabana Inn and started feeling cocky. But Gemini was knocking softly on his mind, and whispers of the night were fluttering through his soul. He never could resist that call from beyond.

Attack of the Spider

Back at the motel the man changed his clothes, and with them, his personality. Garbed in a black karate gi and toting a small black waist-bag with gloves, thumbcuffs, duct tape, a screwdriver, a Taurus 9mm automatic and a Ka-bar knife, Danny Rolling became the Shadow of Shadows. Even his shoes were black.

Dannneee... come to me...
My child... so wild...
I am the Night...
I am ... GEMINI!

Like a Ninja assassin he prowled the neighborhood seeking a victim to unleash his fury upon. In this environment, he felt almost superhuman.

As if some sort of radar directed his course, he was led to the well-lit home of a beautiful young brunette woman. Standing there in the dark peeking through the window, the Eyes could see her lying on the floor with a pillow under her head, watching America's Most Wanted on her color TV. The prowler waited patiently for the magical moment to capture this lovely butterfly and ravish her beauty.

After the program was over, the young woman got up and stirred about the house. Then she walked out the front door and locked it behind her, got into a red and white Chevy and drove off. The moment had come. The Shadow made his move.

He loosened several glass leaves from the bedroom window and removed them. Many Florida homes have this feature, and it is a burglar's dream come true. All you have to do is wiggle the thin panes of glass out of their frames and crawl in through the opening. And that is exactly what this burglar did.

Once inside, he searched for weapons in the usual places — under the pillows on the bed, in the nightstand and dresser — and found nothing. He then proceeded down the hall. There were women's clothing strewn everywhere on the floor. The man could see this girl lived alone. There was only one bed and the second bedroom had been converted into a sitting room with a couch and coffee table. It was in that room that the rapist chose to wait for his victim to return.

Two hours passed before the car pulled into the drive. The pretty brunette turned out the lights on the Chevy, got out, and entered her home, completely oblivious to the danger waiting in a dark corner of her sanctuary.

The rapist made no move to approach the girl. Instead, he kept to the shadows and played the spider, waiting for his butterfly to come to him. The bathroom was the next room off the hallway, a mere step away from the sitting room. Sooner or later she would use it. He would wait... and then pounce on her.

She milled around in the kitchen for a spell, then went into the bathroom. She left the door open, and the man in the dark watched fascinated as she pulled down her shorts and squatted on the toilet. The sound of her peeing filled the still air. Once the job was finished, she wiped herself, pulled up her shorts, flushed the toilet, and washed her hands. As she dried her hands, she stood there admiring herself in the mirror, unaware of the stranger lurking just over her shoulder.

She stepped out of the bathroom and turned the corner. Hearing a slight rustle of movement behind her, she turned to see a masked and gloved man brandishing a huge knife and reaching for her.

"Yeeeaahh!" She screamed and bolted down the hall with the intruder only a step behind. She tripped over some dirty clothes on the floor and fell onto the carpet. The man tumbled on top of her.

"Don't scream!" he growled. "Or I'll stab you!" One hand gripped the knife ready to strike while the other hand smothered her screams.

Panting, she lay on her back watching the masked man with large terror-filled eyes.

"You behave and I won't hurt you," he promised.

"Don't hurt me! I'll do what you want," she pleaded through the hand pressed over her mouth.

The big man turned her over and drew the thumbcuffs from his waist-bag.

As he was cuffing her thumbs behind her back, she protested. "Please, you don't have to do that. I'll do what you want. I have a fear of my hands being tied behind my back." She had calmed down some.

"All right. If you promise to behave, I won't use the cuffs. But I'm still gonna hafta tape your wrists together. It's for your protection as well as mine. I don't want you trying to do anything stupid." And he duct-taped her wrists behind her back.

Then he turned his prize over. It was time to unwrap the fleshly gift before him and enjoy its earthy pleasures. Sitting on her stomach, he ran his fingers through her hair.

"You are very pretty," the rapist murmured as his hand trailed down her soft cheek and found a firm breast to fondle. "Nice... let's have a look at you." With both hands he tore open her blouse, exposing her pointy breasts to the Eyes of Lust. Then he greedily peeled off her shorts. Now she was completely naked, a Greek goddess for him to play with.

"Get up," he commanded, and helped her to her feet. "Let's go back to the bathroom. I wanna get a better look at you." The two left the dark bedroom for the brightly lit bathroom.

"That's it... stand over there." He positioned her in front of the bathtub and shower and pulled off his pants. For a moment he just stood there staring at her while he stroked his thick cock to life.

"Stand up straight. Throw your shoulders back and poke that chest out." She did as she was told.

She was a beautiful sight to behold, standing there erect, shivering naked in the harsh light. The man began to toy with her beauty, playing with her fear-hardened nipples and rubbing on her pretty little pussy.

"Turn around... let's see your ass." She obeyed. "Bend over. Yeah. Uh-huh... ooooh... you're so-o-o pretty. Now be a good little girl and daddy won't hurt you. Come over here."

He maneuvered her in front of the sink. "Get up there." He helped her up onto the counter. Taking his time, he ran his fingers through her silky dark hair, savoring every minute of this rapture of beauty.

"Your breasts are small, but your nipples are perfect," he complimented her as he gently pinched and pulled at the nipples pouting under his touch.

"Thank you," she said, even producing a smile as he looked deep into her sparkling blue eyes.

"Spread your legs. I wanna look at your pussy." The frightened girl obeyed. There before his eyes, the gateway of pleasure parted. She was absolutely *beautiful.*

He examined her, prodding and poking her

opening with his curious fingers. Then he rubbed the swollen head of his cock on her now-wet cunt-lips, and pressed himself all the way into her with one long easy slow stroke.

"Ooooh yeah… good pussy." And he raped her.

She stared at him with a look that said, "I can't believe this is happening to me."

"Say 'Fuck my pussy, daddy.'"

"I'm scared," she whimpered.

"You say it. I want you to talk dirty to me."

"Fuck my pussy, daddy," she whispered as he continued to rape her.

"Again."

"Fuck my pussy."

Finally he withdrew and ordered her down on her knees. "Open your mouth and stick out your tongue."

She did as she was told, and he rubbed his erection all over her face and tongue and forced her to suck on his throbbing veined rod.

"No teeth! You bite me, and I'll stab you," he declared as he held the Ka-bar in one hand and grabbed a handful of auburn hair with the other.

"That's a good girl. Suck daddy's dick. Ooooh, yeah!" This went on for about ten minutes until she gagged, then he lifted her back up on the sink.

For a solid half-hour, he humped her until sweat covered both of their bodies. Her knees drew up to her chest as he held her ankles spread wide so he could take her deep.

"Please, hurry up," she pleaded when she became exhausted.

"I want you doggie-style."

She surprised him by smiling and agreeing in a real sexy voice, "OK, let's do it."

Something about the way she said it and the way she looked at him drove him over the edge. "I'm — I'm — cumming… *Ah!* Ah… ahhhhh!" And he emptied himself into her yawning hole.

The rapist withdrew his spent tool and put on his pants. She asked him to untape her wrists because her hands had gone to sleep.

"I won't call the police," she promised.

For some reason the man was feeling more like Ennad than Gemini, and complied with her wishes. Lucky for her.

She put on a robe and they moved into the kitchen. She cordially asked if he wanted a beer. It was weird, almost as though she was entertaining a welcome guest instead of a rapist.

"Yeah, that would be great!"

She reached into the icebox and drew out a couple of cans of Keystone Gold. They sat at the table and chatted for awhile, the oddest pair you ever saw. She asked him why he raped her. He told her he was a genuine outlaw just like Jesse James, and he had gotten lonely. He gave her the thumb-cuffs as a gift and promised he would never do anything like that again. But he would — and much worse.

The beers didn't last long. As quickly as he had emerged, the masked intruder vanished into the shadows of the night.

He made his way back to the motel, changed clothes again, and went back to the Cabana Inn for a nightcap. He had plenty of money now, so why not?

After a few drinks, it was last call for alcohol. He wasn't ready to go back to the motel, so he decided to stroll the short mile up the road to the Pancake House.

As he crossed the street, a patrol car pulled in front of him and stopped. Two officers stepped out of the cruiser and one of the two — a woman — approached the lone man.

"What's the problem, officer?"

"Let's see some ID," she ordered, and he handed her the only ID he had — a stolen Social Security card under the name of Michael Kennedy.

"Where are you coming from?" she prodded.

"I'm down here on vacation, and I just had a few drinks at the Cabana. It was last call, so I decided to catch some steak and eggs up the street. So I can sober up," he explained candidly, displaying an innocent poker face.

"Have you been up here all this time?" the lady cop asked as she ran the Social Security card.

"Yeah! What's going on?" he asked, seeming alarmed.

"Don't worry about it, Mr. Kennedy. It's just that somebody has been scaring folks, and you match the description given us. Are you sure you've been at the Cabana all this time?"

"Yes ma'm, you can ask the bartender if you

like. I'll be glad to go up there with you, if you'll give me a ride back to the Pancake House."

The card came back with no violations or warrants.

"We're not a taxi service, Mr. Kennedy," she said as she handed his card back. "You can go now."

"Thank you, officer. I hope you catch the bad guy!"

As the man of many faces sat at the Pancake House consuming a platter of greasy steak and eggs, he watched several patrol cars cruise by giving him the eye. They could have taken him down on robbery and rape, but fate chose another day to end the wanderings of his tormented soul.

GAINESVILLE loomed on the horizon, and darker moments of terror awaited.

by Danny Rolling ::
12-13-93

CHAPTER 8

POSSESSED BY THE REAPER

When the unclean spirit is gone out of a man, he walketh through dry places,

seeking rest, and findeth none. Then he saith, I will return into my house from whence I came out;

and when he is come, he findeth it empty, swept, and garnished.

Then goeth he, and taketh with himself seven other spirits more wicked than himself,

and they enter in and dwell there: and the last state of that man is worse than the first."

(Matthew 12:43-45)

WHY GAINESVILLE?

Believe me, I've asked myself that question many times. Danny nor Ennad meant any harm to Gainesville, except robbery of that bank. I never knew Gainesville existed until the summer of 1990.

I have been driven by the winds that rise when the sun sets and the night calls. The spirits take wing and pipe to their lovers, those who have an ear to hear their whisperings. And so they called to me.

Come out Dannneeee...
Come dance with meeee...

The night spirits would take my hand and I would follow where the crickets ring hypnotic tones and the wind plays through the dry leaves of the grandfather oaks.

Through the hollow night...
Where you catch your breath for fright...

It was destiny — I was driven to Gainesville. God as my judge, I was driven there. Spirits can control and put thoughts in your mind. They can even possess you. The Intruder, the Dark One calls. And if you answer, you will be driven like the restless wind. The Darkness called and I answered.

I could have easily gone to any other place in Florida with the cash I had left back then. Gemini wanted it to be Gainesville. The only reason I can think of would be the obvious — because Gainesville is a college town filled with beautiful girls. I suppose it was there in my subconscious all along. The eight souls for every year I was abused by the prison system had something to do with it, and Gemini became the catalyst.

So now we come to why I crossed that bloody bottom line even before Gainesville. That would be revenge against society — revenge for a lousy childhood, revenge for a failed marriage, revenge for years of abuse by the prison system.

I know... I know... it sounds like a cop-out. Well, I'm sorry. That's just the way it is.

I can't explain it, I just know what happened. I was possessed by this THING — driven to these horrific acts. Dear God! I never thought I could commit such horrors! Sweet Jesus Christ, forgive me. Cleanse me so that I might once again lift holy hands to honor the King of Kings with pure worship — not these bloody hands — oh! I am cursed.

Do you think it is easy for me to bare my soul so? Why, Danny? Why did you kill those beautiful people? I've expressed it as best I can: the Powers of Darkness that rule this crumbling world push men to their destiny, and I was possessed by the forces of HELL!

Not a good enough reason for you? Well, tell me this. Is any reason good enough to merit MASS MURDER?

August 19, 1990 was the first night I spent in Gainesville. I remember rolling a joint on the bathroom counter of my room at the University Inn and smoking it while staring into the mirror. That's when I knew it was going to happen. But I had no idea how far it would go.

I saw Gemini's wicked reflection smiling back at me in the mirror and he said one word: BLOOD. From that point on, Gemini became the domineering force in my mind and Danny was out of control — BIG TIME.

Crossed Paths

August 23, 1990. The man registered as Michael Kennedy checked out of the University Inn and set up a campsite in a wooded area within two miles of all of his crime scenes.

At 6:03 P.M. he passed through Register 22 at the Wal-Mart on Archer Road, paying $20.08 cash for tent. He later admitted that he had also shoplifted a screwdriver, two pairs of tight black Isotoner gloves and a fresh roll of duct tape.

At that exact same time, at Register 11, Sonja Larson and Christina Powell placed $51.21 worth of purchases on a credit card.

It is ironic that our paths crossed, but I didn't recognize Ms. Powell or Ms. Larson at the Wal-Mart. They may very well have been there at the checkout line at the same time as I, but if I did happen to notice them, I had no knowledge of their fate at my hand at that time.

The fugitive pitched his new tent in the woods on the eastern side of SW 34th Street at the intersection of Archer Road, in a clearing where the power lines go back into the woods — about 250 yards behind Bennigan's, where Manny Taboada worked as a bartender.

It's possible that I did meet Mr. Taboada at Bennigan's. He may have even mixed a couple of margaritas for me. But if I did meet him, I did not know we would meet again, nor did it register then that he would fall by my hand only nights — possibly hours — later.

A Moment of Silence

Entering a strange house by night is always exciting and dangerous. Passing from the open air into the close, contained atmosphere of a dwelling has its moments. Even though the burglar does his homework and cases the place proper, someone could still be hiding in there with the means to blow his head off!

He had pried open a window with a heavy-duty screwdriver and crawled in. Halfway through the living-room window, suddenly off to his left he sensed a subtle shift in the shadows. Hanging there with his legs dangling just outside, he turned his head and adrenaline spurted into his heart.

Standing a mere six feet away was an elderly woman wearing a patchwork housecoat, her silver hair strewn about in all directions, giving a ghostly effect in the dim light. And in her outstretched hands she held a pistol pointed straight at the intruder's head.

A moment of silence passed as life and death struggled with fate. Then — CLICK! — the aged woman cocked the weapon. She grinned, revealing a toothless maw, and her dark eyes leveled on the target.

"WHOA!" The robber shouted, and pushed himself back out the window. Counting his blessings, he ran off into the embracing shadows.

I Saw What You Did

The young brunette coed was studying in the living room of her second-story apartment, with her books spread out all over the table.

The glass door of the apartment on the ground floor below her slid open, and a man stepped out. He looked up to see a strange man standing on the second-story balcony in the buff. Apparently he didn't think much of this unusual sight, because he just turned around and went back inside.

It was the first time the voyeur had stripped naked like that, and it would be the last. When he was seen, he quickly put his clothes back on and jumped down, disappearing into the night.

Later that night, Gemini emerged at the same location, searching. He was disturbed by a security guard in civilian clothes while standing on top of two large white plastic paintbuckets peering into a second-story window.

As the guard approached, Gemini jumped down and crouched in the shadows. The guard walked past without seeing him, but felt something (a shiver or chill?) and turned about, discovering the furtive figure crouched there in the darkness.

"What are you doing?"

The Shadow stood slowly and whispered, "I saw what you did."

"What — what do you mean?"

"You know what I mean." And Gemini just coolly strolled away. The guard watched bewildered as the figure in black disappeared.

The guard apparently called the cops, because they arrived shortly with their flashlights probing through the trees. When they caught a glimpse of a lurking shadow they hollered, "You! Halt! Come out of there!" But Gemini melted into the darkness as if he belonged there.

Something I Gotta Do

[This section of The Rolling Tape was recorded in Gainesville right before the murders.]

I'm in a different place than the last time I recorded. Now I got the sky for a blanket, the earth for a bed, and some rumpled-up clothes for a pillow, but it's OK. It's just the way it is, you take the good with the bad.

At the first of this recording, my heart was real heavy, and I was totin' a cold, so the guitar-playing wasn't all that good, and my timing was off 'cause I wasn't feeling good, but I just wanted y'all to have something to remember me by.

Listen to those crickets. Man...

I do know this much. I love you. I know we can't ever be together. But, at least there's one consolation. At least I'm free. At least I'm healthy. I know I'll have to run the rest of my life. But I'm gettin' pretty good at it, if that means anything. Shoot, I've been stopped by the police I don't know how many times, checkin' ID's and stuff.

Mom, I love you. I know you're a lot stronger than you make out to be. You'll get along OK without me. I wish it wasn't so, I'd love to be there by your side. But, you know, just like the little lion cubs, they grow up one day and they go off on their own. But I don't want you feeling sorry for me, I'm a big boy. I can take care of myself. I don't want you to worry about me, OK? I'll be all right. We're all down here for just a breath anyway.

Kevin? You better get a dad-gum deer for me with that bow I got you, now. Just go a couple of times, and see if you don't get lucky with it. Take it out in the back yard and practice with it when you ain't got nothin' else to do before deer season comes open this October. And give it a shot. Just make sure that you put on some good camouflage.

Somethin' else too. Aim for the lungs. Straight through the rib cage. Either there or the heart, but the best thing to do is hit the lungs. It's the best shot for a deer. Straight through the lungs. They don't go very far.

Don't chase after 'im, when you hit 'im, when you stick 'im. When that arrow hits 'im, you got to just watch which way he goes, and when he goes out of sight, listen. And you'll hear 'im banging into trees and stuff, and finally, you'll hear 'im either fall down, or you'll hear 'im stop running. He'll stay right there until he bleeds to death, if you don't go and chase 'im.

So what you need to do is, after you stick 'im, just sit right down there for about 30 minutes to an hour. That is, if you're ever going to do any deer hunting. I never could get you interested in it, when you and I was able to go. I don't know, it just didn't interest you.

Well, brother, I'm hangin' in there. Yeah, I'm hangin' in there. I'll say that much for myself. For the moment. Plan on goin' the distance. I'll give it my best shot.

Well, Dad, I hope you're doin' better. You probably don't even want to hear from me. You know, Pop, I don't think you was ever really concerned about the way I felt anyway. Nope, I really don't. You never would take time to listen to me. You never cared about what I thought, or felt. I never had a Daddy I could go to and confide in with my problems. You just pushed me away at a young age, Pop. I guess you and I, we both missed out on a lot. I wanted to make you proud of me. But I let you down. I'm sorry for that.

Whelp! I'm gonna sign off for a little bit. I got something I gotta do. I love you. Bye.

The Gainesville Murders

It was murder and rape — rape and murder from the beginning. Gemini led that fateful night... and Danny followed. The mind of Gemini seeks only to destroy the wonderful creation of

God, because we can feel God's Love... but the Powers of Darkness cannot.

[On February 13, 1994, the State of Florida accepted Danny Rolling's guilty plea to the five Gainesville student murders. The following Statement of the Facts was read into the record by the prosecution at that time.]

In the early morning hours of 24 August, 1990, the defendant, Danny Harold Rolling, entered an apartment which served as the residence of Sonja Larson and Christina Powell. The apartment was Number 113 in the Williamsburg Complex, 2000 Southwest Sixteenth Street in Gainesville, Alachua County, Florida. The defendant entered the apartment by breaking in through the rear door. At the time he entered into the apartment, the defendant was armed with both an automatic pistol and a knife, to-wit: a Marine Corps Ka-Bar knife. The defendant entered into and/or remained within their apartment for the specific purpose of committing sexual battery with great force and murder.

Upon entering the apartment, the defendant observed Christina Powell asleep on the downstairs couch. The defendant stood over her but did not awaken her. He then crept upstairs, where he entered into the bedroom where Sonja Larson was asleep. He paused to decide which of the girls he desired to rape. He then, from a premeditated design to effect her death, stabbed Sonja Larson. The first blow was to the upper left chest area. At the same time he struck the first blow, the defendant placed a double strip of duct tape over Sonja Larson's mouth in order to muffle her cries. He continued to stab her as she tried to fend off his blows. She was stabbed during the struggle on her arms and received a slashing blow to her left thigh.

The State would prove through the testimony of the Medical Examiner, that Sonja Larson died as the direct result of the stab wounds the defendant, Danny Harold Rolling inflicted upon her.

After having murdered Sonja Larson, the defendant returned downstairs where he found Christina Powell still asleep. He pressed a double strip of tape over her mouth and taped her hands behind her. He used the knife to cut off her clothes and undergarments. The defendant then committed sexual battery with great force upon Christina Powell, a person seventeen years of age, by penetrating her vagina with his sexual organ without her consent and in the process of the sexual battery with great force used and/or threatened to use a deadly weapon, to-wit: the same knife the defendant used to effect the death of Sonja Larson.

Upon completing the sexual battery with great force of Christina Powell, the defendant put her on the floor near the couch, turned her face down, and with a premeditated design to effect her death, did murder Christina Powell by stabbing her five times in the back.

The State would prove through testimony of the Medical Examiner that the cause of death for Christina Powell was the stab wounds inflicted upon her by the defendant Danny Harold Rolling.

The defendant then posed the bodies of each victim and exited the apartment.

During the evening hours of Saturday, August 25, 1990, the defendant, Danny Harold Rolling, did enter the apartment which served as the residence of Christa Hoyt. The residence was located at 3533 Southwest 24th Avenue, Apartment M, Gainesville, Alachua County, Florida.

The defendant broke into Christa Hoyt's apartment by using a screwdriver to break or dislodge the locking mechanism of the sliding glass door at the rear of her apartment. At the time he entered her apartment, the defendant was armed with both an automatic pistol and a knife, to-wit: the same knife used to murder Christina Powell and Sonja Larson. The defendant entered into or remained within the structure with the intent to commit sexual battery with great force and murder.

Upon entering the apartment, the defendant, Danny Harold Rolling, moved a bookshelf from the alcove area adjacent to the front door. He placed the bookshelf in the bedroom at the rear of the apartment. The defendant then returned to the living room area and awaited the arrival of Christa Hoyt, a young woman in whose bedroom he had peeked a few days earlier.

At approximately 10:00 p.m. to 11:00 p.m.,

Christa Hoyt returned to her apartment. Upon entering her apartment, the defendant surprised her from behind and placed a choke-hold upon her. After a brief struggle, the defendant was able to subdue Christa Hoyt. He then taped her mouth and her hands behind her back. He then led her to the bedroom where he cut and/or tore off her clothing and undergarments.

Danny Harold Rolling placed Christa Hoyt on the bed and did then and there commit a sexual battery with great force upon Christa Hoyt, a female over eighteen years of age, by penetrating her vagina with his sexual organ, without her consent, and in the process thereof did use and/or threaten to use a deadly weapon, to-wit: a knife.

Upon completion of the sexual battery with great force, the defendant turned Christa Hoyt face down on the bed and did then and there out of a premeditated design to effect her death, stab Christa Hoyt through the back with such force that her aorta was ruptured and she died.

The State would prove through the testimony of the Medical Examiner that the cause of death of Christa Hoyt was the stab wound inflicted upon her by the defendant, Danny Harold Rolling.

After posing Christa Hoyt's body, the defendant exited the apartment.

At approximately 3:00 A.M. on 27 August, 1990, the defendant, Danny Harold Rolling, broke into the Gatorwood apartment which served as the residence of Tracy Paules and Manuel Taboada. The apartment was located at 2337 Southwest Archer Road, Apartment 1203, Gainesville, Alachua County, Florida.

The defendant broke into the apartment by prying the double sliding glass door at the rear of the apartment. The screwdriver was the same screwdriver he had used at Christa Hoyt's apartment. At the time the defendant entered into and/or remained within the residence, he intended to commit sexual battery with great force and murder. The defendant was, at that time, armed with an automatic pistol and a knife, to-wit: the same knife used to effect the deaths of Sonja Larson, Christina Powell, and Christa Hoyt.

After breaking into the apartment, the defendant entered into a bedroom occupied by Manual Taboada. He found Manuel Taboada asleep. The defendant did then and there, with a premeditated design to effect the death of Manuel Taboada, stab said Manuel Taboada with such force that the knife entered the victim's solar plexus region and penetrated through to the victim's thoracic vertebrae.

Manuel Taboada, awakened by the first blow, struggled with the defendant. During the struggle, the defendant repeatedly stabbed Manuel Taboada on the arms, hands, chest, legs and face.

The State would prove by testimony from the Medical Examiner that the cause of death of Manuel Taboada was one or more of the stab wounds inflicted by the defendant, Danny Harold Rolling.

The commotion caused by the struggle between the defendant and Manual Taboada caused Tracy Paules to come towards Taboada's bedroom. Tracy Paules saw the defendant and fled towards her room and attempted to lock her door. The defendant followed, breaking the bedroom door open. While still covered with the blood of Manuel Taboada, the defendant then subdued Tracy Paules. There was a brief verbal exchange and the defendant taped Tracy Paules' mouth and hands behind her back. He then cut or tore off her t-shirt and committed sexual battery with great force upon Tracy Paules in the same manner as described in the indictment, without her consent and in the process of said sexual battery with great force used and/or threatened to use, a deadly weapon, to wit: a knife.

After completing the sexual battery with great force upon Tracy Paules, the defendant turned Tracy Paules over on the bed and with a premeditated design to effect her death did then and there stab her three times in the back. The defendant then moved, cleaned, and posed Paules' body and left the apartment.

The State would prove by testimony from the Medical Examiner that the cause of death of Tracy Paules was one or more of the stab wounds inflicted by the defendant, Danny Harold Rolling.

Apartment "M" for Murder

August 25th, 1990. Time 7:30 P.M. Christa Hoyt, 18, was enjoying a brisk game of racquetball with her friend Paul Daniel Schwartz. She was the epitome of all we admire and love — moving gracefully as a swan and swift as a tigress to score points. Ah, but alas. This would be her last night on the courts.

If we could see Death approaching, where would our thoughts take us? God only knows. When our loved ones step into that mist beyond the vale of tears they become but a memory we carry forever — and forever is only a heartbeat away.

At a campsite in the woods, this night of woe took on a different face. It was the face of a madman struggling with the forces that drove him.

"Not tonight! No! Not again!"

Zzz-it... zzz-it... zzz-it... we piped...
Zzz-it... zzz-it... and you came...
Dannnneeeee... you came...

The crickets beckoned.

We called... zzz-it... zzz-it...
And you answered

The wind rustled through the trees rising from the earth like dark behemoths of old.

Come dance with us...
Through the hollow night...
Where spirits sing and fireflies fling
Their tiny lanterns of light

And he could not resist.

The bike crossed S.W. 34th Street at a fast clip, wheeling into the shadows. Its destination — Apartment "M" for Murder.

The place was familiar to the possessed man. Several nights prior, while on a night hunt for the window to his fantasy, he stood on the back porch, peering through the blinds in the sliding glass doors.

Christa had just taken her shower and was moving about naked. She was a real beauty any man could appreciate, and the voyeur had to have her.

She was close enough to touch. Only the glass separated her from the madman lurking in the dark masturbating.

"I want her, Gemini," he whispered. "I must have her."

And so you shall... Dannnnneeee...
But not tonight... another night...

Two murders later, the night arrived.

Danny parked the bike behind a housetrailer and made for Apartment "M." He unlatched a wooden door and passed through the alleyway between the duplex and a stack of lumber. A chain-link fence stretched across the end of the alley barring access to the back yard.

As the demented man unhooked the chain links hung on a tree by a driven nail, he sensed a presence.

"There's someone here — in the shadows — staring." The hairs on his neck stood out as he let the fence fall forward. Slowly he turned to discover what troubled him.

Two beady black eyes caught the starlight in their dark orbs. The fat gray and white possum sat still on the wooden fence that ran the length of the alleyway, its attention aimed at the stranger intruding into its environment. Animals and deranged people have something in common. They both possess a sixth sense — the animal instinct.

"Well, now! What do we have here? Are you spying on me, little fella? I'm gonna getcha, you peeping tom!" He reached for the possum's long bare tail, but the rodent wouldn't have any of that! It scampered down the fence, hopped on the woodpile, and scurried for safety.

"Oh, no you don't!"

The man grabbed a 2'x4' about two feet long and brought it down hard across the critter's back, as it entered a large conduit pipe buried under boards of different sizes.

CRACK! GOTCHA!

The blow broke the possum's back, but it managed to crawl into the pipe anyway.

The crazed man stood there in the dark, listening to the wounded possum's scratching and hissing death throes until the pipe grew silent.

"Thought you could get away, didncha?"

The operation began. He unbuckled the bag of goodies strapped to his side, placing it on the woodpile. He unzipped the bag and drew out the Ka-Bar knife, screwdriver, mask and gloves, Mini-Mag penlight and duct tape — laying out his instruments of pain on the wooden planks.

He stripped off his shirt, laying it with the tools before him. He felt the cold blade of the Ka-Bar against his skin as he slid it under the waistband of his pants on the right side. He grabbed the roll of duct tape, flattened it, and pushed it into his pants on the left side.

He donned the mask and gloves, took driver and penlight in hand, and moved to the backyard, leaving the bag behind.

The Eyes peered intently through the sliding glass doors of Christa Hoyt's apartment. Once he was satisfied no one was home, the intruder wedged the driver between the frame and glass door and pried. It opened easily.

A calico cat sprang free from behind the open door, bounded a safe distance from the intruder and sat eyeing him suspiciously.

"Well, little fella, looks like tonight is your lucky night. Jailbreak time, huh?"

The cat flicked its tail, twitched its ears, dashed over the 6' wooden fence and was gone.

Danny looked up at the twinkling stars in the night sky, took a deep breath, gave a sigh, and ducked into Apartment "M."

At that moment, Christa was elsewhere, batting balls at her friend across the racquetball court as the countdown to murder began. She was a lovely, good-natured girl, the essence of youth. How could she know? Soon she would be swept away from the land of the living by a madman possessed.

That fateful night in August, the Evil moved through her apartment staging the drama about to unfold. She the damsel fair, to stumble into the arms of a dragon lying wait in its lair.

The man tore two strips of tape approximately six inches long, stuck them together, and pressed the lot to his bare left arm. He looked about the place to see how it would go, using the Mini-Mag to probe the darkness.

There was a large bookcase in an alcove by the front door. This would be the ambush point. He muscled the heavy thing into the back bedroom, closed the door, and returned to the living room.

The stage set, he positioned himself by the color TV, using the window as his observation point. And he waited.

The spider had spun its web. As the minutes ticked on, the butterfly was drawn closer to the sticky thread of her impending demise.

Time: 10:15 P.M. The silence was broken by a ring from the telephone causing the intruder to snap, draw the Ka-Bar and assume ATTACK POSITION!

The phone rang several times, then ceased.

"Whewwww-WEE!" He returned the blade to its place and tried to still his racing heart.

He didn't have to wait long. Christa appeared, walking casually down the path towards her apartment, completely oblivious to the danger that waited her behind — THAT DOOR.

Party time!
Now... wait and see
Who is with her, Dannnneeeee....

But Christa was alone — as alone as she had ever been in her life.

The crazed man pressed himself against the alcove where the bookcase had been, making himself as small a target as possible.

Keys rattled. Lock clicked. The door opened.

Christa entered, closed the door behind her, locked it, and placed her keys, racquet and balls on the table.

She felt a shiver and sensed someone was there, but it was too late. As she turned, the Shadow leaped from the alcove and seized her around the neck.

"Yeeeeeah!" she screamed as racquetballs and keys went sailing across the table, strewn about the room.

She was flung to the floor like a rag doll, her assailant landing atop her! He snatched the deadly knife from his side with his right hand, while cupping his left over her screaming mouth.

"You've got one chance! Do you hear me? One chance! Behave and live — or fight me and I'll kill you!" He waved the menacing blade before the terrified girl's face. "What's it gonna be?"

Christa settled down a bit, but her breathing labored heavily under the forceful hand.

"Mmmm... bah... hav... mmm day wha ya wan..." she mouthed as best she could.

The attacker released his grip.

"How did you get in here?" The only and last words she said.

"You don't worry about that. I've been watching you."

He ripped the tape from his left arm, pressing it over Christa's mouth.

Then he turned her over on her stomach, drew the roll of tape, bound her wrists behind her back, and rolled her over. He paused to admire the catch and fondled her breasts through her shirt.

"Get up!" She was yanked up by the arm, led to the back room and flung on the waterbed.

It was a NIGHTMARE — just a bad dream — ah, but no. It was all too real.

"Sit up!" She obeyed.

"My, you're a pretty thing, aren't you?" And the masked psycho ran a gloved hand through her lovely hair, brushing it away from her left ear. He leaned in close and whispered, "I'm gonna fuck you, little princess."

The Hand worked its way down the terrified girl's cheek, along the length of smooth neck to her shoulder, to her breast... and squeezed.

"Feels good... I wonder what's under there? Let's have a look-see, shall we?" And the maniac ripped off her t-shirt exposing a tan sports bra. Rough hands cut away the straps and unhooked the latch in front.

Two perfect firm breasts, nipples erect with fear, presented themselves to the hungry wolf drooling over them. The animal pinched and pulled, teasing her with anticipation of what would follow.

Close inspection revealed a single wild hair protruding from the edge of her right corona, the only flaw to an otherwise perfect set of tits.

"Why don't you pull the hairs out from around your nipples?" the rapist snarled, striking a sensitive nerve, which brought tears to the captive woman's frightened eyes.

He cocked his head to one side as if puzzled by this development. Extending a gloved finger, he gently touched her tear-streaked cheek. A single salty tear glistened on the end of his glove, catching the light and reflecting rainbows in the heart-squeezed liquid emotion. He touched the tear to his tongue, tasting his victim's shame and fear.

"Tears are good. It's OK to cry," and Danny regained himself for a moment.

The evil spell broken, he looked around the pitiful scene and wanted to run away. But the powers that drove him were strong in his mind. The personalities struggled for control within him. Good against Evil, Right against Wrong — which one would sing his song?

Ah, but alas. Once again Danny lost the battle when GEMINI reared its ugly head, taking center stage.

The Evil grabbed the damsel by her ankles and drug her to the bed's edge. It pulled off her tennis shoes, but left her socks. Then slowly, painfully, it eased her shorts down to where the pubic hair began.

"Oh! Lookie here!" The Creature teased, searching for emotion in her eyes. They spoke volumes of shame. Her eyes were pleading for dignity when her voice could not. She was brave — very brave — as the Horror stripped her bare.

She was naked now except for her pink socks — the only shred of dignity that remained.

"You're a goddess, a Greek goddess. Look how flat your stomach is! I'll bet you exercise a lot." The Glove gently stroked her smooth belly.

"Get up! I wanna get a good look at you!" And she was lifted from the bed.

"Stand up straight! Throw your shoulders back — that's it! Stick them tits out," he commanded, pinching and pulling downward on her nipples, toying with her.

"OK, turn around." She did. She was beautiful — so beautiful — his little private dancer.

"Good girl. Now back on the bed." And he maneuvered her to the left side of the bed and laid her down.

Deranged eyes peered from behind the mask, blazing with emotions of lust and hate that would not be satisfied until he took her... ravished her... and then murdered her.

The Gloves took a perfect ankle in each hand, and opened her box of charms.

"What's this?" A single white thread hung from her vagina. She was obviously on her period.

A glimpse of hope filled her pleading eyes: "Maybe he won't? Cause I'm on my period?"

But the Creature read her thoughts. He took hold of the thread and eased the stained Tampax out.

"This only makes it better," he taunted, waving it before her. He tossed it over his shoulder onto the floor.

"RAPE TIME!"

He stood, peeled off his pants, and left them with the knife on the floor.

His cock sprang free, fully erect with throbbing need. It had a mind of its own, and all it could think of now was — PUSSY!

Christa closed her long silky legs bashfully, as if she could prevent the inevitable. Ah, but alas. When the dam breaks, how can one hold back the flood of strange fish that tumble out?

"Spread your legs, bitch! Wider! Draw up your knees. I want you deep." In shock, she obeyed.

He rubbed the helmet of his swollen pulsing spear over the mouth of her bloody orifice, and plunged it into her.

The sex act didn't last long — fifteen minutes and it was over. She was so sweet. He couldn't hold back the flood that ached to be released, and he shot his seed deep into the folds of her.

"Ah... Ah... Ahhhhhh." And he withdrew.

He stood up, put on his pants, picked up the knife, and moved towards the helpless ravaged girl.

The bedroom light was bearing down on Christa, and she sensed what was next. Then... the Evil filled the room, like dark clouds boiling over the graves of gotten grief.

Danny was there — but it was as if he was not a player in the drama, merely the audience observing his appendages acting out the orchestrated horror conducted by Gemini.

The reel in Danny's mind turned slowly. He could see Christa being turned on her stomach... the Knife rising... then plunging into her back. But there was no sound — only the slow-mo strobe flashing horrific images in his mind.

The blade burst the A-artery and she died quickly. Ten seconds and her life leaked out, leaving her still.

The man removed the tape that bound her, turned her over again, and stripped the tape from her blood-filled mouth.

She lay looking at him with accusing lifeless eyes. THOSE EYES! He would never forget the way they bore into him. He reached out and closed them, turning away.

You're not through...
Dannnnneeee...

The Demon commanded:

There's more to do...

And the horror movie continued.

The Knife poked into the corpse's belly just above the pelvic and sliced upward, eviscerating her. Gray guts emerged from the bloody opening.

The Knife continued its terrible work — slicing off both nipples. Each were placed perpendicularly on top of the guts bulging from the abdomen.

Finally, the Demon was satisfied. The butcher gathered his things and left.

Danny crossed the lawn, hopped on the bike, and peddled away. He felt ill. His stomach turned over, announcing the need to move his bowels.

Finding a vacant house, he ditched the bike. He trotted around back and dropped his pants. He grabbed hold of the fence, squatted and relieved himself. He opened the bag, drew out a wad of toilet paper he carried for just such emergencies, cleaned up, and resumed his journey.

Navigating the bike into a gas station and convenience store off Archer Road, he went inside for a soda. His throat was dry and he felt ever so thirsty. But when he searched the bag, his wallet was missing.

NO! Red lights went off in his mind. Already troubled, now he became FRANTIC!

"Whatsa matter, bub?" The attendant asked, observing his customer's odd behavior.

"I seem to have lost my wallet. Damn!" He dashed out and sped away on his bike.

"Did I leave it at the scene? Maybe it fell out of the bag when I fished out the toilet paper after taking a dump." His thoughts were only of loose ends that could not be tied.

"Oh, bloody HELL!" He muscled his bike with all his strength, backtracking to the scene of the crime.

An hour later, Danny entered the apartment cautiously. The smell of Death greeted him. The bloody body lay where he had left it.

In a panic, he searched the apartment from top to bottom using the Mini-Mag as guide. But he never found that wallet. Exhausted and disgusted, he gave up the search and proceeded to leave.

From the shadows it slithered into his mind, turning him about.

Dannnneeeee... wait...
Leave them something to think about...

He stuck the burning Mini-Mag in his mouth, freeing his hand. He drew out the Ka-Bar and approached the corpse, penlight showing the way.

He couldn't believe what he saw. Somehow, some unearthly way, her eyes had opened and she lay staring back at him.

"I closed 'em. I — I know I did! But — how...?"

The halogen beam caught the opaque gaze of eyes that reflected only DEATH, coldly accusing the murderer who took away their sight.

Danny thought Christa would rise and strangle him right then and there! He wanted to run away. He didn't want to touch her again. But... Gemini bade him stay.

DO IT! Dannnnneeee...
Cut off her head!

The reel turned frame by frame. And the Blade drew across her throat while she looked on with eyes fixed in death.

The Ka-Bar designed for just such work cut through flesh, muscle and arteries like a razor cuts paper, until metal met the bones of the spinal column.

Blood thirsty! The Demon cut 360 degrees around the column and twisted.

She loves me... She loves me not...
She loves me... She loves me not...

And the head separated from the stump.

The madman grabbed it by the hair, lifted — and the eyes closed.

Put it on the shelf...
Dannnnneeeee...

He did, but it wouldn't sit up. It just flopped over and fell to the floor. THUMP!

He picked it up by the raven hair and used a counterweight to prop it up facing outward towards the hallway.

Insanity is like a warped record. It plays only twisted and tormented songs. Once the volume is turned up — you go BLOODY MAD!

The bodeeeee...
The bodeeeee... Dannnneeeeee...
Leave them something to think about...

He grappled with the stiff lying in a congealing pool of blood. It was like molding a block of Playdoh — just a lifeless lump of clay.

He sat it upright on the edge of the bed. A stream of blood spurted from the wound where the left nipple had been and splattered, pooling at its feet planted on the floor.

The arms were placed over the spread legs, resting its elbows outside the knees, hands drooping. It resembled "The Thinker," fashioned by Rodin, the famous artist of the roaring twenties.

Ah, but alas. 'Twas a grotesque replica carved from human flesh and bone, its sculptor the devil's advocate — GEMINI.

The day will come when the Creator of Heaven and Earth shall wipe clean this world, like one wipes refuse from a filthy plate. Oh, that glorious day! All that offend — Lucifer and his wicked imps — will be cast into the bottomless pit, no more to mar the works of beauty. The smoke of their torment shall ascend forever from the midst of hell. And all things will once again be beautiful, pure and good.

Danny left Apartment "M" troubled and spent emotionally, his mind swirling down the whirlpool of insanity.

THOSE EYES — those staring, dead, accusing eyes — for the rest of his days they would haunt him. Christa Hoyt's lovely body had been dismantled like a Tinker Toy by a madman possessed, but her loving spirit shall live forever in the hearts of those who knew and loved her. Christa walks the streets of gold now, beyond this vale of tears where angels sing praises to the King of Kings.

Expert or Very Lucky

Dr. Edward Copeland, Dean of Medical Students at the University of Florida, commented that the incision he observed in the abdominal area of Christa Hoyt's body was centered in a manner he characterized as either "expert or very lucky." He then commented that the incision was in the medial area where the abdominal muscles attach, and that the bowel did not appear to be perforated by this incision. The perpetrator had been "very meticulous" with that incision, as well as the removal of the nipples.

I have studied human and animal anatomy. I witnessed an autopsy while employed with LSU Medical Center. I have also been present during dissection of cadavers by med students at the Veteran's Administration Hospital in Shreveport, Louisiana. Also, I'm an expert deer hunter and I have field-dressed many a felled doe or buck.

The incision performed on Christa Hoyt was not a stroke of luck, but rather the result of knowledge acquired. For someone who lacks this knowledge of anatomy and hands-on skills, it would have been extremely difficult.

But take into consideration, Danny never intended to harm his fellow man with this knowledge. Gemini used Danny's hands to work his terrible will.

Dr. Chip Souba offered the opinion that decapitation is especially difficult because the bones overlap in the cervical column, and the vertebra have to be disarticulated. He concluded that for the decapitation to be so clean, the knife would have to be very sharp.

The knife was razor sharp. The force in that place took the head off easily, cleanly, quickly — just as the bookshelf was moved from the living room to the bedroom without even causing a single item to fall from its shelves. When Gemini surfaced, the elements of the night made Danny physically stronger. So much so, it's hard to believe myself.

I will say this much. Once a knife's blade has tasted human flesh, it becomes transformed from mere metal and leather to an entity which thirsts for more... and more... BLOOD. In fact, it even smells different — sweeter, the sickening sweet smell of power to take life poured out on its tempered edge.

The Last One

August 27, 1990. The gut-wrenching blows of a murder spree that paralyzed Florida with fear crescendoed to its final horrific scene.

Manuel Taboada and Tracy Paules were both college students. He pursued architecture; she business. He worked nights tending bar at Bennigan's; she loved to dance. They were a lively pair, both 23 years of age, who shared the same apartment: #1203 at the Gatorwood Apartments, a large complex located on Archer Road.

Not far away, Danny Rolling lay naked, sweating out the daylight hours in his small tent. It had been a scorcher, and he slept fitfully, swatting an occasional determined mosquito that wormed through the netting to feast on his hot blood.

Dusk brought little relief as the blistering sun

slid grudgingly behind the fading horizon, bathing the sky in red. Darkness soon swept over the town and HORROR took to the shadows.

It's time... Dannnneeeee...
Night embraces day...
Come out and play...
Rise and slay...

He unzipped the netting over the door flap and crawled out into the new night. He came to his feet, stretched, yawned, took a piss, dressed to kill... and rode off into the night on his stolen bike.

Wheels turned silently down darkening streets as the man pumped the pedals propelling the vehicle on. Like a dark predatory bird searching for prey, the Evil swooped down over the Gatorwood Apartments.

The man left the bike leaning against the backside of the complex and began to prowl. The hour was relatively early, approximately 11:00 P.M. as the Darkness crept from shadow to shadow, peering in windows.

The search ended at the corner apartment. Tracy Paules lay on the bed in her room chatting with a girlfriend over the phone when the Eyes appeared above her in the window.

"I wish Manuel was here. I'm worried about these murders. Oh, that's all right, I'll be OK. It's just sort of spooky, ya know," Tracy spoke into the receiver.

She was wearing only a nightshirt — no panties — and the Eyes could easily see her bare bottom.

Seconds turned to minutes to hours, and the clock struck 1:30 A.M. Tracy hung up the phone and rose from her bed. She stood before the mirror, pulled off her nightshirt, and admired her youth in the reflection.

Turning this way and that, she was oblivious to the Eyes of Lust watching her every move. Like a ballerina in a music box, she danced naked before the mirror, her beauty and grace obvious.

"I must have her," the man in the dark whispered as he felt a shift in the elements.

Quick!
Dannnneeeee...
Behind the bush!

Instinct warned and he immediately fell prone behind the bush by Tracy's bedroom window, just as two young males rounded the corner.

"I heard one of the girls was beheaded."

"Naw... yeah?"

"Weird stuff. Looks like a serial killer."

"Aw, it was probably some poor slob who couldn't take the pressure." And the teenage students passed right by the very serial killer they were discussing, entered a stairwell and disappeared.

The prowler rose slowly to his feet from behind the bush and pondered what he had heard.

"The heat's on, buddy! You better get out of this town after tonight," he spoke to himself, turning his attention back to the window and his fantasy. The ballerina had left.

The Eyes searched, wondering where she had gone. He had to find out.

The man in the dark unzipped his black bag, drew out the brown ski mask and black leather gloves, donning both. Then he jumped over a wooden railing onto the back porch of Apartment #1203 and peered through the curtains hanging behind a pair of sliding glass doors.

"Nope! Not there. Could she be in the bathroom?" But there was no bathroom window in this apartment. So the prowler just waited on the deck.

Suddenly! A Siamese cat poked its feline head between the curtains and glass. Instantly it saw the dark figure lurking there. Sensing danger, the alarmed cat pranced back and forth, meowing and disturbing the curtains.

The masked prowler knelt on all fours mimicking the upset cat. He stared deeply into its green eyes and hissed, "Hssssst! Go away!"

Animals can't hold intense eye contact with humans. The cat hunched, bristling its back. Hissing and baring its fangs, it ducked behind the curtains and hid.

The man sensed the girl inside had been alerted by the pet's odd behavior. He quickly jumped back over the railing and lay prone in the dirt between the bush and apartment, just as Tracy pulled back the curtains to investigate what disturbed the cat.

"Is anyone out there?" she tested, searching the deck and surrounding yard from behind the glass. Satisfied no one was there, she checked the lock on the double doors, arranged the curtains so no one could see inside, went to her room and crawled in bed, leaving the table light on.

Someone was out there. She couldn't see him, but he could see her.

Time: 2:45 A.M. Manuel Taboada returned after a night of tending bar. The Eyes watched the husky young man corral his red and white Honda Superbike into its parking space, turn it off, leave it crackling hot on its kickstand, and go inside.

Exhausted, Manny threw his keys and helmet on the kitchen table. He went straight to his room adjacent to Tracy's, pulled off his shoes and pants, and dove onto his waterbed.

The Eyes watched as Tracy awoke. She went to the door and looked across the hall into Manuel's room to make sure it was he had come home.

"Manny, is that you?"

"Yeah! I'm beat. Gotta get some sleep. See ya in the morning."

Relieved and feeling safe with her burly roommate home, Tracy closed her door and returned to bed.

Time: 3:00 A.M. The clock counting heartbeats as the Grim Reaper chipped away at the seams of life remaining.

The masked killer unzipped his bag of deadly toys and drew out the roll of duct tape, the Ka-Bar knife and the screwdriver, leaving the bag with the fully-loaded Taurus 9mm automatic on the rail. Then he began work on the locked door, trying to pry it open as quietly as possible.

Pop! The driver slipped from between the aluminum seam and frame.

The man froze motionless, extending every fiber of his being like the feelers of some primitive creature. Yet he detected no movement or noise within the dark dwelling.

He continued, focusing his energy on the security pin wedged through the frame where the doors overlapped.

Pop! The driver slipped again, this time making a more noticeable noise.

He reached into the bag, drew out the loaded Taurus 9mm, crouched and waited.

The curtain moved! He aimed, ready to fire.

Manuel Taboada's cat emerged, strutting her stuff as if to say, "Purrr... I know what you're up to! But you can't get in — purrrr... say?" And she flicked her bushy tail, sat down and watched.

"I'm gonna huff... and puff... and blow your house down! Then whatcha gonna do, little kitty?" And the pin popped out.

The Siamese sprang to its feet anticipating the next move. All that was left was to free the locking device from its latch.

Pop! The door slid open and Manuel's anxious cat scampered away into the night without glancing back.

Inside all was still. Not a creature was stirring, not even a mouse. The cat had seen to that.

The killer moved to center stage, and Act Three began.

He crept silently down the dark hall towards the light emanating from under Tracy's closed door.

Once there, he turned towards Manuel's room. The door was open. Pale blue light from the parking lot spilled through the window and beamed across the bed where he slept.

The masked killer eased into the room closing the door carefully behind him. The only sound was Taboada's heavy breathing.

The Evil fell into Danny's mind like mercury settling to the bottom of a glass of water, and it was Gemini who inched towards the sleeping man.

Taboada lay on his back, deep in REM sleep.

The Knife paused over the victim's chest as the Demon marked the spot. Down it came slicing the air, plunging through the solar plexus and driving upward, hunting spleen and heart.

"Ahhhh! I've been shot!" screamed Manuel, his eyes bulging in shock as he was yanked from his dreams.

Both men stared into each other's eyes — one demented, the other desperate, held together by a single deadly thorn embedded in Taboada's chest.

"You bastard!" Manuel spat in pain, as the Horror twisted the thorn deeper into the center of his being, wiggling it to scramble his insides.

"Ahhhhh!" The dying desperate man swing at his attacker, landing a fist. This brought on a flurry of lightning blows — stabbing and cutting — blood spurting and splattering on the bed — splashing the men and the walls.

"Ahhhh! Tracy!" (his last words). Life gushed out as he left the land of the living, staring blindly at nothing, drenched in his own blood.

The Bloody Mask backed away from its horrid work, withdrew before Tracy's closed door — and listened. Nothing. No stirrings came from behind the door.

There in the dim glow, Danny looked at the blood running down his arms, dripping from his gloved hands. And he came to himself.

He hurried down the hall into the kitchen, turned on a small light over the sink, and tried to wash off the blood.

"No more! Never again!" he whispered, watching the blood swirl down the drain. His head throbbed, brain ablaze, struggling for some sense of sanity in this nightmare he was cast. Ah, but alas. Hopes of his humanself disappeared, swirling down the funnel of dementia in rivers of red.

He turned from the crimson-stained sink and tried to get away from the madness, only to make it as far as the sliding glass door.

Waaaait... Dannneeee...
There's more to do...
The girl! Remember?
You said you wanted her...
Well...

The possessed puppet of flesh crept down the dim hall, pulled along by an angry, twisted master — his own insane mind.

Tracy's door creaked open and she emerged frightened, brandishing a curling iron. Instantly she saw the Terror coming for her.

"Yeeeee... ahhhh! Go away!" And she leapt back into her room, slamming and locking the door behind her.

The Demon took three steps, kicked, and SMASH! The door splintered away from the frame. The Creature of Lust pounced on the screaming woman. He flung her onto the bed and pressed one hand over her mouth while drawing the Ka-Bar with the other.

"Shut up! Scream one more time and you're dead! Understand?"

"Uh-huh," she nodded behind the weight of his hand.

"I'm gonna take away my hand, and if you scream, I'll stab ya." He let go.

"You're him, aren't you?"

"No, lady, I'm not."

"What happened to Manuel? You — you hurt him! Didn't you?"

"Nah. But he won't be gettin' up any time soon. You see? I'm an ex-Green Beret with a black belt in Tae Kwon Do. I just knocked him out."

"I don't believe you."

"Well, hell, lady, I wouldn't worry about it. He ain't gonna be botherin' us. Now turn over!"

She did as bid. He taped her wrists and rolled her back over again, facing him.

"My brother was a soldier too. He — he was killed in Vietnam," Tracy tried using reverse psychology.

"Really? Vietnam was a bitch! I'm tempted to let you go. But then again? I guess not."

"They'll catch you! You know?"

"Perhaps. But not tonight. Look! If you behave, I won't tape your mouth."

He stood, keening in on the night sounds without. "I wonder if anyone heard you scream?"

"I doubt it. These walls are pretty thick," she soothed, hoping someone had indeed heard.

"Well, kid, for your sake you better hope not," and the madman knelt and ripped off her nightshirt.

"Nice tits," he admired, fondling her appreciatively as she grimaced under the gloved touch.

"Open your legs."

She refused, and the rapist grabbed both knees, spreading her.

"Look at that! A shaved pussy! Oh yeah! Baby, it's party time!"

He dropped his pants, standing over the bound, naked woman, and stroked himself to life. Then he knelt and probed her vagina with gloved fingers.

"That's a pretty pussy," and he drove his swollen pulsing need deep into her yawning hole.

"It hurts!"

"Take the pain, bitch!"

"But... but... it HURTS!"

"Shut up! That's a good little girl. Now say 'Fuck my pussy, daddy.' Go on, say it!"

Tracy looked into the crazed eyes behind the mask... and refused.

"I said, say 'Fuck my pussy, daddy!'" A rough hand squeezed hard a breast.

"Fuck my pussy, daddy!"

"Good girl. Now keep saying it. Don't stop!"

"Fuck my pussy, daddy! Fuck my pussy, daddy! Fuck my pussy, daddy!"

"Ah... ah... ahhhhh," and he reached the cliff of tormented ecstasy, falling over the edge of emptiness.

"That was sweet. Now roll over. I want some of that pretty ass."

She obeyed and a leathered hand caressed a naked shoulder, stroking the length of bare back.

Darkness filled the room, releasing the genie from the bottle in his mind. And once again GEMINI took center stage.

The Knife rose as the terrified girl's face was pressed into her pillow. Down plunged the iron thorn piercing supple flesh! Again and again the Knife stabbed into her back, as her screams died in the pillow.

"OK! Mmmmmm... ah! That's enough," her last words strangled through the pillow.

Life dwindled, wheezing from gaping wounds, and she went still. Blood streamed down, saturating the bedsheets, turning them red.

The demented psycho wiped the baptized blade on the bed and sheathed it to his side. He grabbed the corpse's feet, turned it face up, and pulled it off the bed. He dragged it across the carpet, leaving a trail of blood in its wake.

He left it by the bathroom, turned on the light, and stood there looking down in Tracy's face. Even in death, she was a beautiful and elegant sight.

Trickles of blood ran down the sides of her mouth. Her eyes were closed, her hair strung out helter-skelter. She appeared almost peaceful, as if she were merely resting, but the gray tint of cooling skin betrayed the illusion. She was dead.

Danny came to himself. He took a washrag from the bathroom, wet it, knelt, and gently cleaned the damsel's face, wiping away the traces of blood. He did the same with her hair and arranged it in a loving manner.

The last one...
No more...
You're the last...
And so she proved to be — the last one.

Manuel Taboada and Tracy Paules were an inspiration to all who knew them, even those who did not. They met a terrible fate. Yet they faced the dark void with courage beyond their tender years.

They never saw the face behind the mask or knew the reasons why they had to die. Their voices cry out from the grave, "Why, Danny? Why did you murder us?"

The answers are not easy.

The Reaper stands center stage, takes his final bow, and the curtain falls — thus ending the horror play. We bury our dead and walk away. And the circle of insanity is complete.

Plays will come and go, but when the drama is presented on the Theater of the Real — the blood is hot, the screams sincere. Such a drama continues to haunt us long after they bring the curtain down.

It MEANT Something

Lt. Spencer Mann, Alachua County Sheriff's office: "That image. Incredible. I mean far different from and exceeding anything I've been exposed to in my life."

Gainesville Police Homicide Detective Chuck Jempson: "I've been a policeman for 27 years and I've seen all kinds of things in my time, but I never saw anything this cruelly done. It made a permanent impression. These were just kids. They were like lambs led to the slaughter, and they were slaughtered."

Officer Ray Barber: "I think he's somebody who likes to do it. It's one thing if you're so mad you lose control and shoot somebody or stab somebody. He's sick. The guy's just a very, very sick person. I don't mean sick in a mental way. I mean sick in a disgusting, shocking type way."

Police Spokesperson Sadie Darnell: "I was ill. There was some decomposition and the apartment was warm, musty. And there was the 3-D of it — not just a picture kind of thing. A lot of sensory things were occurring at once. It was an unusual death situation. Evil."

Criminologist Ron Holmes: "The outstanding thing I see is the rage expressed. So many killings in such a short period of time. It looks like utter hatred and rage directed toward young women. The mirrors used are for him to see what he's done. It's a theater to see for himself."

Dr. Michael West, Mississippi crime scene analyst who spent a day and a half combing the scenes with a light intensifying device that attaches to a 35mm camera: "I thought I'd seen everything. This is the most difficult crime scene I've ever seen. All the areas the killer touched or manipulated were free of prints. Nothing. I've never seen so many incidents of violence at a crime scene without leaving any evidence."

Gainesville Police Capt. R.B. Ward: "In the scene, the setup, there was a message — to authorities, to law enforcement, to whoever. The primary purpose was not the deaths. It was organized vio-

by Danny Rolling 4-9-93

lence. This whole thing was packaged in such a way as to make some sort of statement. The person doesn't necessarily want you to say why? as much as he wants you to be shocked by the way he committed the crime. Although we didn't realize it at first, this person is leaving us messages or signals. He's saying, 'You're not stopping me. Catch me if you think you can.' He enjoys the control he is exercising and the confrontation with authority."

J.O. Jackson, Florida Department of Law Enforcement: "He had set up a play for us, and when we walked in, we saw the play."

Sadie Darnell: "It was strange — very quiet and very different. And it MEANT something."

What's the Message?

You are not going to be satisfied with my answer here. I really don't have a message. It's a tragedy — a terrible, terrible TRAGEDY. I regret it. I wish it had never happened.

The terrible thing that happened to these beautiful young people is something I just can't explain. Gemini is a sculptor from hell. I am only a mortal. How can I fully understand all the immortals think or plan? I only make observations of my part in this and try to pick up bits and pieces of the puzzle left behind in the crimson wake of these terrors. I am not Gemini — Lucifer and his imps belong to that exclusive club. That Dark Spirit seeks only to dismantle the wonderful beauty created by the Almighty.

Any message left in Gainesville came from the voice of Gemini through the flames of hell. It was a message left to mankind that Evil walks among us like a natural man.

CHAPTER 9
NO PLACE LEFT TO RUN

Nice Fucking Day

August 27, 1990. A bare-chested, ski-masked Danny Rolling robbed the First Union Bank one half-mile from Christa Hoyt's duplex on Archer Road. Two eyewitnesses later could only pick him out of a lineup after he removed his shirt. They recognized him by the muscle definition of his chest.

The hyperkinetic robber vaulted over the counter, smashed the video camera with his gun, and talked constantly, ordering the stunned robbery victims around. As he exited, he snarled sarcastically, "Have a nice fucking day." Fleeing the scene, he removed his ski-mask and several eyewitnesses got a look at his face.

August 28, 1990. A white man walking towards the woods behind Archer Road with a black man was recognized by police as matching the description of the bank robber. When police ordered the pair to halt, the fleeing felon escaped into the woods, but Tony Danzy stopped. He told the cops he had known Mike for a few days, and eventually revealed that their relationship was based on Tony's selling Mike marijuana and crack cocaine.

Following the fugitive into the woods, police found Danny Rolling's campsite. They seized the items they found there, including the stolen money, dye pack, 9mm Taurus pistol loaded with hollow-point bullets, ski-mask, and gloves used in the bank robbery. Police also found the screwdriver that pried open the sliding glass doors at the last two murder scenes, along with tape recorder and an audiotape.

Even though efforts to identify and apprehend the Gainesville slasher eventually cost the State of Florida over seven million dollars, it took police almost a year before one investigator finally listened to the tape the killer had left for them, giving his full name and linking him the scene of the crimes.

Police initially charged Michael J. Martin with the bank robbery. He bore a slight resemblance to Danny Rolling and had been camping out in the same woods. Three months later, when it became amply clear that the culprit was safely in custody, Martin was released. Michael Martin was the first in a series of hapless suspects detained, arrested, and publicly identified as suspects by Florida law enforcement in the crimes committed by Danny Rolling.

August 30, 1990. University of Florida engineering student Christopher Osborne returned home from a game of tennis to find the TV on, dirty dishes in the sink, and the door to the house wide open. The thief had come in through Osborne's bedroom window by popping the screen. He had apparently made himself at home, helping himself to some of Osborne's cookies and a bowl of Quaker Instant oatmeal. He also left evidence that he had watched a Playboy videotape, played with Osborne's puppy, taken his car keys, and stolen his 1978 tan Buick Regal.

August 31, 1990. On Labor Day weekend, thousands of students left Gainesville. Fearing further attacks, over 700 students did not return.

September 1, 1990. Tampa residents Larry Dale Lawrence and Holli Jo Paula returned home from a weekend camping trip to find their home had been burglarized. The thief had ripped the entire rear kitchen window from the frame, knocking over several house plants in the process. Inside, the entire house was ransacked. The dead-bolted door between the kitchen and the garage had been kicked open, and virtually every file in a desk in the garage had been searched. Files in a desk in the master bedroom had also been disturbed. Missing were a Nikon 35mm camera, $10.00 in change, an unused knife sharpening stone, a black leather wallet with credit cards, and two birth certificates for Anthony James Lawrence. Numerous fingerprints were left. The stolen items were recovered from Chris Osborne's Buick Regal when Danny

Rolling was finally arrested.

On Labor Day Weekend, I broke into and burglarized an entire block — roughly 15 to 20 homes — looking for a pistol. I finally took a large rock out of a rock garden behind one house and smashed a basketball-size hole in the back door. Letting myself in, I found the .38 cal. revolver I was later busted with.

Ode to Jesse

Well, I guess this song depicts the way my life really is. In a way Jesse James and myself, we're both having to live the same life, the life of an outlaw — even though I really don't believe in Jesse's heart it was what he wanted. So maybe I was really writing this song about myself. Well, anyway, here's "Ode to Jesse":

This is a story without a reason, without a rhyme
About a man named Jesse
Who chose a life of crime
His six-guns he wore by his lonely side
With the taste of desert dust
And the hot sun in his eye.
So ride, Jesse, ride
Into the setting sun you cry
You were born to be free
But tomorrow where will you be?

September 2, 1990. It was a hot September afternoon. As the white Florida sun slipped lazily behind the horizon, a tan Buick Regal entered the Tampa Save-N-Pack parking lot at the corner of Nebraska and Fowler, and began to prowl.

Behind dark sunglasses, the man now known as Jesse cruised the area.

Dead broke and on the run
From the Lawman's gun.

He parked the stolen Buick, got out, and walked across the filled lot. He stepped on the electric sensor and the glass door swung open with a *whoosh*.

Walking tall, Jesse entered the cool supermarket. He pulled a shopping cart from its stall and began to browse. Pushing the cart along nonchalantly up one aisle and down another, he cased the place for armed security. He grabbed a couple of cans of soup, dumped them into the basket, and strolled on.

In the middle of Aisle 6, an odd couple were arguing over what Poopsie, their French poodle, would eat. "I'm telling you, Homer, Poopsie won't eat that stuff!" the tall red-dyed frizzy-haired woman spat, pointing her finger in the old man's face.

"Hell! Ethel, that dog eats better'n I do!" the short dumpy bald-headed man replied, his face flushed with frustration.

"Excuse me, folks," Jesse said, as he reached between the two for some Chow-Chow dog food. He eased around the corner. "I'll betcha he's as henpecked as he can be," he mumbled, placing a box of Capt'n Crunch in the cart.

Moving on, he surveyed the environment. "Hmmm. No security in sight. Still, it's a big place." He weighed the risks in his mind and decided to go for it. Deserting the shopping cart in Aisle 4, he left the store light-afoot. He drove the Buick into an alleyway across from the parking lot and began to prepare.

Jesse robbed his first train
In the driving rain
As the posse lost his trail once again.
While he warmed his bones by the campfires
His mind began to dance
Cause he knew in his heart
He lived by chance.
So ride, Jesse, ride...
Into the setting sun you cry.
You were born to be free...
But tomorrow where will you be?

At the same moment, officers Delanoit and Wooten, representing Tampa's finest shining shield of law and order, sat down at a local restaurant to have their supper.

Jesse got out of the car and placed the keys on top of the front left tire. He shoved the stolen .38 cal. revolver in his pants and pulled his shirt over it. Gloves dangled from his left rear pocket and a rolled-up ski-mask was perched on his head. He crossed the parking lot and stood against the far right wall, watching the flow of traffic. People were coming and going, nobody paying much attention to the lone man with the funny-looking brown cap leaning against the wall.

Jesse gazed up at the pearl-shell sky and gave a sigh. How he hated to live this way, from moment to moment not knowing whether he would survive another day.

He heard his fate calling
On the wings of the wind.
One day soon
It would bring a bitter end.

He pulled the white leather sports gloves from his left rear pocket and put his hands into them. The adrenaline throbbed in his temples, his breath quickened, and a million thoughts flooded his mind at once. It was always this way before a robbery. The muscles in his neck tightened. He pulled the ski-mask over his face, drew the .38 from its hiding place, and stormed into the customer-filled Save-N-Pack.

Elsewhere, a waiter brought the officers their food.

They savored the aroma,
But would not taste.
For they would soon
Leave in haste.

Bounding in front of the checkout counter, the masked bandit shouted, "This is a holdup! Nobody move, nobody gets hurt! You, you, and you" — pointing the .38 in the cashiers' direction — "take all the money out and put it in the sacks!" He pointed to the brown grocery sacks folded there. "Move it!"

The cashiers began to fill the paper bags with the contents of their registers. "That's it, hurry up," he demanded. "I don't want anyone to get hurt."

One of the checkout girls was having trouble opening her register. The outlaw sprang into her aisle and shouted, "You! Get that register open!"

The frightened young black woman was obviously near panic as she answered, "I can't! It won't open. I — I..."

The robber was aware time was running out. He knew he must be in and out in less than three minutes. "OK, forget it!" he hollered, and scooping up the now-full sacks sitting at the end of the counters, he turned and dashed out.

His robberies he planned
With passion and joy
As he and the boys
Cleaned their deadly toys.
The Lawmen couldn't catch you
And you escaped the hangman's noose
Till a friend took aim and shot you
Turned your weary soul loose.
So ride, Jesse, ride...
Into the setting sun you cry.
You were born to be free...
But tomorrow where will you be?

"Unit Alpha, robbery in progress, Save-N-Pack, your 10-20." Officer Copeland grabbed her field radio and keyed in, "Central, this is Unit 290 responding." The three officers jumped up, left their hot suppers to grow cold, and scrambled out of the restaurant.

The running outlaw raced across the parking lot, his lungs heaving. He could call on an amazing burst of speed when in need, and the time had come. Several customers followed behind at a distance to see how it would go.

Little did they know
It would be quite a show.

The officers converged, but the outlaw did not see them yet. He sprang over the 7-foot brick wall separating the alley from the parking lot, and landed with his feet in motion. He reached the getaway car instantly, snatched the keys from under the fender well, opened the door, tossed the money sacks in, jumped in, slammed the door, and pulled off the brown ski-mask. As he started the engine, two policemen filed in front, blocking the exit with weapons drawn.

Jesse put it in reverse and peeled rubber, but the alley was too narrow. The left side of the Buick ground against the concrete dock and wedged itself there. Someone in the gathering crowd shouted, "Good for you, asshole!"

Officer Copeland appeared on the dock just above and twenty feet behind the now-stilled Buick. She unholstered her 9mm service revolver and leveled it on the man behind the wheel. "Get out of the car!" she screamed. The outlaw did not respond. "I said get out of the car! *NOW!*"

Inside the Buick, Jesse pulled his .38 caliber revolver and zeroed in on the lady cop. For a long moment, the two were transfixed on each other's desperate faces. Then Jesse yelled, "Lady, I don't want to shoot you! Don't make me shoot you!"

Startled, with her weapon kept on target, she backed around the corner hugging the wall.

The jammed Buick now leapt forward towards the two cops barring the way with weapons aimed at the approaching vehicle.

Wildly, Jesse plunged ahead in a do-or-die effort, with his right hand on the steering wheel, foot heavy on the gas pedal, and left arm hanging out the window pointing the .38 in the direction of the matadors awaiting the charging bull. And so the bullfight began.

All hell broke loose! *POP-POP-POP!* The windshield exploded on top of him, as he ducked below the dash. With his left hand out the window, he answered their volley with two reports of his own. *POW! POW!* He was firing and driving blind.

The matadors emptied their weapons into the charging bull. Hot lead slammed into its metallic skin. Glass and parts of the dash and interior splintered everywhere.

Officer Delanoit was almost mashed as he got between the runaway Buick and the concrete wall. The driver was dodging bullets, driving blind, and did not see him. But it was close. So close in fact, that his partner rushed to aid his comrade, thinking the worst.

As the tan Buick left the alley, it screeched sideways and crashed into a mobile home, knocking it off its supports — and stalled.

There amidst the broken glass, Jesse raised up and immediately tried to restart the Regal. *Whrrr... whrrrr...*

Finally it came to life with a popping protest. The once-regal Buick limped off smoking with nineteen holes drilled into it.

The fugitive's mind was racing ahead now. *Escape... elude... survive.* The Buick drew its last breath twelve blocks away from the shootout. The robber grabbed the money and the gun, and left the car hissing and smoking in the middle of the street.

Running for all he was worth, he came to the end of the street. A ten-foot chainlink fence barred his way. The interstate was just beyond.

Quickly he threw the brown sacks of money over the fence. With one hand clutching the .38, he climbed the fence with the other, swung over its barbs, and free-fell down onto the other side. Landing like a cat, he picked up the money sacks and dashed across the highway, outrunning an oncoming sports car full of joyriding. One of the youngsters stuck his head out the window, shot the finger and yelled, "What? Are you crazy?" as they sped off, missing him by inches.

Jesse bounded across the median and the opposite lanes, reached the next fence, and went through the same maneuver — climbing, dropping, scooping up the money — and continuing his flight.

He fled through a residential area, salty sweat stinging his bloodshot eyes. Then overhead in the evening skies a helicopter began its search. Closer and closer it circled, tightening the noose with every pass.

Jesse came upon some old trucks parked in an overgrown lot. He hid himself between two of the junkers and watched the copter circle him like a shark homing in on its prey.

A patrol car pulled up and stopped. Jesse held his breath, certain that he would be discovered. He could hear them talking on the radio about him. Inexplicably, they left.

After he was sure they were gone, he began running strong. Further and further the helicopter faded into the approaching darkness, and once again the outlaw disappeared into the arms of his lover, the night.

He Thought He Was Going to Die

September 3, 1990. After the Save-N-Pack robbery and shootout, Jesse was looking for a place to hide. He broke into Janet Bos' home through a window and stole a bike, a bag of gym clothes, and a canceled check. He took the canceled check and wrote on the back, "In case of emergency, call Claudia Rolling," and listed the Rollings' home phone number. He also placed four long-distance calls to Shreveport, speaking to his mom one time for 20 minutes and Bunnie Mills three times for 2, 3 and 2 minutes each.

"He thought he was going to die," said Assistant State's Attorney Cass Castillo later when the robbery came to trial.

It was a pretty stupid thing to do, but I was having a bad day, and I needed someone to talk to. I told my mom and Bunnie about the shootout. They didn't know where I was and were very worried for me. I didn't mean to upset them, but I guess I did. I was running wild and not thinking clearly.

The night closed in on the lone gunman escaping with the loot. Like a vampire bat seeking a cave, he crept through an unfamiliar neighborhood searching for a place to rest. A well-lit Tampa home presented its haven as a gift. Desperate and on the run in a strange area, the outlaw cased the house for occupants. It was Labor Day weekend and nobody was home.

CRASH! He broke a window with his fist wrapped in a t-shirt. For a tense spell he stood there in the dark waiting to see if the noise had alerted a neighbor to the burglary in progress. Then he carefully extracted the jagged pieces of glass wedged in the sill and let them fall to the green grass below.

The man searched the house for weapons. He found none, but he still had the .38 he had used in the Save-N-Pack robbery. He took a small navy blue athletic bag and dumped the stolen cash into it. As he was leaving, he hijacked a ten-speed bicycle leaning on its kickstand by the back double-glass doors leading to the screened-in porch.

Off into the darkness he pedaled, changing gears on the ten-speed, breathing in deeply the cool night air. Ahhh, it was so good to be alive, free, and rolling-in-dough — a couple of thousand dollars worth.

He spent the night in an unfinished house. The raw beams resembled the backbone and ribs of a whale's skeleton. Rest was fitful at best. The mosquitoes making kamikaze runs on his exposed face and arms kept him busy most of the night. He left early, before the sun came up, not wanting to be caught there when the construction workers came back in the morning.

A Quiet Evening

September 4, 1990. His eyes were blood-shot and he had been stretched past the limit of his endurance. Mounting the bike, he pedaled on down the road in search of a safe place to hang out. When he chanced upon Lowery Park and Zoo, he stashed the bike and strolled up to the main entrance to the park. He approached a woman waiting on the bus across from the arcade. He was to drift in and out of her life like a warm summer breeze, barely ruffling her hair. The two got acquainted rather easily.

"Hi! Name's Jesse — Jesse Lang."

"Hello. I'm Diana." She was a free-lance artist drawing portraits in the park. She showed Jesse one of her pastel sketches.

"Hmmm... you're pretty good. Would you do one of me? I'll pay you. How much do you charge?"

She told him. He agreed and Diana drew him leaning against a fatherly oak with branches sagging from years of gravity pulling it earthward.

"Finished!" She proudly presented it to him.

"Yes, and it looks just like me!" He handed her two twenties and a ten.

"Oh no! This is too much!"

"No, you take it. Just mail the portrait to this address." He gave her a phony address in Dallas, Texas.

Diana asked Jesse if he had a place to stay for the night. He told her no. She offered to let him stay over at her place, and he gladly accepted. They rode the city bus to her duplex apartment. She let him take a shower and wash his clothes in her washer.

They spent a quiet evening together, eating Chinese food and watching "Good Morning Vietnam" on TV. Later he slept on the sofa and she slept in her bedroom. The next day when he left, she gave him written directions on how to get back to her place. But he was never to return.

The Robbed Robber

September 5, 1990. Fading into the seedy side of Tampa, Jesse spent a lot of money on meals, movies, alcohol and crack cocaine. One night at a strip joint called the 2000 Club one of the pretty blonde dancers asked to dance privately for him. Taking him by the hand, she led him upstairs, where they danced one-on-one in a special room with a jukebox.

"Give me some quarters for the box," she said, smiling seductively. He gave her some change and she fed the machine, punching up her choices.

Jesse had been drinking all afternoon. His new kick was Captain Dee's Spiced Rum. It wasn't the best, but if you drank enough of it, you could get a pretty good buzz going. At this point he had about two pints stirring in him.

The dancer was completely naked. She rubbed her body up close to the man sitting in a comfortable padded chair. Her body moved with grace and ease as she turned around, straddled his lap, bent over, reached around her ass, and spread her pussy, giving him a close-up view of her insides. Mercy sakes and a bag of rattlesnakes!

The outlaw reached out to stick a finger up her snatch, but the dancer politely slapped his hand down gently.

"Uh-uh! You can look, but you can't touch!" she smiled.

"Ah, too bad. It looks pretty good in there," he grumbled.

She bent back over and wiggled her ass in his face. He began to gently scratch the back of her legs, starting from her buttocks to the back of her knees, surprised that she allowed him to do so.

Then she turned around and gave him a frontal of her beautiful body. She squeezed her perky breasts, saying, "That was nice. I've been on my feet all night and my legs are tired. Scratching them felt good. Say, I know what!" And she leaned over and put her exquisite breasts right in his face. Well, you don't stick a firm pair of ripe peaches in a hungry boy's face and expect him not to take a taste, do you? Jesse grabbed both tits and sucked on them until the music stopped and the dance was over.

He asked her if she knew where to get some crack. She said her friend did, but they had to work all night.

"How much to get you and your friend the night off?"

"Two hundred apiece."

He forked it over. They got dressed and the three of them got into a white Jeep and drove out to the projects to get some blow. Jesse produced another two hundred dollars cash, they scored the rock, and the three of them split.

"Let's get a hotel room and party!"

"OK... but no sex."

"What do you mean, no sex?"

"Just that! We'll party with you, but no sex."

"Well OK, whatever. Let's get high."

They rented a hotel room and drank and smoked their way into the wee hours of the morning.

Danny came to with the pounding on the door matching the pounding in his head.

"Who is it!"

"It's the manager!"

"Uh-huh?"

"It's past checkout time. If you wanna stay another day, you'll have to pay the bill."

"All right. Thanks. I'll be down in a minute."

His head was half a mile thick and he was sick to his stomach. He staggered into the bathroom and threw up. He washed his face and looked around the room. The girls had disappeared and — his moneybag! It was gone! The strippers had robbed him and run off.

"Damn! The money's gone! What am I gonna do now?"

He left the hotel with a sinking feeling lodged in the pit of his uneasy stomach. As his head cleared, he remembered the .38 he had used in the Save-N-Pack robbery. He had stashed it in the bushes behind the 2000 Club.

The next night he went back to the club, mad as a Brahma bull with a burr under his saddle. The head barmaid waddled up, a big fat ugly bitch.

"Where's those two girls I left with last night?"

The bitch spat, "We heard about you, loverboy. We don't want your kind in this club ever again. Now get lost and don't come back."

"Oh, I'll get lost all right, doggie-breath. But I'll be back! And you ain't gonna like it!" He stormed out, seeing blooming bloody blasted *RED!* He went around in back of the club and retrieved the .38. It felt so good in his hand. He stood holding it, visualizing waiting on the two whores who robbed him — but it was not to be.

Instead, the robbed robber broke into an apartment, and while Reynaldo and Patricia Rio slept in the next room, he ate a banana, then picked up the car-keys and a couple of watches off the table and eased out. He started the Rio's Silver 1983 Ford Mustang and drove off into the night.

He made it as far as Ocala, where his money and his luck finally ran out.

The Last Arrest

September 7, 1990. The barechested gunman burst from the grocery store in Ocala, Florida, a.38 revolver in his right hand and a jeweled bag of folding green in his left.

The young woman leaving the gift shop at the corner of the shopping center dropped her bag, screamed, and scurried back into the store as the robber raced by and turned the corner.

A quick spring, and Jesse reached his getaway car — an old silver Mustang. It sat running, engine firecracker-hot under the boiling Florida noonday sun. He yanked the driver's side open and tossed the money bag and the revolver onto the empty passenger's side. He dived in, slammed the door, threw it in gear, and burned rubber!

Jesse sped off, the vinyl backrest of the Mustang blistering his flesh. The adrenaline was throbbing through his brain and sweat stung his hazel-green eyes.

In the distance, a wail of sirens gathered in strength. A voice told him, "This ain't gonna go down right." Suddenly police cars emerged from everywhere!

Look to the left... look to the right...
No place to run... no place to hide...

One police car screamed past the Mustang, then another. Then one stopped and let out a big black man in a brown uniform and sped off.

The black cop crouched with his big hand resting nervously on his service 9mm automatic. He looked over at the Mustang now waiting at the stop sign and approached cautiously, stalking his prey like a big black panther.

Jesse read the scene playing out before him. The cop stopped at the corner and screamed, "Put your hands where I can see them!"

Jesse reached over and grabbed the .38. With an innocent smile like the cat who ate the canary, he called out, "What's the problem, officer?"

The cop repeated, "Put your hands where I can see them!" and unsnapped the strap on his holster.

The moment was tense. The two men looked into each other's eyes. It was a matter of who moved first.

The outlaw weighed the chances. "I could drill a hole in him as easy as fallin' off a log." But he decided, "No, not this time," and he floored it.

The old beat-up Mustang came to life. The carburetor sucked air as the 4-barrel kicked in, the tires smoking on the hot pavement.

The policeman was left standing behind, pointing his automatic at the departing vehicle and waving his free hand at his comrades to give chase.

The Mustang was weaving in and out of noon rush-hour traffic, reaching speeds of a hundred plus miles per hour. Looking in the rearview mirror, the fugitive saw many red and blue flashing lights trying to pursue, but heavy traffic slowed their progress. "Well, Jesse," he said to himself, "the chase is on!"

Foot off the gas, on the brakes. Tires screaming, the Mustang almost rammed the rear end of a 1990 tan Buick. Turning hard left, it cut in front of another car in the center lane with only inches to spare. Jesse put his foot on it and watched the speedo climb from fifty to ninety. "Man! This thing has sho-nuff got some *HEART!*"

Leaping ahead, he approached a busy intersection. As the light turned red, a tractor-trailer pulling a load of fresh-cut trees for the sawmill pulled out and stopped, blocking the intersection.

Foot off the gas, on the brakes. Skidding 170 feet, then hard right, barely squeezing between the logs hanging off the end of the trailer and a stopped vehicle. It was so close he could have grabbed the red flag dangling from the end of the log-laden tractor-trailer. The rampaging Mustang jumped the curb, tore down a street sign, and sped off again.

Then from a side street, a motorcycle cop pulled in behind him, sirens blaring like on TV, a regular Evel Knievel in a cop suit.

The motorcycle cop sped in behind the runaway Mustang.

Inside the fleeing felon's mind was panic, pure and simple. He drove like a maniac, slamming on brakes, cutting in between people on their way to lunch with nothing on their minds but pizza and computers.

Eventually, the man eluded the CHiPs from Hell. "Whewwwww-*WEE!*" A moment of ease.

Then! From both sides of the road, two new tormentors appeared, lights blinking madly and sirens spitting obscenities.

"Damn!" Jesse said. "This has got to stop!" Brakes again, leaving ninety-something feet of Goodyear on the hot asphalt. Speed reduced to about fifty, trying to power-slide to the right down a side street.

Suddenly out of nowhere, a long blue whale of a car appeared with two nice little old ladies coming from the flea market. The blue whale beached itself at the stop sign — too late for the silver bullet to change course.

The ladies turned their heads and looked on helplessly, astonished as the silver Mustang moaned and groaned toward them on burning rubber, and finally smashed into their whale.

The impact threw the money and the .38 onto

the floor of the Mustang, and the driver into the steering wheel. Dazed and disoriented, Jesse looked for the pistol but could not find it. "Must be under the seat."

Just then the motorcycle cop showed up with siren howling.

Daaaanneeeeeee!
Come to meeeeeee!
Daaaanneeeeeee!

The fugitive grabbed the sack of money, opened the door and stepped out, unsteady on his feet for a moment. Suddenly he dashed across the parking lot packed with cars.

Cat and mouse time. The bandit dashed between the parked cars trying desperately to get away, but the Robocop sped ahead of him. An army of police cruisers arrived — motorcycle cops, state troopers, and whatever else Marion County could throw at him. Sirens and blue and red lights everywhere.

Look to the left... look to the right...
No place to run... from the Lawman's gun...

He felt like Custer in the print that had hung by his bed as a boy. Still, he didn't give in. He chunked the bag of money into the pale blue sky. "Who says money don't grow on trees? Why, lookie here, it's raining tens and twenties! Money, money everywhere! Across the parking lot, under cars, stuck on windshields!"

Sprinting, legs reaching out in quick strides, his athletic heart and lungs pounding in his chest, he outran the motorcycle cop and ducked into an insurance office, where one man sat at his solitary post.

Bursting in, breathing hard with sweat pouring down his desperate face, Jesse felt the cooled air but it did not soothe him. His mind was ablaze.

The insurance man jumped to his feet. "What on earth is going on here?" The running man never stopped. On his way to the back he yelled over his shoulder, "The cops are after me!" and smashed through the door into the back driveway.

Lo and behold, the driveway was blocked by a trailer. And wouldn't you know it? The back lot was packed with sweet little blue-haired ladies. It was the flea market the ladies in the whale had just left.

Dodging between tables full of old clothes and whatnots, the man dashed across the driveway into a back lot coated with lush green grass.

Look to the left... look to the right...
Nowhere to run... nowhere to hide...

The police converged. The motorcycle jockey sped ahead, blocking escape. Cops were coming at him from every angle now.

Nowhere to run...

And so he stopped. And to the amazement of a hundred or so sweet little old ladies, the serial killer who had terrorized the entire state of Florida dropped to his knees, raised his hands, and surrendered.

Now, for those of you
Who are taking all this in,
If you've never been taken down
By the Law,
Let me fill you in.
It's like someone pulled a plug
On your life.
All the sounds
And tastes
And feelings
Drain from your soul,
And leave you empty and numb.
I don't recommend it
For anyone.

Someone behind him yelled, "Get down on your face!"

He did.

Someone — a woman — put a gun to his head and screamed, "You move and I'll blow your fucking head off!"

"Don't worry, lady," he answered as they handcuffed his hands behind his back, "I ain't budgin' an inch."

And thus Danny Rolling was finally dragged away.

Louisiana Law is after me...
for the things I've done...
Now they've surely found me...
nowhere left to run...

CHAPTER 10
THE LAST DANCE

A Mysterious Woman

It was a roasting summer day when the white prison van entered the east gate of Florida State Prison. It wheeled down the drive and parked at the base of the long concrete ramp.

The back doors of the van swung open and Danny Rolling emerged, shackled hand and foot and squinting at the glaring sun. The climb seemed to take forever under the weight of the chains that hindered his progress. As he struggled up the lolling concrete tongue that protruded from the yawning doorway, it seemed to him that he was about to be swallowed up by some terrible monster.

The escort marched him to a special strip cell and he was greeted by two captains. "Welcome home, Danny, you're gonna die here," was his reception. He was immediately strip-searched, a bend-over-and-spread-'em indignity that goes with the territory. Then he was hustled down the main hallway and deposited in the last cell at the far end of W-Wing.

Slam! Clink! It was a sound the prisoner would never adjust to — his cell door closing behind him, driving home the bleak impossibility of ever leaving such a stronghold.

Later that day two porky guards banged on Danny's cell door. "Hey Danny! Get up and come over here!" He did. "You piece of shit! How could you take an innocent life? You piece of shit! We're gonna take a rope and hang you with it! Better yet, why don't you just kill yourself and save us the trouble? Whatcha think about that, you piece of shit?"

Danny just stood there and stared at the guards having their little fun for the day. Once he got the general idea, he simply turned his back on them and before long they left. But the scene was to repeat itself over and over again every day at the same time for weeks, until the sergeant over the wing caught wind of it and put an end to the pork-and-beans fun.

It wasn't long before another face appeared at Danny's door — the swollen, beefy chops of an inmate named Bobby Lewis, who wasted no time buddying up to the new arrival. He showed Danny every consideration and soon gained his confidence. Bobby was the type of guy who could make you laugh at anything, even yourself — a born storyteller and entertainer. But Danny would find out Bobby was not the jolly character he appeared to be.

One day Bobby was unraveling a stretch of yarn about his famous escape from Death Row. "Yep, I just walked right out the back door," he boasted, failing to add that he had betrayed a friend in order to accomplish this great feat. He made it seem like he was such a hero. "Here," Bobby said. "Let me show you something," and stuck a wad of paper through the food slot in the cell door.

"What is it?"

"It's a screenplay I wrote. Read it and tell me what you think."

"OK, Bobby, I'll do just that." Danny read the manuscript entitled Redbone nonstop front to back. It was fantastic, absolutely fascinating! That screenplay was the beginning of a journey into a world he knew nothing about — the world of writing. That evening when Bobby brought Danny his supper, Danny asked him, "Who is this Sondra London I see listed on the manuscript?"

"Oh, she's just my editor."

"Uh-huh. Say, Bobby, how's about letting me have her address? I'd like to write to her and see if she would be interested in doing my story."

"Sure, Danny," he replied and eagerly gave him the address he wanted. That night Danny wrote to this mysterious woman, and it was not too long before he got her response. From that very first letter there was magic, pure and simple. A flame began burning in Danny's heart that day, and each letter thereafter fanned it higher until it was a beautiful glowing bonfire!

A steady correspondence of poems, songs, stories and artwork flowed between the two. It soon became apparent to Danny that Bobby Lewis was not the mastermind behind Redbone, but rather it was the talents of Sondra London that gave it life. This endeared Sondra to Danny all the more, and a lifelong friendship was formed.

As time pushed forward, Danny and Sondra drew steadily closer. They reached for each other, pouring out their very hearts and souls with pen and ink on fallen pine. Their hearts became as one, and Sondra was granted one visit with Danny behind the glass. For two and a half blessed hours they were as close as the divider allowed. That meeting was supercharged with emotion, and the couple hardly noticed the glass separating them until it was time to say goodbye. Then the obstacles between them became all too real. As they kissed on either side of the unfeeling plexiglas, it was painful to be so close, and yet so far away. They gazed into each other's eyes until the last moment, their hands pressed against the glass.

"I love you, Sondra."

"I'll be back."

Soon after that visit, Danny asked Sondra to marry him. Though she accepted, the State denied them the God-given right to become man and wife. But that's another story, and it remains to be seen if the ending will be a happy one.

Sondra

You Can't Run

February 13, 1994. Danny Rolling pleaded guilty to five murders and all related charges. The clean-cut and clear-eyed defendant, dressed in a beige sports jacket, blue shirt and striped tie, addressed the Court in a soft Southern drawl: "Your honor, I have been running from first one thing and then another all my life, whether from problems at home or with the law, or from myself. But there are some things that you just can't run from, and this being one of those."

In pleading guilty, a huge weight lifted off my shoulders. Now even my prayers feel more sincere. Regardless of what people think, I know in my heart that my Lord God has forgiven me. "If we confess our sins, he is faithful and just to forgive them, and to cleanse us from all unrighteousness." (I John 1:9)

The Gemini Defense

On the day Danny Rolling pleaded guilty to the Gainesville murders, his public defender Rick Parker told the press, "Mr. Rolling has emphasized honesty and his belief that the pleas of guilty are the right thing to do. An important consideration in this decision has been Mr. Rolling's concern for the families of his victims. These last comments may sound bizarre to many people because of their difficulty reconciling them with reprehensible acts like rape and murder. The best explanation lies in the fact that Danny Rolling is, and has been since before these crimes, mentally ill."

At trial, several psychiatrists testified as to the nature of his mental illness. "Danny Rolling has magical thinking," observed Dr. Robert Sadoff. "I can give you two or three examples. One is the expectation when he went up to one of the homes here in Gainesville and the door was not open. He said, 'I want the door to be open,' and when he tried it again, it was open. So that was a sign to him that he could go in.

"When he first became affiliated with the Pentecostal Church after he came out of the service, and the man picked him up on the highway, took him to church to pray, and he found that this was a good church for him. Then Danny said, 'Lord, I need a wife.' And there was Omatha, and that was the sign for him. It wasn't just coincidence. It wasn't that she was an attractive woman that one of us might say, 'OK, that's somebody I may want to marry.' No, this woman was literally a gift of God. Because this is the magical world Danny lives in.

"The same with these spirits he saw, when he was with his wife and this smoke came into the room and he believed it was an evil force. He didn't put the name Gemini on it then, but it was an evil force, he knew it was evil, and the way to get rid of that was to magically state the words, 'Jesus Jesus Jesus,' and it went away. To Danny, that was a sign from God that this was an evil devil kind of thing. That was part of his religious belief, but it's also part of his borderline personality. You're either from God or you're from the devil. So he has this magical thinking, if you will. He's looking for the signs that he believes come to him supernaturally.

"I interviewed Mr. Rolling on the 19th of November. The purpose of that interview was to find out for sure, did Mr. Rolling have multiple personality disorder? When he talks about personalities such as Ennad and Gemini, do they really exist? Could they be drawn out under hypnosis, could he relive experiences, and could I talk to Gemini or Ennad? I've examined a number of people using this special technique, and I have been able to talk to other personalities on occasion. If I could, it would help us in the diagnosis. If I couldn't, at least we could rule it out. My conclusion was that he does not have multiple personality disorder. I was not able to talk to Gemini or Ennad. It was just Danny Rolling.

"What he does have is a variety of dissociative disorder called possession syndrome. This is a syndrome wherein a person believes he is responding to the will of either another person, or another being or a spirit. He feels that he has certain obligations because of his relationship with that spirit, or entity as the case may be, and he acts accordingly.

"I have found Danny to be totally honest in reporting his experience. There is no evidence he is malingering. There were signs of exaggeration, of distortion, of other kinds of communications that Danny may have believed through his perception, but may not have been based on fact. But malingering is a conscious deception, lying. A malingerer is one who purposefully deceives the interviewer, knowing that he is doing so. It's not that he has a distorted view of the world and gives that distortion believing it to be the truth, because there's a difference between truth and fact. So what he may believe is the truth may not be based on absolute fact or corroborating evidence, but he may believe it's the truth. Malingering is when a person says something they know to be false. I didn't find any of that. I did find omissions, I did find exaggeration and distortion, but I didn't find deception, not absolute falsehoods or lies.

"Danny had experienced these different personas earlier in his life. He experienced a part of himself early on which he had some difficulty controlling. He didn't give it a name then, with that smoke coming in through the window that he got

Danny

by Danny Rolling :: 6-28-93 ★

out by saying 'Jesus Jesus Jesus.' Subsequent to that he saw that same force when he was parked at a cemetery. And I believe he saw something he identified as that a third time as well.

"Danny deals in magic and fantasy and he had these experiences before seeing Exorcist III. Seeing the movie confirmed for him that the signs were right, that this was what has happened to him. There it is in the movie, so it must be true. And so he puts a name on that evil spirit within him, and he can then say it's real. It's real because Gemini is my sign and therefore this is a sign from the movie. Now, most of us would have taken that as just a coincidence. But not in the magical thinking of the borderline Danny Rolling.

"He is mostly rational, but there are times when his thinking is not so rational. It's based on fantasy, wish fulfillment, unreasonable expectations. He has a very serious illness.

"At the time of the offenses here in Gainesville, he was suffering from a serious emotional disturbance, and he lacked substantial capacity to conform his conduct to the requirements of law. I'm not saying he lacked ability, because no one's saying he could not conform. But he lacked substantial ability because of his borderline condition, which included the rage and the anger, and the need he had for the persona of Gemini that he believed was in control at the time that he acted out these events. Now, could he control himself? Yes, he could. Did he have difficulty controlling himself? Yes, he did."

Awww, come on, guys... there's nothing wrong with me that a good piece of pussy and a fifth of tequila wouldn't cure.

In the considered opinion of Dr. Elizabeth McMahon, "Danny has a dissociative disorder which is known as a possession disorder or possession syndrome. He has talked about Gemini. Danny was raised in and became very active in a fundamentalist church. He studied the Bible very intensely. It's an integral part of his life. Although that may seem contradictory, the borderline tends to be very contradictory in that way. Danny can accept the sexual urges within himself that led to the voyeurism and that even led to the rapes. But Danny to this day doesn't understand rape as an act of rage, hostility, degradation. In no way can he come close to acknowledging the rage within him. If you ask Danny to describe himself, he will very genuinely give you a picture of a gentle, loving, caring, passive individual, which he is a good part of the time. As long as that door isn't opened, he is that way. He has kept that door closed on the rage. It has become compartmentalized or disassociated. It's out there, it's somebody else, it's not Danny, it's Gemini. So he will say it's Danny that is the voyeur, it's Danny that robbed, it's Danny that raped, but it's Gemini that killed. Because that's what he cannot accept. And I don't mean he's saying the devil made him do it or he's not responsible. Danny has said repeatedly, 'It was my body, my hand, I was the one that was there, I did this.' He has not varied from that, so it's not that this is a way of getting out of anything in terms of society or the law. It is a way of not acknowledging internally for himself his own rage, which he just can't look at. So when you ask him, 'Danny, tell me what you were thinking when you went in that apartment, what were you thinking when you approached this woman? What were you feeling?' Danny can't get close to that. 'I don't know, that was Gemini.' I mean he can get right up to that point — and then it's 'I don't know, that was Gemini.' Can't get him there even now. Because he still can't look at that horrible bottomless pit that's the reservoir of rage within himself. The only way of dealing with the urges that come from that, and the behavior that has resulted from that, is to encapsulate it out here and call it Gemini. That is the dissociative part.

"Now, possession per se is when an individual experiences something that is in accord with their cultural beliefs. The way it's manifested, a number of people might have it, and it would look the same in all of these people in a particular culture, and it's accepted by the culture from which the person comes. Now, spirits influencing one's life is a principle accepted by Danny's culture in the sense of the church in which he was reared, yes. But the possession syndrome is unique to each individual for two reasons. One, it's going to be manifested in terms of that individual, not in terms of a cultural norm. In other words, you're not going to find a lot of people walking around with Gemini. Nobody's saying that there is in fact some independent entity that has anything to do with Danny. Danny says that, but the rest of us are not saying that. Possession syndrome is a psychological defense mechanism whereby one dissociates that aspect out that one cannot accept. There are all kinds of dissociative disorders. It's not in the form of a multiple personality disorder or of fugue states where a person has amnesia, and winds up in another town with another identity. This is when that part of the individual that they can't accept takes on a supernatural description, way of being, even a name. Danny will say. 'Gemini is a spirit, it's mainly intellect, it doesn't talk to me in terms of words, I can feel it, I can sense its presence, I know when it's here, it loves the dark not the light.' He can tell you all about it in supernatural or religious terms. So in that sense, that's why it's called a possession syndrome or possession disorder, not simply possession."

Man! Is He Crazy!

I gave the names to the characters that run around in my head. Ennad was part of my makeup even before Parchman, although I didn't really realize it until then. He is a part of my character even today. But Gemini, well, that's another thing altogether. He is a spirit — a demon from HELL.

This thing that entered my bedroom while my wife and I had gone to sleep did not give its name, nor has it ever. I do not enjoy speaking about it. Even though I have heard it calling in the middle of the night, it has not addressed itself as Gemini. I gave it that name.

Only Danny can look into the mind of Gemini. But that's like looking into the flames of hell. I don't like what I see. So… I don't look.

I told Dr. McMahon as much. When she asked me if I had an imaginary friend as a child, I told her I didn't.

"Where did Ennad and Gemini get their names?" she prodded.

"I gave them their names."

"Was Gemini summoned or did he just appear?"

These are the kinds of questions she asked me. Although I tried to be as honest and frank as I could, I'm afraid I am poorly equipped to open up every door to the dark corners of my mind.

"I suppose he was summoned, I don't know. Although he was summoned at Parchman, he also just appeared that night in my bedroom."

I never lied or put on with Dr. McMahon or anyone else about this. GOD AS MY JUDGE. I have been as honest and cooperative as I could be.

I realize sometimes it seems too melodramatic to be true, and gives the impression of something I've just made up. But I mean, I'm not a babbling idiot (although some would dispute that). So how could an intelligent human being allow himself to become so entangled that his sense of reality becomes vague and distorted? I don't have the answers. Tell me, can you turn your eyes inward and see all the working parts of your mind? Does anyone here on earth possess such insight? I think not.

I have been confused. But what I know, I DO KNOW. There are things afoot and winged that drift between the natural and the unnatural. Spirits, if you will. I have seen such things. But I don't expect the narrow-minded to believe me. Hell! I'm liberally-minded myself, and it still strikes me as unbelievable. If I hadn't seen it with my own eyes, heard it with my own ears, I too would have my doubts. But I have no doubts, and I don't care what doubts the shrinks may cast on my sanity. They weren't there. I WAS.

God help us. There are things out there you can't see with the naked eye. But sometimes you catch a fleeting glimpse of a shadow that shouldn't be there. And on a special night a soul is born with eyes that can see BEYOND.

Those who haven't seen or experienced it, just can't comprehend it. To them it is either mystery or myth. Reality and fantasy, these are opposites to be certain. Still, why do we choose to entangle the two? TV is a prime example of escape into a world totally unlike our own. But when the real and the unreal collide, the result can only be confusion.

For instance, take the dark and strange power known as GEMINI. Can you envision Danny possessed, prowling down a lighted city street? When the wind blows, rattling the leaves in the trees, BLINK! One street light after another winks out as Danny and Gemini stroll past each light pole, darkness following the two, one walking inside the other, into the engulfing night. And so it happened.

The fact that I did see Exorcist III at the time I was in Gainesville is an unfortunate coincidence. Still, the fact remains that I did tell my mom about Gemini long before I ever ended up in Gainesville. In fact, I don't even think the movie was produced during this time frame. I tried to tell my mom about what was going on inside me and about Gemini long before I saw the movie.

When I did see the movie, it made quite an impact on me because I already was dealing with this force in me that I had been calling Gemini for years. I saw the movie stoned-out on some killer weed, and yes indeed. It did make an impression on me. I was already dealing with these elements and when these similarities flashed on the big screen — I freaked!

If you will recall, there was a beheading in the movie. The decapitation was done by a Dark Spirit, a Grim Reaper, if you will. During those horrific acts, I was under — and Gemini was about. He wants only one thing: BLOOD.

The murders were like being in a movie — a horror movie. Gemini the puppet master was pulling the strings and I was the possessed leading actor.

I've told the shrinks who pick my brains as much. Ah, but alas. They cock their heads to one side and give me the evil eye, as if to say, "Man! Is he crazy!" Yeah, sure! Maybe I am! Call me crazy if it makes you feel better. But still, these things and many other strange occurrences really have taken place around me.

I've lain Gemini to rest now. Well... at least I have gained some control over the forces within. I didn't one day just wake up and tell Gemini to get lost. It was anything but easy. I took a lot of prayer on my knees to put him away, and I know he is still out there, scratching on the window of my soul. But I pray, oh dear sweet Jesus, please keep Gemini away from my soul! For his desire is to destroy not only Danny but Ennad — who is still an important part of me.

These two are in agreement these days, and the glue that holds it all together grows stronger with the passing of each day. I know my angel protects me and guides me along this troubled path my feet must tread.

Believe me, Gemini will never ever hurt anyone again. Ennad and Danny won't let him. Gemini is no longer a part of this man Danny Rolling, but I'm afraid that same killer demon is out there somewhere, seeking out another soul to possess.

I want to warn the public. Beware! There could be a Gemini gently knocking on the door of your mind. Don't let him in! For God's sake, don't open THAT DOOR!

Death for Danny

March 19, 1994. Jury's deliberation: 7 hours. Decision: 5 death sentences. The atmosphere in the courtroom was as still as a graveyard but heavy with emotion, until the jury presented the judgment concerning Danny Rolling's punishment. Then the dam broke and people wept out loud as DEATH... DEATH... DEATH... DEATH... DEATH for Danny was announced. They were not weeping for pity's sake. The tears that fell from their eyes came from JOY!

The condemned man stood and looked across the courtroom. Justice must be served, and it's best served cold.

I suppose I must have appeared under control in court that day, but under the surface, restless drums pounded in my soul and rang through my head. I felt like a roach under someone's shoe. It was all I could do just to stand.

Demons Rear Their Heads

March 30, 1994. In the little white house on Canal Street, Claudia Rolling, in the final stages of terminal liver cancer and no longer able to care for herself, sat immobilized in a recliner chair with three tubes coming out of her body. When James Harold came home, he was outraged to find her watching the coverage of their son's murder trial on TV. Attacking and brutally beating her, he threw his dying wife out of the house. He was arrested for misdemeanor simple battery and released, whereupon he promptly filed for divorce. Claudia went to live first with her sister, then with her son Kevin. It was there that she died ten months later, without seeing Danny again.

Not only did my dad rough up my dear ailing mom, he viciously ripped out the tubes surgically implanted directly into her liver, damaging the vital organ further. He tried to kill her. Had Claudia not been rushed to the hospital, she would have bled to death. Nice guy, huh?

That's the kind of cruelty we had to live with under James Harold's roof. We weren't his family. We were his possessions. We lived in terror in that house — terror of James Harold and his uncontrollable fury. Eventually one's demons rear their ugly heads and make themselves known. Dad tried to bully me one too many times and I put a bullet between his eyes. But he is so mean not even a .38 slug blown through his skull could stop him for long.

I was afraid Dad would hurt Mom, and I have lived to see my fears came to life. If I had been there, he never would have harmed her. At least he can't hurt her any more now.

When I heard what he did to my mom, I began to see Dad for what he is, and I don't like what I see. Oh yes, I see James Harold in an entirely different light these days. He is a very sick man, and he has a poisonous effect on those around him. As a child I was never allowed to just be Danny. I was never good enough to be James Harold's son. Instead I was to bear the brunt of his fury and displeasure.

Believe you me, I am very angry at my dad for this! Claudia had to go to the hospital all the time to get her tubes refixed because of the damage Dad did yanking them out. She suffered to her dying day because of James Harold.

The judge ordered him to give Claudia her car, and do you know what that asshole did? He took all four of the new tires off it and replaced them with old worthless recaps. Even that wasn't enough. He ripped out the carpet and trashed the interior. It wasn't enough he beat Mom half to death. He had to trash her brand new Buick LeSabre as well.

But Dad doesn't care. Hell! I hear he's already got himself a new girlfriend.

Die, Danny, DIE!

April 20, 1994. Upon hearing Judge Stan Morris pronounce his five death sentences, Danny Rolling stood and addressed the Court: "Your Honor, there is much I would like to say about our world, my beliefs, and the destiny of man. However, I feel whatever I might have to say at this moment is overshadowed by the suffering I've caused. I regret with all my heart what my hand has done, for I have taken that which I cannot return. If only I could bend back the hands on that ageless clock and change the past? Ah, but alas, I am not the keeper of time, only a small part of history and the legacy of mankind's fall from grace. I'm sorry, Your Honor."

I have been under an enormous strain. On whose scale do you measure my suffering? The past? Tortured! Flesh ripped off with red-hot pincers! I know there are those who would pay dearly for the pleasure of seeing me boiled in oil and my head served up on a silver platter. I have looked into some of their eyes and seen the hatred there.

Day after day for hours on end, I had to sit rooted to the adjudicated chair, slapped time and time again with the words "BURN HIM" shot like flaming arrows of hate from the mouths of people who never knew me. I wonder how many of those who judge me so have a pure heart and conscience before God?

As they flung their burning hatred at me, I looked into the eyes of animosity, but returned not the flames of anger. Instead I tried to see the situation from their point of view.

I always try to detach myself from the heavy atmosphere that settles over a courtroom during such tense and emotional moments. But when I witnessed such touching sights as the two ladies on the front row of the jury box crying while viewing the crime scene photos, I found myself becoming entangled in spite of myself.

On the outside I may have appeared devoid of emotion, but inside I was weeping right along with them. Why? Because I regret with all my heart that they ever had to look at such hideous suffering. I prayed for those people that God Almighty would give them strength and not allow what they saw to inflict injury to their tender consciousness.

I have learned a great deal about humanity by going through this ordeal. Even though the jury box was filled with people who looked at me with hatred and disgust, I could not return their hatred. I love them as the Creation of God they are (Genesis 1:26). I will not hate them that condemn me, lest I happily reject the handiwork of God. We are the craftsmanship of a loving and powerful Creator, and I will love and respect what my Lord and Savior has made with his mighty hands.

As I sit here in my cell on Death Row, the wind brings the smell of freedom. Ah, but alas — not for me. I am branded to take my last breath in this house of woe.

No more will I embrace my guitar and make love to the night — the songs of my soul flung towards the stars and the moon, my private audience. Never again — at least not in this life.

No more long distance running with the wind in my face, the sun setting behind me, moving cross-country, running, running, powerfully galloping forward, eating up the distance.

It brings tears to my eyes. I'm a caged bird that longs to fly again, but it seems the only thing I can do is die — DIE, DANNY, DIE! Then perhaps my soul will fly beyond the reach of this tomb that suffocates me. Only in Death will I ever be free again. Then Death is my friend — not to be feared. The key that sets Danny free... free. No more running... no more pain... no more loneliness... no more suffering.

Ah, how could my life have ended up such a tragedy? I never wanted to come this way. Something... some force drove me to this place. I fought against it all my life, but each time I ended up in prison, I lost a little more ground, until I slipped over the edge and fell down a deep dark well.

A young black man in his early twenties was the last prisoner in this cheerful cube. He hanged himself and strangled to death rather than face the ordeal of his own execution. Oh, the horrors I must face.

The Feds have come up with a new bill that once a Death Row prisoner's state appeals are exhausted, the appeal must go directly to the United States Supreme Court. This will shorten my life by several years. So my fate draws ever nearer with each breath.

Dear Lord God of Heaven and Earth: Have mercy on this, the least of your children, and grant me the grace and strength to face Eternity with my head held high and my spirit prepared. Amen.

The Death Penalty

The earliest form of execution is described in the Old Testament in Genesis 40:9-22. This classic tale is known to every Christian. Several thousand years before Christ, we see beheading as the common cause of execution, because Joseph said that Pharoah would lift the baker's head from off him and hang his lifeless body on a tree for the birds to peck on. Quick, to say the least — but messy.

Later, in Numbers 15:32-36, we read of the Jews stoning their condemned. They found a man gathering sticks on the Sabbath, and the Lord said to Moses, "The man shall surely be put to death." All the congregation stoned him, and he died.

The Romans were a bit more creative. They developed crucifixion, the same method that brought us salvation through the suffering of the Lord and Savior Jesus Christ. Praise his Holy Name, and thank God above for his great love towards us sinners that he gave himself as ransom for us all (I Timothy 2:5-6).

As time ticked on, gunpowder was discovered, and so the firing squad soon followed: Kaa-POW! OOOW!

Hundreds of years later, Christopher Columbus sought out America, and it wasn't long before we were burning accused witches at the stake. If your neighbor got on your nerves, hey! All you had to do was point your finger and cry WITCH! That'd take care of 'em. Hmmmm. Maybe we could use that one today? Just kidding, folks.

During the French Revolution, the guillotine was constructed — a grisly sight to behold. Marie Antoinette said, "Let them eat cake," and they stretched her neck below the guillotine's heavy blade and relieved her of her head. Gasp!

And you know how the West was really won? If you were apt to rustling cattle or stealing horses, well, you sure as shootin' better not get caught at it! Cause they would throw a scraggly old rope over a tree limb and put the noose around your neck. And you guessed it — hang 'em high! Whew-WEE! What a way to go — left for buzzard bait.

After the Civil War painted the American countryside red with the blood of our own, we Americans began to diversify and expand our means of execution. The gas chamber and the electric chair were added to our gallows.

In "Public Enemy Number One," James Cagney played a real tough gangster type, but towards the end, you caught a glimpse of his humanity on his sorrowful face. It was spine-chilling when the guard said, "It's time." As Cagney hung down his head and walked the last mile into the awaiting arms of the electric chair, it was so sad. There's no other way to describe it.

The death penalty has not accomplished anything other than sweeping our dirt under the rug, and the electric chair is inhumane. We don't even electrocute stray dogs. The Humane Society won't allow such cruelty to animals, yet we will fry our own.

You can raise a child to become a decent law-abiding pillar of the community, or you can drive a child to become as uncontrollable as a whirlwind. Many of our criminals began this way, driven by cruel uncaring hands, destined to smash into the society that spawned them like a tornado slams into a trailer park. "For they have sown the wind, and they shall reap the whirlwind." (Hosea 8:7)

The death penalty is not the answer. It is not even a viable deterrent. No, the answer lies deeper than that. It goes far back into the dawn of man himself. The day we chose to become wise, we became fools. Since the first man Adam and the first woman Eve, we have rejected the counsel of God and chosen rather to lean upon our own understanding, and there has been nothing but death and confusion ever since.

We rejected paradise for knowledge, and look

where it has led us. Now we are all under the death penalty. Great and small, young and old — we must all return to the ground from whence we came. Ashes to ashes, dust to dust. But there is hope for us all in our Lord Jesus Christ. Death for one who believes in Him is only a step into Glory.

We all must die, my friends, and as long as man refuses to seek the Lord God Almighty Jehovah for the answers to our violent world, greed will persist, hunger will remain, and the Death House will fill to the brim. Such is the wisdom of man, whose eyes have been opened to the knowledge he was not meant to retain.

God help us all.

How Many Days?

How many days till the hollow wind blows through your soul and takes you away from this world?

That question keeps tick-tick-tickin' like the grandfather clock in the Twilight Zone that goes on day after day, until someone fails to pull the chain to set the hands and suddenly, the old man's heart stops.

Most of us never see Death coming. Sometimes a soul is keen enough to hear the engine of that life-crushing steamroller called mortality easing up behind them, but more often than not, it just mashes over us before we even know it's coming.

Not so for a condemned man. For those who dwell on Death Row, the Grim Reaper pays daily visits. He grimaces and extends a bony, white, lifeless hand and coldly says, "How ya doin, fella? Oh, don't worry, I was just in the neighborhood and decided to check in and remind you. Up the road a-ways, I'm gonna stick my sickle in you and reap your soul. Ha! Ha! But not today. Maybe tomorrow? Till then... it was so nice to see you again." And so it goes on the Row.

The thing is, you don't mind old Grave-Breath dropping by to say hello, so long as he moves on and doesn't decide to stay over. Then he outwears his welcome real quick, know what I mean?

Time is short! Shorter still when your days dwindle before your eyes like a kite soaring high in an azure sky. Suddenly someone cuts the string. And even though the wind holds it up for a spell, eventually it sinks away earthward. You see it falling, helpless to retrieve it. Down it dives until it crashes on the rocks, broken beyond repair.

How many days till then? Who's counting?

The Last Dance

Another day, another dollar, huh? It's sort of like dancing. There you are on the dance floor and your partner is looking at you like you are suppose to know what you are doing — but you don't. It's your first time, see?

Well, you fake it because you figure it's high time you learned. After awhile it's cool, because it seems everybody else is faking it too. So you learn to dance.

Life is sort of like that. We are all dancing to this tune or that. Take your partner and do-see-do. Some people dance alone, others in a crowd. It's the Dance of Life, you know, and everybody is invited. But there is another dance — the final song piped to those who reach the outer edge of existence in this dimension.

It is the Dance of Death, and we are all drawn into its cold embrace at the appointed time. The Grim Reaper comes calling as Death knocks on our door. Peculiar as it seems, we pretend not to be at home. We say, "Go away! Come back another day!" But he comes in anyway. And it is the Last Dance.

The Grim Reaper comes for us all. Whether rich or poor, great or small, one day you are born and the next — mourners are standing over your grave. It's out there waiting for me... and you... and all of humanity: The Beyond.

Beyond what? Beyond the moon and stars? Beyond the galaxy and past the universe? Beyond your last breath taken in agony? No one has ever come back from the Land of the Dead and said, "Hey, man! Death is where it's at!"

Everything we see and beyond was designed by a powerful Master Mind. It is all His handiwork. He controls the universe and destiny. So why worry about it? I say, "Praise God! He is wiser than I."

The key to the universe and eternal life is Jesus Christ. His sacrifice on the cross of Calvary gives us hope and a promise that there is more out there than just cosmic dust and darkness. There is life — even after the Last Dance.

The End of Murder Road

I'll tell you what's at the end of Murder Road: a toxic waste dump where mankind's rejects end up. I've been in and out of the meanest, nastiest prisons in the South ever since I was 25 years old. My teacher was PRISON. Behind bars of solid, cold, unforgiving iron, my metal was tempered. It is here my mind became bent and my perceptions warped.

Prison does something to a man — it changes him forever. Ninety percent of men who do time repeat their criminal behavior and end up back in the joint. Most convicts are extremely immature and throw temper tantrums if they don't get their way. They are a selfish lot — schemers out for what they can get. Most convicts are not what they seem. They are little children in men's bodies and that is what makes them really dangerous.

And they never... never... NEVER... are WRONG. Oh no. If something goes amiss with a plan they have, automatically it's someone else's fault. It's someone else's fault they got caught. It's someone else's fault they ended up in prison. It's someone else's fault, PERIOD. When you're talking convict, you're talking the bottom of the trash-can where the maggots live.

I must live with rough... ugly... sneaky... dirty... smelly... freaky... rotten... bad... spooky... kooky men — those the world has cast aside. I have to be capable of defending myself in a scuffle — and I am. When it comes to fighting, I know every dirty trick in the book. I can get down with the worst of them. That's why they call me MANIAC. I will walk away from trouble if I can, but if it is brought to me, I will fight with all my might. In the jungle, you don't play kitty-cat with the tigers. Respect is earned by the way you carry yourself, not by push and shove. That won't just get you into deep shit, it can get you killed.

So now I'm on Death Row. But I have found that even though the most infamous characters are housed here, they are better behaved and respectful of each other than the majority of inmates in a maximum security prison — and I have had the grand tour, to be sure.

Myself... I am what I appear to be — a man who will be imprisoned for the rest of his short life. I have five death sentences and ten lifes, with a couple hundred years running wild behind that. I'm in here for some heavy duty crimes. I make no bones about that. I am paying for my wrong against society and I will pay and pay and pay until the life within my heart can pay no more. This is the State's wish, and so it is.

I have many regrets, but I have become such by my bloody deeds against fellow human beings. Being tagged a serial killer ain't no picnic. No sir. I never thought I'd end up this way. God as my judge, I'm not proud to fall so far from a state of grace that I have become a messenger of sorrow and pain. How deeply I have plunged into the darkness!

Still, I'm not like my fellow prisoners. I've been told so by several. I may be down here with the maggots, but I am not one of them. A convict will bullshit you, use you, then throw you to the dogs. But I won't.

How can a man convicted of such terrible crimes make such a statement? Because I am what I appear — Danny Rolling. And I can be no other.

Reality Jolt

How does Danny sleep? Not very comfortably, but he tries to make the best of it. His bed, if you want to call it that, consists of a 6-1/3' long, 2-1/2' wide steel bunk protruding from a bland tan concrete wall, suspended one foot above a bare concrete floor. The "mattress" is approximately 3-1/2" thick and is composed of some uncomfortable man-made substance. The "pillow" he rests his head on is 3" thick. It's made out of the same ungiving material as the mattress, some sort of light gray fire-resistant plastic. Obviously there is not enough room for a man of Danny's size to stretch out on this chunk of unforgiving metal. He is 6'3" and the clump of steel is only 6-1/3" feet long. He sleeps on his right side in the fetal position, but often he just tosses and turns, drifting in and out of fragmented dreams.

There is a realm beyond the past, present and future — this being the land of dreams. Sleep is the only freedom I know, and when I drift off to Never-Never Land, I almost always dream.

I love to go places my subconscious mind takes me. There are so many other worlds to visit and explore. My favorite one is when I can fly like a bird or Superman! These are fantasies that lift my inner soul above this dungeon where I am cast.

More often, though, my dreams turn into nightmares. I twist and turn in my sleep as I wrestle with every kind of demonic creature you can imagine.

I had this awful dream last night. I dreamt I was searching for my mom. I had heard she was dying and I had to find her before she was gone. I looked high and low, and after climbing a twisting, turning flight of dirty, dark, unfriendly stairs, I found them — my mom and dad. They were living in a rat and roach infested building crumbling from neglect.

I was standing just outside their door. I paused a moment listening for sounds of life inside, but there were none. Only their noisy neighbors gave life to the place. Knock! Knock! Knock! I rapped on the dingy apartment door.

My dad answered the door, wearing a solemn expression on his haggard face. My heart went out to him, but he regarded me lightly. Then he led me to where my precious mother lay. As I stood there looking down at my mom Claudia, the pitiful shell before me who was once vibrantly filled with the exuberance of life, my heart broke into a million pieces.

She looked up from her deathbed, which was merely a mattress on a cold, dirty, barren floor, and she smiled at me. Oh, how that beautiful smile still lit up her tortured face! Even through her pain and misery, she recognized me.

In my dream, she was desperately reaching for me, trying to tell me something. Ah, but alas. Her voice had left her. I fell down on my knees beside her frail body and cradled her in my arms like a child... and she died there in my arms.

Oh! That dream really hurt me. I woke up in this stinking prison cell with tears running down my face. I had been crying in my sleep. Lord only knows, dreams like that rip your heart out by the roots and leave you tired and spent. It haunted me all day.

Suddenly! The prisoner is jerked from a deep sleep. When the smoke detector from hell goes off unexpectedly in the middle of the night, it's one hell of a jolt back to reality! You know those hand-held boat-horns people take to football games? Well, they're like cherry-bombs compared to this thing. It's more like an H-bomb when it jump-starts your heart to trick-hammer in the dead of night!

Visiting Day

I'm sitting on a pillow on my green steel locker looking out the steel mesh and iron barred window at the sun going down. Sigh... I'm so blue. Today was visiting day — but not for me. Nobody ever comes to see me.

Early this morning I pretended I was going to get a visit from my Lady London. So I took a hot shower, brushed my teeth real good, and put on my best prison blues — thinking of my Lady. I even borrowed a splash of $40/oz. cologne from one of the cons. Then I stood outside my cell door with a cup of black instant coffee in one hand and one foot propped up on the railing on the second tier and watched the other fellas get called out to be with their loved ones.

I drank the coffee in my hand, turned and stepped back into my little world of 9x7. I looked in the plastic excuse for a mirror that sticks to the tan steel wall of my cell, and said, "Damn! You're looking good this morning, Danny. It's a shame no one will appreciate it!" Out of frustration and hurt, I grabbed the mirror and flung it across the room, crashing it into the steel mesh window. Ha! The damn thing didn't even break.

I'm baby-sitting tonight. Yep. Betcha wonder what the devil I'm supposed to be taking care of? Well, here's a hint. It has two beady black eyes, a long snout, a long tail, and it's about 10 inches long. It's a pet rat. Ha! That's right — a furry, beady-eyed, curly-tailed RAT.

I've been so lonely all day, I asked a friend of mine if I could keep his pet rat for the night. The little critter is completely tame. My friend raised him from a baby. In fact he or she — I don't know which — has better manners than most of the yo-yos around this dump. The little potato-eater just stuck its head out from the locker I'm sitting on. Earlier today, he crawled up on my shoulder to take a look out the window. Ha! What a trip!

I Saw His Feet!

We just had another tour group come through. This one was fairly large, about two dozen women in their twenties.

Before I came to Death Row, the guards always closed the solid steel doors to our cells, so we couldn't see them and they couldn't see us. I recall some girl begging the officer, "Aw, can't we see him? Come on — let me talk to him!" The officer said, "No." Then one of the girls got down on her knees trying to look under my door. "Do you see anything?" one of them asked. "I can see his feet," the other one squealed. "I SAW HIS FEET!"

Now they get to see everything. They stand there gawking at me like I was a trophy or prize the State parades for the curious, or some sort of wild animal gone mad. They just stand there... and stare. It's unnerving.

For hours after a group leaves I feel terrible. My emotions get all torn up. I get so angry and depressed I get ill.

Don't Step on the Blood

"There's a bad moon on the rise." Creedence Clearwater Revival so adequately chose those lyrics to express a warning. Well, sometimes there is no voice to alert one to danger. Such was the case today.

I was looking forward to a couple of games of volleyball with the guys here on The Row. You put twelve Death Row prisoners together, stretch a net between them, and you've got one mean game of volleyball. Yesterday two arguments came a hair's breadth from developing into an all-out free-for-all. Must be something in the food.

Today there was no sense of anything amiss. I went on the yard to exercise with the rest of the guys, when out of the blue, two men were stabbed up pretty bad. Blood spewed everywhere, and the word on The Row is ONE DEAD and the other in critical condition. I can't elaborate, because I don't want to get involved. All I can say is — it was BAD.

There's a hush on The Row when something like this happens. It affects the prisoners each in a different way. Each man just has to deal with it and get on with his business.

Everybody on The Row here knows what went down. You can't keep something like that a secret. It's just see no evil, hear no evil... and don't step on someone else's blood.

Timebomb

May 8, 1993, 9:26 P.M. Exactly 34 minutes from now, Larry Joe "Timebomb" Johnson will be strapped into the electric chair and 300 amps, 2,000 volts will race through his body, burning his existence in this world away. I have just prayed for Timebomb that if it must be so, God give him the strength to walk the last mile with courage to face the inevitable that reaches for all mankind: DEATH.

The Grim Reaper hovers over Florida State Prison, and it is a dark night indeed. The entire prison is locked down, each prisoner confined to his cell. The protesters have gathered outside the tall, forbidding barbed-wire fences, lighting candles as they bid a fellow human being farewell.

9:40 P.M. The lights just went out over the whole prison. The power company refuses to supply the prison with the electricity it seeks to execute Timebomb, so the prison switches to a generator for the duration.

9:50 P.M. My heart begins to squeeze within my chest as my pulse quickens. I feel a sickness in the pit of my stomach. It is almost as though I am sitting in the Chair myself.

9:55 P.M. I can't move. The leather straps hold me fast to the wooden iron maiden of death. The metal cap has been placed on my now-shaved head. An electrode is attached to my leg. The black hood is placed over my head. It's hard to breathe! I wait for the moment to come.

10:18 P.M. The lights just blacked out again as the prison generators were switched off and the regular power came back on.

Larry Joe Johnson is dead. Now the state's blood lust is satisfied for the time being. And so the endless cycle of an eye for an eye, tooth for a tooth, continues.

Today I finished another ink drawing. It is a man reaching toward the heavens, head lifted, eyes full of hope. I dedicate it to Timebomb.

Hate Factories

When you enlist for military service, they indoctrinate you by a process known as basic training which breaks you down, dehumanizes you so you are no longer an individual, but a part of the collective machine that rolls into battle warring against its enemies. The same principle applies to the prisons which dot our land like scabs on a leper's back. The machine seizes the offender, binds him hand and foot, and strips him of his basic human dignity in order to gain control of him.

The difference between the two is profound. The military does break you down, but it builds you up again, making you stronger, wiser, better. But our prison system just continues to push its working parts deeper into its ever-grinding, inward-turning machinery. After years of neglect, what is left? Bitter, hot dust, corrosive to anything it comes in contact with.

Every day thousands of brand-new human beings are drawn from their mothers' wombs — naked, vulnerable, and completely dependent on those who hold their destiny cradled in their arms. So begins life on this tiny blue planet. The light shines for the first time through an infant's bewildered eyes, illuminating a once-blank mind. And so begins the learning process.

All the child experiences, beginning with that first beam of light, will inevitably mold what he or she becomes. Children cannot see the future, or compare beyond the scope of what we teach them. As children grow in mind, body and spirit, those who have charge over that process have a great responsibility to nurture a healthy environment for these ever-learning tender souls, so they can expand and develop into productive, creative, beautiful human beings, unique and special in their own rare forms.

Ah, but alas. There are hate factories that churn and grind a troubled mind into something so hideous that we refuse to even study the causes that create such a beast. In our flawed society, if it can't be understood, we either remove it from our sight, take it apart, or destroy it. We think ourselves so mature, so sophisticated. And yet, under the vast expanding stars of the universe, we are all but children reaching for understanding of ourselves and the world we live in.

What is the flaw that turns a little innocent wide-eyed baby into a robber, a rapist, or even worse — a serial killer, capable of the most heinous of crimes? Is it a violent upbringing? An unstable home? Or is the child a bad seed at birth? I think not. Something this serious must be cultivated over a period of time.

Love and understanding go a long way in the development of a young pliable mind. Not the belt, not harsh, hateful, damning words, and certainly not a slap in the face. Remember, that little one is a person too, with the same feelings and emotions of an adult, only magnified tenfold.

The only way to prevent crime is to treat the cause, not the symptom. Violence erupts in our streets, and there are more prisons now than ever. As you read these words, another son or daughter has been swept away, prison-bound. Human souls are sucked in one end of these hate factories and fire-breathing dragons are vomited out the other end.

Why don't we build special housing for lawbreakers and put them to work building highways, bridges and hospitals? Why don't we teach them to be responsible and reward them for progress in that direction? If all else fails, then remove the offenders that refuse to comply from the mainstream and lock them away — but only after they prove to be unreachable. And even then, why not give them a means to express themselves in a productive manner?

Because of legislation recently passed in Florida, some day in the near future they may take away the limited access to TV's that prisoners are allowed. Anything that makes convicts suffer pleases society.

One thing is certain. Without a means to vent the frustration and ho-hum drudgery here towards something positive, I predict this prison and others like it will become a living HELL! Possible scenario: If prison conditions decline to the point that there becomes little distinction between population, lockup, close management, and Death Row, then what does one have to lose?

Honest, decent taxpayers should not be penalized by having to shoulder the burden of providing adequate housing for healthy prisoners, when industries could evolve behind prison walls that could give to the common good. There are no quick remedies to this problem, but if we could put our healthy prisoners to work, at least they could flex their hardened muscles to build a better world for us all.

The Destiny of Man

Doesn't look too good. There's trouble afoot on every shore. Wars and rumors of wars. You see it on TV, you hear it on the radio. Our world is filled with violence.

Society points their fingers at those behind bars and blames all their ills on us. What they fail to see is that we have problems, yes — but society's most pressing problems are not behind bars. They exist out there on the streets. To hang the woes of a moth-eaten society on its locked-away prisoners is a cop-out in the first degree.

Mankind never learns. We are constantly shifting our energies into negative veins and blaming our failures on imprisoned criminals. Why doesn't society quit dumping all its frustrations on the result of its failures? Wise up and treat the cause of social decay. Then the path will look brighter for everyone.

You can judge a tree by its fruits. The trees that grow these treacherous days (the nations of the world) bear only evil, violent, bitter fruit. Therefore, the not-so-distant future will hold torture, mass executions, and horrible times for mankind. To dwell on it means to go insane.

Often those who sit in their ivory castles choose to condemn and destroy, rather than to preserve and heal — but can you heal a wound by knocking off the scab? Mankind will never learn to heal its wounds. No, we choose to make the wounds greater because of greed. It's inevitable. History repeats itself. One day society's ills will be too great for it to recover. When entire families are dragged off to the death houses — then what?

Let's see. Hmm... the Zulus are kicking up African dust in Jo-han-is-burg... the Serbs have declared all-out war on anybody and everybody... Bosnia-Hurts is going up on flames of torment... in Somalia, Africa's warlords are at it again, looks like another bloodbath in the making... Russia is acting funny, moving troops and equipment to its borders... North and South Korea are eyeballing each other with steam boiling out of their tiny ears... and the 80,000 American GI's caught in the middle of that family feud have as much of a chance of holding their ground against a million-man NK Army as a bullfrog has crossing a 4-lane highway at high noon on Labor Day weekend.

A thousand years from now, who'll care anyhow, right? Well maybe so, but for now you'd better dig yourself a real deep bomb shelter and stock it with enough provisions to weather a 7-year nuclear winter. As for myself, I am more concerned about meeting Jesus Christ.

It will happen on a day just like any other day on Planet Earth — people running to and fro, going about their daily tasks, while on the other side of the globe little ones lay dreaming of tomorrow's delights that will never come.

Suddenly! There in the eastern sky, a gloriously bright figure will appear in the clouds — Jesus Christ clothed in pure dazzling white. Following Him will be a multitude of heavenly hosts. He will raise his arms and send angelic winged beings known as cherubim to flock over the four corners of this blue orb, gathering His chosen to take them away from this hellhole that was once a paradise, leaving it to burn at the hands of the Rulers of Darkness of This World! He foretold these things coming to pass over 2,000 years ago in Matthew 24:4-8.

It will happen in the blink of an eye, and then... He will be GONE, along with all his faithful. If you are left here on earth, you will live to see all Hell break out! I'm talking nuclear war, baby. The Big One — hydrogen bombs and missiles doing a tap dance over the inhabitants of Mother Earth.

Here's a prediction, for what it's worth. Bill Clinton will be the last President of the United States, and in the very near future nuclear war will be raising its ugly head. After China, Russia, France, England and the U.S. of A. slug it out with their nukes, there won't be enough left of the civilized world to support any government.

Any weapon forged by man's destructive hand that has been used in war and still exists solely for that reason — what are the odds of that weapon being used again? World War III will happen soon! It's a war that will not be fought in years, months, or even weeks. Nope! Once those buttons are pushed, the lights are gonna go out and overnight it will be OVER, dude. Of course, the aftermath will take years to dissipate.

So I feel it my duty to warn you. Search the deep corners of your heart. We will all face our destiny soon, but you still have a choice as to which fate befalls you. CHOOSE JESUS CHRIST NOW — before the tribulation passes its dark shadow over this world and perilous days find you terrified and alone.

Those who accept Jesus Christ as Lord and Savior will escape the wrath to come while the thunderbolts of man's inventions strike the earth's mantle like jagged fingers of searing destruction.

The Children of God will be partying down at the marriage supper of the Lamb, while hellfire ravishes this blue-green planet earth. Hallelujah! What a bash it's gonna be! It'll make a Rolling Stones concert look like a game of bingo at an old folks home. We're talking major good times! I mean, how much better can it get, when you've

got the Key to the Universe?

You know, it's a mighty huge cosmos out there. Yep! You betcha! And I plan on boarding the Galaxy Express. But the only one giving away tickets is — you guessed it, amigo — Jesus Christ the Righteous.

So what's it to be for you? Myself, I'll choose Jesus over this doomed world any old day of the week.

Whelp! I don't rightfully know how you have received these words from the thought generator in Danny's head. Coming from a convicted serial killer, my ideas probably appear slightly out of the Twilight Zone. But I assure you, the truth coming from anyone is still the truth. If you look to man for the answers that tug at your being, you'll be sadly disappointed. This world is going to Hell in a handbasket — sooner than you think!

My Prayer

It has been said, "The most difficult thing for a man to do is to recover himself after a great fall."

In the end, my life is required. But before I pass from this mortal world, I pray I will be able to recover Danny from the mire of dark deeds.

Only through the blood of Jesus Christ and His mercy shall I overcome the demons that scratch at the doors of my mind. By facing them head-on with my Lord's help, I hope to purge my soul of its sins.

On my knees I bow before my Lord and Savior Jesus Christ, and in the dark solitude of my prison cell I pray before my angel, who bottles up my prayers and takes wing to Heaven's throne to pour out my worship and complaint before the Alpha and Omega.

My Prayer: Oh! Son of the Great Creator Father God, grant me the courage to loose the fiery dragons from their secret places beneath the earthen strongholds of my heart, that I might face the truth and slay the evil that dwells in the folds of my soul.

I pray of you, Lord, that when the mighty archangel Gabriel blows that glorious trumpet on Judgment Day, this wounded soul might stand before his Maker, whole and pure, tried in the Holy Fire and purged of its terrible sins.

Master of the Universe, so vast and almighty, I pray that you may find pleasure in thy humble servant. After I shed this mortal vessel for an eternal body according to thy wonderful design, may my spirit seek out the mysteries of the cosmos on angels' wings by thy command and everlasting plan. Amen.

Fly, Elestria, Fly!
Immortal being of power and beauty
Take my hand and embrace my spirit.
Take the lead, and
Fly! Fly! Fly! Fly! Fly!
Flutter your heavenly feathers
And wing Eternity
Holding your candlestick
To lead the way
Standing at the portal
Between Death and Forever
In the Valley of the Shadow
Whether peace or sorrow
End or tomorrows
Drawn in or cast out!
Fly, Elestria, Fly!
Fly! Fly! Fly! Fly! Fly!

I Don't Do Lucifer

Have you ever come in contact with demonic Evil in its darkest form? Oh, I don't just mean serial killers — I mean the dark spirits of the netherworld. I can't recall ever meeting anyone else who has been touched by the imps of that parallel dimension.

Well, Hell's bells! You think my question is a bit out in left field? Truth is, I'm all the way out there past the Twilight Zone. Once you have been touched by a cold hand reaching from the descending caverns, you are never the same again.

You see, I have been drawn into the realm of the fallen angels. I have often answered the voices of the night calling out my name. How sweetly they sing — until they begin to SCREAM! It happened to me when I wasn't even looking for that door to open. It's a door I wish I had kept shut.

There are demonic spirits roaming this world in search of an open door to a soul to possess. If you open the door to these forces, they will enter and influence your mind, even dominate you to do things you never thought or dreamed of doing. I'm not making excuses for my behavior. God only knows there could be NO EXCUSE for what my hand has done. But I am here today to bear witness that Evil walks among us.

Lucifer is good at covering up his presence. He doesn't want people to see him for what he is, because then they would have to turn to Jesus and God the Father for protection, and that would put the Powers of Evil out of business once and for all.

In my writings and drawings I portray the Evil that has invaded my life, but this does not mean I am akin to these forces. I hate what the Forces of Darkness have done to me, and to all mankind, and I do not side with the Devil. I side with JESUS. He is my sword, my shield, my hope, my love. Praise His Holy Wonderful Precious Name! Praise Jesus! Down with Satan!

Let's get this straight once and for all: I AM NOT A SATANIST. I don't do Lucifer. I never did and I ain't about to start. I have not, do not, and will not ever belong to any cult or Satanist group. I'll die before I'll give my soul to Lucifer. I hate Lucifer. He is no friend of mine. He is my enemy. He doesn't own me.

Jesus Christ our Lord owns my soul by the precious blood he spilled for my sins on Calvary. Prayer and faith have delivered me from that Evil Spirit that had a death grip on my mind and soul. I am a Christian. I believe in Jesus Christ as my Lord and Savior. Period.

Writing About the Murders

When you turn over your own past in your mind, it's like standing on a rock looking at your reflection in the pool below. You never know how deep the water beneath the surface is until you dive in. You probe your own subconscious thought, reflecting visions of past-present-future on waters stirred only by diving deep into reality.

Writing consumes your energy at levels you can't even fathom. You throw your mind, heart and soul into it, and then it demands even more — reaching for parts of yourself that you can't imagine. My fingers are hurting from all this writing... writing... writing. Over the last two and a half years I've spent virtually every waking hour writing and rewriting this book.

Let me explain what it's like for me to write. I have obstacles to overcome that the average person never experiences, and the average writer would go hair-pulling NUTSO over.

There's the negative environment. While writing this book my accommodations have varied from The Hole to the Nuthouse to Death Row. My home is a tiny, cramped sauna bath nine feet long and six feet wide. "It's a small world after all." Ha!

There's the limited equipment — just a pen and a legal pad, an envelope and a stamp. That's it. No tape recorder. No clippings. No reference books. No typewriter. No computer. No desk. No chair. I sit cross-legged on a solid steel locker two feet high, four feet long, and two feet wide. I mean, even Adolf Hitler had a table and chair to complete his infamous Mein Kampf!

Right now it is so quiet, I can hear this pen scribbling out these words. And whenever there is a noise, it is so abrupt and loud! It jars me from my thoughts. Buckets banging... police radios squawking... people yelling... iron gates slamming... brass keys rattling. And so it goes.

I don't have an air conditioner. And it's HOT! Humid. Sometimes it's an effort just to stir in the stew of this heat and humidity. Right now I've got a ka-thobb... ka-thobbing headache pounding in my temples. I feel so confined. Everything closes in and I get irritable. To top it off, I am allowed only three hours to breathe fresh air per 168 hours, and I only get three showers a week. This blasted Florida humidity is ungodly. I just got out of the shower a few minutes ago and I'm already covered with sweat again.

There's my damaged vision. I stared into the sun when I was in the Marion County Jail and literally burnt holes in my retinas. There's a blue dot about the size of a pencil eraser right in the center of my field of vision. When my eyes get tired, I actually see double. In fact, it's a wonder I can see at all. Can you imagine having to write and draw that way? After a while you get used to it. You just have to pick the point between two illusions and go for it. So long as I don't overwork my eyes it's OK. It's just something I have to live with. Like counting down the remainder of my days on Death Row.

Then there's my mind. Let me explain how that works. If I'm disappointed, my mind goes into neutral, and I'm disappointed every single day. I mean, I wake up in the morning... I'm disappointed. I go to chow... I'm disappointed. I get a visit from my lawyers... I'm disappointed. I line up for whatever... I'm disappointed. Disappointments on top of disappointments. I just go into neutral. It's my way of dealing with it. My mind can and does shut down during extreme moments, sort of like you're watching a movie and someone turns off the picture but you can still hear the sound. Each time I am forced to take my mind out of gear, I might coast along for days, sometimes even weeks or months before I can get back on line again.

And depression? Mercy! You ought to try on one of these bottomless pits I fall into for size. It's like my heart just keeps sinking and sinking beyond my grasp. What makes it so bad is I haven't been able to cry lately. So it just keeps bottling up, pushing my spirit down that old dark well I know so well. My only real therapy is writing.

I am not even close to a professional writer. I am just a beginner with an ardent desire to reveal myself to the world that has rejected me. I know I shall never be a part of this world. But I just thought... what if I could produce something worthwhile? Maybe — just maybe — it could make a difference to someone. I don't know. All I know is, this work is my life, and it is IMPORTANT.

Does anyone know themselves inside-out totally? I'm not a psychologist, and I don't have all the answers. I've been as open and objective as I possibly can — beyond the point where most people would have bolted the door and turned away. Everyone has secrets. Yet I have not withheld my darkest secrets that nobody would want to share.

It's true, there are views of Danny I don't like to see in the mirror. There are many sides of me that are shameful and perverse — even monstrous. But still I have tried to reveal the truth unflinching and portray every facet of my being.

The Gainesville student murders were a sickening tragedy. The cameras broadcast the misery for the delight of the horror-and-tragedy seekers who stayed glued to Court TV and the evening news. They did their front-page news articles, magazine stories, TV and radio broadcasts. They've even written a couple of books about it. But when all was said and done, when the mad-dog killer was sent off to die five times over, what did we learn about why it happened?

For me, the trial was not half as bad as writing about the murders. To set these sights before the world as they really happened has been VERY DIFFICULT. I have bared my tortured soul in this book, digging out my heart and nailing it to fallen pines. It is both physically and emotionally exhausting to pen such pain.

Once I set out on that journey through the terrible maze of tragic events that occurred in Gainesville — Oh! What bloody footprints I have followed, enduring the shame of their senseless murder. My head pounded. It made me physically ill. I didn't sleep well.

I just wanted to put the whole bloody mess behind me. I wanted to portray the victims as the fine people they were and leave them some dignity. It's so difficult to honor those you have dishonored. They obviously deserved to live and enjoy the future they were working towards. And I am the one who took all their dreams away from them. God help me, God have mercy on my soul!

There have been times while writing about the horrible suffering of those fine people murdered in Gainesville that I just wanted to break down and cry. I have accumulated more gray hair with each line I write, but still I have pushed forward to finish the task set before me. Though it is painful to relive, my mind has returned to the place of bone and blood, screams in the hollowed night and tears of shame, the conversations with the victims, the terror, the shame, the loss, the mystery, the blood and guts and gore of it all — the entire nightmare. God forgive me. It is such a terrible thing I have done — sick and disgusting. How could I have gotten so far out there?

There are still moments I struggle with myself. Sometimes I say something or give a certain expression and I get these strange looks. I don't know. I can't see myself as others do. Still, I struggle again and again to look into the mirror of my troubled past and confront the demons lurking there. As I wrestle with my demons, shining the light of confession into the dark corners of my complicated mind, I feel a powerful healing taking place.

So here's to our odyssey deep into my soul. It's all out there now. I have opened the flood-gates of my mind and all the strange fish have tumbled out. Swim around with them long enough, and you might just see… the mystery.

The Word is Love

Sondra London, your creative magic sparkles. It easily stands out against the backdrop of the ho-hum run-of-the-mill journalism that is force-fed down the throats of the reading public these days. Your talent as a writer brings a breath of fresh air to a polluted and stale craft which once freed the reader to enjoy the magic and wonder of a well-written story. Ah but alas. During these uncertain days of haste, the magic has been trampled underfoot by narrow-minded employees of assembly-line journalism.

This striking contrast is what makes you such an amazing find. I compare it to walking down the beach and stumbling upon a perfect, flawless white diamond. You are not the average journalist, not a 9-to-5 punch-clock writer, but a gifted talent! Anyone who has an eye for thought-provoking, rare material would treasure working with a masterful writer such as yourself.

In a world full of prototype androids who crank out the same old earthbound rusty rot day after day, you pilot your course amongst the stars, always seeking to discover one hidden planet after another, unlocking hidden mysteries with your pioneering brand of journalism. You are among those who launch their imagination beyond this troubled earth in which we dwell — even beyond the starry heavens above.

The universe is yours, Sondra. Explore, conquer, harvest! And thank you for sharing your extraordinary self with us. I am honored and blessed to have you in my life.

I recall the day I first saw you.
I reached out to say "I love you."
But it was hard to say
Cause I couldn't touch you.
So tell me… what were my words?
All my tears run together, baby, just like rain.

Someone said to me,
"You can't run from your shadow,
And all you wanna be, deep or shallow
And all you wanna see
Along the path you follow."
So tell me… what were my words?
All my tears run together, baby, just like rain.

No one seems to know
Or even care why,
How the real story goes.
They'd much rather lie.
Now on goes the show, do or die
So tell me… what were my words?
All my tears run together, baby, just like rain.

Sondra & Danny's Tree

Sondra, the way you have completed this difficult and mysterious work is first-rate. My words are only the raw material. I love the way you have reworked them. In some places, your touch is ever-so-light, like the wings of a butterfly fluttering from petal to stem. In other spots, you have had to wrestle a sentence, word or phrase onto the anvil of clarity and hammer it into shape with the weight of experience — all for the best. I couldn't be more delighted.

Looking back over the years we've been working on this together, it's amazing to see how far we have come! Many veins bleed into the heart of this book, and only you could have woven them together into one river flowing through the heart and mind of the reader.

You see how my love for you brings out the artist in me? That's what made this it all happen from the beginning. I piped… and you came. You called… and I answered. You have touched the deep places hidden in the dark corners of my soul.

My writing, my songs, my artwork — all this creativity is spurred on by my emotional and intellectual link to you. The past two and a half years have not slipped through our fingers. We have much to show for it, in terms of art — for Danny & Sondra are art.

I like to be creative and touch my love in special ways. Sharing my talents with you helps me cope. When I paint or write, I'm emotionally involved with you. I reach for you in this manner, because they deny me your physical touch and presence, and it is all that I am allowed. I wish I had a magic potion we could both drink, smoke or drop, and you could crawl into my mind and I could drive into yours.

I don't ever want to sink into a non-creative rut. The only way I can rise above the ugliness and drudgery of this ho-hum daily existence on Death Row is to dive deep into the arts of my talents and create a legacy.

I've always liked the idea of Sondra & Danny working on this story together, contributing their own individual styles and talents. I really enjoy the magical time we spend together in our fantasies, the easy flow of creative words that stroke and provoke the intellect. Without your voice, this book wouldn't even be half of what it could be.

From day one, I joined hands with you in a combined effort to bring out the tragedy of this story in a shocking and magical way. You are the vehicle I sought after, to come along on this Rolling Coaster Ride with me. Of course you are much more than merely a means by which I express myself.

You are my inspiration, my beloved, the soulmate of my pilgrimage through this temporal realm and beyond even the mortal. I cling to the

Sondra Honey, You are the wind through my Tree. Without you… where would I Be? I look in the mirror and I see… a man with a dream. Don't take away that dream BAbydoll! Danny truly Loves Sondra. No one else can fill the spot in my heart where you dwell.

hope of an eternal plane where Sondra & Danny can explore the vast expanse of the universe! When we shed our fleshly shells, join spirits as children of the Forever Jesus Christ.

No one could have brought me this far or inspired me as much as you have. You give me purpose, you fill up my life. I would have given up long ago, if it weren't for the encouragement and support you have given me. Your probing questions have rooted out many deeply-seated problems that once disturbed me, and brought the ugly things into the light where the healing begins. I am all the better for it.

I bare my soul before you, my Lady Love. The good, the bad, the ugly — it's all in my own words — the truth, the bloody shameful truth — and God help me after all is said and done. I've stayed within the boundaries of how it went, but when it comes to what happened those balmy nights in Gainesville, truth is much stranger than fiction.

To open up my soul like a book for you to thumb through Danny's past, present and future is not an easy thing to do by distant correspondence. It means real pain for me. Being as I love you so fiercely, I give you as much of myself as possible under these adverse circumstances.

This page cannot contain the words needed to adequately express how special you are to me. You are the holder of the key that fits the door to my thoughts. My love for you is real — as real as the tide that caresses and strokes the sandy shore.

How do we explain love? Webster's tells us it is a feeling of intense affection, enthusiasm or fondness. In truth, love can't be narrowed by vowels and consonants. A mere look or touch from one's lover conveys a thousand unspoken words in an instant.

God only knows you mean so much to this downcast man. My aching, caged heart beats only the words, "I love you! Marry me, darling, and make me happy."

I am already joined to you, my soulmate. You are the true extension of myself. I will never leave or forsake you. As I live and breathe, you are the fountain from which flows my life's desire! Every other earthbound desire pales in comparison. I can't offer you my physical self — only my intellect, the core of my being.

A name symbolizes what an individual consists of — flesh and bone, thoughts and feeling, awareness of time and space — the sum total of one's self. And to this man, the name Sondra London means true love.

I am so sorry I have come to you this way — drenched with blood, dressed hand and foot in shackles and chains. Ah but alas! I cannot be other than Danny Rolling, and that name means bitter regrets and deep pain. Because I am a prisoner, I can't provide the closeness only the warmth of touch can give.

Sondra Touches Danny

Oh!!! What price of misery must I endure for just one kiss from my Lady Fair? I weep and rend my soul because the State of Florida refuses to allow me embraces from the one I love.

O my captors! Take from me my music... take away the blue sky... string me up by my thumbs... hang me on the tree of woe and beat my back bloody with a cat of nine tails... stretch me on the rack of pain... burn me with hot pokers... lock me away and throw away the key... even take away my life that I should die... the breath of my living soul burned from my body to please the state — only allow me to embrace my Heart, my Love, my Lady London, still kept from my empty arms.

Rose petals cast
into a fast-moving stream
Plucked from the heart
one at a time
Like hopes snatched
from a dream
Become memories
in the back of your mind

They have plucked the living rose from my hand, and now I am a prisoner indeed. We were so close, only an inch thick glass separated us. So close... and yet so far away. The one thing I long for in this life is to be with my love. Now she is adrift on that forever blue sea and I am marooned on this deserted island, alone — Captain Castaway without his queen.

My Lady, my Love, they can prevent us from being close bodily, but nothing can prevent you, the princess of my caged heart, and I, the prisoner of your dreams, from sharing our hearts and souls.

Can the moon forget the stars or the sun the heavens? Does the winter turn from the spring or the mocking bird refuse to sing? My Lady London, you are in my heart constantly. I bow before you, princess of my love. Will you kiss this desperate dragon and change him with your magic into your handsome prince?

Yes, my sins found me out and chained me to this life, so I cannot touch or feel your warmth to comfort me even from a distance. But I pray the good Lord in his mercy will allow us to meet and embrace in the hereafter. I love you, Sondra. I always will.

There is a room, a special place I keep just for you, where we swirl in each other's arms and dance off into our dreams. You once told me I sprang from the wellsprings of your imagination. I see you as the woman I have longed for all my life. And though I am forbidden to see you — woman of beauty and song, of bright expression and fire, so unique, so lovely, so exciting and warm — oh how I love you! My one, my only… Sondra.

In a dungeon deep, with chains about my feet, what of life? What of purpose and creative energetic passion? Like the blood red sun disappearing beneath the restless sea, I see… Sondra.

And even after I draw my last breath, when this world fades away and my spirit is drawn like a well that gives its last drop of crystal clear water, I remain true to only one… Sondra.

Sondra, my sweet Lady Love, can you feel it? The music I play for you — drummings of my heart, guitar strums of my soul, songs of my spirit. I sing just for you, just for you, my Love, and there is none other that shares the best of Danny Rolling.

Now let me take a new penny… warm it over the fire of desire… and press it against this frosted window that separates me from my Sondra.

S-sssst!

There, can you see me now, peering at you through the peep hole in the window? The snow is falling between us now and the cruel winter wind howls. But can you see me smiling at you? Hi, baby! I love you!

Oh! Something got in my eye! Ouch! What was that pricked my heart? Last night the Snow

Queen came and took me away. Now I am imprisoned in her castle of solid crystallized ice.

It's so cold here, so empty. In my heart of hearts, I long for freedom to play with my lovely Sondra under the kind sunshine. Ah, but alas. The Snow Queen has kissed me once to blind me, twice to bewitch me, and the third kiss (the kiss of Death) awaits me in her dungeon of devices.

Sondra, before the third kiss of Death befalls me, reach me, my Love so fair! Wash my eyes and cleanse my heart with your hot tears, that I might see again and know the warmth of Love that melts the heart of ice!

The Snow Queen I speak of here is not the one in Hans Christian Andersen's creation of fantasy, but the cruel prison bars that keep me from my betrothed, Sondra London the Lady Fair, and the kiss of Death is the electric chair. Before I die, I want to know Love again… my true Love… my Sondra.

I saw a black crow flying over this prison the other day as I walked the yard in chains. He cawed his way across the gray overcast sky. My heart grew heavy and I cried out to the crow, "Take word to Sondra. Tell her Danny is still alive. My heart beats strong — the love I have for her…" and so I watched the black bird wing his way beyond this prison of pain. Fly, crow, fly to my Sondra!

So here I am, bound in chains within the Snow Queen's cold crystal prison. The Queen said if I could spell Eternitas correctly, I could go on my way in the wide world — but I think the word is really Love.

Dear Lady London, Writeress of the Beyond, do not let this story flee capture! Grasp it! Embrace it! Let it burn passionately through your very heart and soul, blazing beyond what others have even dared to dream.

Only the Lady London possesses the magic to scratch the dragon's horn and tame the savage beast. So grab hold, my princess, and woo the dragon's fire into angel's breath. Take your dragon to the mountain top and leap over the edge, that we may soar together as eagles above the abyss of pain and despair, hand in hand… into Paradise.

190

Beyond the Keyhole

Come, Lady London
Open the dungeon
With your key… come see
The mystery you seek
In the corners
Of my mind.

Take my hand and follow
Into the hollow
Night
Where you catch your breath
For fright!
Where your mind will reel
From the hideous sight.
That is your desire
Is it not?

I will show you reflections
Horrible and ghastly
Painted on a bloody tapestry
And splashed with insanity.
Come now, my Lady
Let me lead you
Down the staircase
To Horror.

Turn the key and speak to my soul
With your inquisitive eyes behold
The deeds of my past
Reflected in your looking glass
Ah, but alas
You must hold fast
To what you find
With the key that unlocks
My mind

APPENDIX A
SECURITY TIPS

1. Park your car in the light.
2. Buy yourself a.38-caliber revolver. Get a permit to carry it on your person, and put it in your handbag, where it's easy to get to.
3. Buy some mace on a keychain and have it ready when you get out of your car.
4. If your bedroom window doesn't have a screen, get one and nail it to the windowsill.
5. Place a bunch of empty glass bottles in the windows.
6. Get you some curtains.
7. Buy a dead-bolt and put it on your bedroom door so you can lock yourself in.
8. Sleep with your .38-caliber revolver under your pillow. It won't go off by accident.
9. If someone bothers you, don't ever let an attacker get control. Fight for your life. Scream as loud as you can! Spray mace in his face. Kick him in the balls. Scratch at his eyes.
10. Pull your .38 caliber and blow him away!

Take it from one who knows:
It pays to be paranoid!

Now I'd like to take a moment to share my insight on a new product they have been advertising on the tube. It's called a Myotron, and Pulsar Technology drives it by lithium. It's a self-defense weapon you can attach to your keychain. It never needs recharging. You can use it over and over without waiting in between strikes delivered. On contact, it delivers a knockout one-punch charge that is like something out of a sci-fi flick!

No scream — just uhhhh... and then lights out. With only a brief touch of this device, you can render the baddest of the bad helpless for up to 3 hours. It's also a tragedy just waiting to happen.

Why? Because they fail to mention the offensive capabilities of this weapon. Can you imagine being able to take anyone out of action instantly and quietly with just a gentle touch of your hand? And it works through up to 1-1/2 inches of clothing.

Can you imagine the power of such a device in the hands of a serial rapist? Or worse — a serial killer? It defies imagination and in my opinion poses a real threat to society. It should not be made available to the public domain through standard channels. Even the commercial content of the advertising reaches directly into the psychopathic mind and says "BUY ME."

Scenario: You cross the parking lot holding shopping bags of merchandise. It's dark; you reach your car and open the driver's side door with your free hand. As you get in, the attacker comes at you quickly from your blind side, and merely touches you with a Myotron. Immediately! You lose all voluntary motor functions — but silently you remain conscious. You just can't cry out or move.

In the wrong hands, such a device makes a Ruger Black Hawk 44 magnum revolver look like a lollipop. Anyone can obtain such a device. All I have to do is write or call and send a check or money order, and they'll mail me one. Now that's scary.

APPENDIX B
A PACK OF LIES

Reader, there have been a lot of things said about this man Danny Rolling that are just not true, and if I am to share the haunts of my past with you, then I want to take this opportunity to set the record straight right now.

During the hearing, I encouraged my lawyers to rebut the misconceptions, but with all the gory facts surfacing, they were swamped. Being as I confessed before a trial could commence, I can see the logic in letting certain facts waive then — but not now. Now I must bring the full-strength truth to light.

I know you want to know what's fact... what's gossip... what's lies. But if I attempt to clarify every misconception about Danny Rolling I will have no peace, and I have very little of that at present.

I am the first to admit I do not know all I've done. I do the best I can to recall events and things I have said and done, but there are blank spots in my memory and perhaps I have gotten some facts confused. I'm not always 100% correct.

Take for instance the allegation that I said I wanted to chop off Madonna's head and place it where she could watch me have sex with her corpse. At first I denied it, but I've been thinking about that one, and perhaps it is true that I did say that. I was taking Thorazine while I was at Marion County Jail, and a great deal that went on during that time frame is foggy to me. It could be true.

I just can't put my finger on each and every accusation slung at me. I mean, you are talking to a man who has lived a double, even triple life for as long as I can remember. I can only see windows in the fog of my past. So it is possible some of these people coming up with wild stories about Danny Rolling are telling the truth.

I am not going to waste your time and mine responding every single one of the pack of lies that has surfaced. But there are a few that merit a moment's attention.

Of course, whether you choose to accept or reject what I say is entirely up to you, but God as my Sovereign Judge, whom I will stand before in the great Hereafter, I speak truly.

They Lied

I, Danny Rolling, did not — repeat, did NOT — confess to the Gainesville student murders because I was put up to it. My decision to plead guilty was strictly a matter of conscience — and you heard it directly from the horse's mouth.

This bullshit about Danny confessing because guards trashed my cell is ridiculous. The truth of the matter is, I had already spoken to the authorities before the shakedown and had already made arrangements to meet with them again. So the guards trashed my cell! Big deal, but it had nothing to do with my confession. I sense a cover-up here to hide the fact that one of the main reasons for the little talks we had was to have my fiancée put on my visiting list. They said they didn't see any problem there. They lied.

The State did indeed reject a plea bargain, but only after I turned down life for all the murders with a promise not to write about them - except Christa Hoyt's. They intended to seek the death penalty for that one, no matter what. I said I would only plea for life across the board. They refused... I confessed... and that's the way the song goes.

The State said Danny made up the story that a little bird flew on his window sill at Parchman and died, because he saw it in a movie. That's a LIE. I never said that. What I did say was that a sparrow flew down and landed in the snow on the ground behind my cell and I watched it freeze to death while I was in the cell that flooded with sewage. I tried to get my lawyers to say, "Hey! Wait a minute! That's not what Danny said," but I was told it wasn't important.

The State said Danny's cell in Parchman never flooded out two or three times a week with raw human sewage. That's a LIE. It damn sure did, and the only thing Agent Ed Dix relied on to support this fabrication was hearsay from that institution covering up its dark spots with little white lies.

She Lied

That fateful day my ex-wife took the stand and outright LIED, she did it so cool, calm and collectedly I couldn't believe it! She traveled over 700 miles just to nail my coffin shut.

Omatha said I never caught her with John Lummus while we were married. SHE LIED! I did catch them together, twice.

She said I beat her. SHE LIED! I never beat her.

She said I punched her in the face and gave her a black eye. SHE LIED! I slapped her once and all she had to show for it was a little red spot under her eye that went away in a day.

She said I threatened her with a shotgun. That's true. But then she said I didn't turn the gun on myself. SHE LIED! I did turn it on myself.

She said she never saw James Harold yank the covers off me while I lay sleeping in bed and jump on my chest and put a knife to my throat screaming, "I'm gonna kill you!"

SHE LIED! She did see that. She would have to be blind not to see it. She was standing along with my mom at the bedroom door looking directly at me. When he ripped off the covers, they both saw me naked.

To this day, I cannot put my finger on why James Harold invaded my home and attacked me that day. He was on-duty and in uniform. He had come in his squad car. Omatha and Claudia apparently followed in Mom's Buick.

It was my day off. I wasn't skipping work, and I wasn't smoking pot, as the State's Attorney implied. I was sound asleep in the nursery in the guest bed. It was hot and Kiley's room was the only one with an air conditioner. Omatha had taken Kiley to visit Claudia.

I was shocked by the whole scene and to this day I don't understand it — my mother and my wife standing at the door watching my father pull a knife on me.

Why did Omatha testify in court under oath at my trial that she didn't witness this event? I do not know the answer to that question, but I do know that it happened, and Omatha knows it too.

No Dental Instruments

This black prostitute I supposedly had kinky sex with at the University Inn, whoever she is? The one who says in John Donnelly's book that I rubbed cold metal over her after paying her $40 to undress? The one I was supposed to have told over and over, "I'm not going to hurt you" until I jacked off on her leg? HA! HA! HA! That's a total lie — NO truth to it whatsoever.

If I had such a wild time with a black prostitute, DON'T YOU THINK I'D REMEMBER IT? Why would I lie about something so insignificant as a $40.00 crack whore as compared to five murders which I have confessed to? I NEVER MET THE BITCH!

I did not — repeat, did NOT — and have not EVER — had sex with ANY black woman, least of all this Denise Taylor, whom I have never met. I have nothing against black folk. I have just never had the opportunity to have sex with a black woman. Years ago, while I was taking a Greyhound bus to New Orleans, I sat next to a real pretty black girl. We talked for awhile, and I asked her if I could kiss her. I told her I had never kissed a black woman and I just wondered what it was like. She agreed, and so we kissed. And that was the only time I ever got that close to a black woman. It wasn't a bad experience, just the only one I've ever had.

I don't know who this Denise Taylor is. All that stuff about paying her $40 for services rendered and playing with knives and something about dental instruments in a little velvet-lined case and four or five small mirrors positioned here and there around the lying bitch and lah-dee-dah-dee-dah — all that is pure BULLSHIT. The bitch is LYING! No doubt about it.

If I did pay the black bitch and do all the shit she said I did, then how come no dental instruments were ever found in my property? I mean, everything else was. Don't you think I'd keep something like that if it had ever interested me? Which it doesn't.

No Mirrors

Besides the mirrors I supposedly used in this kinky sex scene, it has also been reported that I arranged several mirrors to project the image of Christa Hoyt's severed head out the window, or to reflect the faces of whoever discovered the scene. Nada. The only mirror I recall seeing was the one on Christa's dresser, facing the bottom of her bed. I did not use that mirror or set up any other mirrors at this crime scene or anywhere else.

No Satanism

This woman who says I was on a mission from some Satanist church and she has hundreds of letters I supposedly wrote? And I was supposed to be well known by some guy named John Wheaties Carr? Boy is that wild, because I've never met this

Wheaties guy. I've never written hundreds of letters to anyone but Sondra London. I have never met any David Berkowitz. I don't know a damn thing about the Process Church or the Hand of Death or the Sisters of Asteroth or any other cult. If this woman ever does publish a book about me stuffed with such lies, I will SUE THE SHIT OUT OF HER, because IT AIN'T TRUE! Once and for all: NO... NO... NO... NO... NO... NO... NO... NO! I AM NOT INTO THE OCCULT!

The star I place at the end of my signature is only my seal of approval of the best I can offer. It is merely a star, nothing more. It is not a pentagram, which is a sign of the Devil. I will continue to use the star in my art to represent GOOD WORK. If people out there misconstrue my symbolism to mean something other than intended, I can't help that. If it's not the star, it will be something else, like the toes on my fallen angel looking like 666. Blahhhh... pure poppycock. Sometimes a star is just a star, and toes are just plain toes.

No Sodomy

Forensic experts placed in the stand testified that semen was found present in Tracy Paules' rectum, implying sodomy. That may be so. Regardless, I can't remember doing that to Tracy. I have argued that very subject with doctors and lawyers alike. Still, I must speak honestly in order to clean the slate once and for all. I have probed the fog of my memory, and I just can't recall sodomizing Tracy Paules. I don't even believe in sodomy. You'd think I'd remember something like that if I had done it, but the truth is I do not remember it. Medical examiners have been known to make mistakes, and maybe that is what happened in this case, I don't know.

Who's Conning Who?

Bobby Lewis is a pathological liar. He lied on the stand in order to make himself look good. He lied to the media just to make a play for the spotlight. So many lies have spilled from his mouth, I can't possibly deal with all of them. But let's take a look at just a few. Consider how he switches from truth to lies:

Bobby to WTVJ Channel 4: "The things he's done are so horrible that when he tries to talk about them he gets real emotionally tore up, he goes to crying and gets real, real messed up. He don't understand all the why's. He has a lot of problems that go back a long time, sexual problems, child abuse problems, but none of them problems justifies the things he done. He knows that, he admits that."

FDLE Agent Ed Dix to the Gainesville Sun 11/16/93: "He had been up praying all night and he wanted to confess his sins to God and man."

Bobby to the Gainesville Sun 2/19/93: "He said, 'Look, you know I'm guilty, I can't live with this. I've got to get right with God. I need to get this out.' He's literally laying it out for everybody and letting the justice system decide what his outcome is going to be."

Bobby to the Florida Times-Union 2/20/93: "He's trying to understand it himself. Now he's trying to do the right thing. He can't talk about the families of the victims without breaking down. Part of the reason why, he told me again and again there's no way to pay back to them what he's done. He realizes that, but he doesn't want to make it worse for them throughout this."

The Gainesville Sun 2/28/93: "Part of the reason why Lewis and Rolling are not disclosing details about the murders is because of the families. The horrible details will come out at trial, and that alone is painful enough," Lewis said. "He tells me again and again, there's no way to pay back to them what he's done. He realizes that, but he doesn't want to make it worse for them throughout this."

Then you see Bobby on WTLV TV 12 two months later going: "Danny Rolling is a big con man and you can't believe what he said about the victim's families, because he used to laugh about it to me, it really used to make me sick."

What happened? Obviously there are severe inconsistencies. The Toad changed his tune to suit his purpose, because his ticket out of prison got cashed and there was no longer any reason for him to play the role of "Top Con Gives Cops a Break."

Let's get this straight. Bobby Lewis has been

lying through his yellow teeth about this man Danny Rolling. I do not — and I have not — put on any acts, and I never told him I got pleasure from what went down in that college town.

Bobby has a way of twisting everything he hears to fit his own designed thoughts. He told the press that I said I had a seance with the spirit of Ted Bundy in the woods. He was always talking about Ted Bundy this and Ted Bundy that, because he met him in prison and I guess that makes him an authority. Once when he was telling another Ted Bundy story, he said that Ted had told him he was possessed by some kind of murder demon or spirit.

All I said was, I felt the same spirit present during the chain of events in Gainesville. I am not — nor have I ever been — a fan of the late Ted Bundy. I really don't know that much about him. In fact, I didn't even know Ted Bundy had ever been in Tallahassee until Bobby Lewis told me.

Then Bobby said that the reason I went to Tallahassee was because Ted Bundy had murdered two college girls there in 1978. That's a LIE. I passed through Tallahassee because I spit on my finger, tested the wind, and that's where the Greyhound took me.

Bobby Lewis is scared to death of me. That two-faced coward could never even WISH he had the heart to take my life. That's why he checked out of V-Wing, to get a safe distance away from me. Because he knew that sooner or later, I would discover what a RAT he is.

Bobby says he comes from the old school of convicts. He should have said "the old school of SNITCHES and RATS." Ever since I pulled up here on the Row, all I've heard about The Toad is what a low-life SNITCH he is. That's why he hadn't been in population here at FSP for years. Because all the real convicts can't stand him. He is a con, not a convict. Convicts don't drop dimes on their fellow prisoners. There isn't even a thimble full of honor in that toad. Anyone who really knows him will tell you as much. Scum, pure scum.

The worst liar is one who befriends in order to betray and promote himself. He pulled my strings in order to launch his own agenda and to make himself appear such an outstanding hero and stand-up guy, when in reality he is nothing but a conning bucket of swill. And that's the truth about your "Beautiful Bobby."

No Superstar

I never told Bobby I committed these terrible acts of violence in order to become a SUPERSTAR AMONGST CRIMINALS. What kind of sick joke is that supposed be? My artistic talents may reflect the dark struggles of my inner self, but I never meant to end up a BLOODY SERIAL KILLER.

No Bundy Seance

Bobby Lewis told the press that I said I had a seance with the spirit of Ted Bundy in the woods. He has a way of twisting everything he hears to fit his own designed thoughts.

Bobby was always talking about Ted Bundy this and Ted Bundy that, because he met him in prison and I guess that makes him an authority. Once when he was telling another Ted Bundy story, he said that Ted had told him he was possessed by some kind of murder demon or spirit. All I said was, I felt the same spirit present during the chain of events in Gainesville.

FACT. I am not — nor have I ever been — a fan of the late Ted Bundy. I really don't know that much about him. In fact, I didn't even know Ted Bundy had ever been in Tallahassee until Bobby Lewis told me.

Then Bobby Lewis said that the reason I went to Tallahassee was because Ted Bundy had murdered two college girls there in 1978. That's a LIE. I passed through Tallahassee because I spit on my finger, tested the wind, and that's where the Greyhound took me.

No Sexual Abuse

Another story making the rounds through Bobby Lewis is that I was sexually abused as a child. All right, yes. When I was very young, maybe 8 or 9 years old, a cousin visiting from out of town did get me to jerk off with him. It happened once, and it has never happened since. Although the thought of what happened does upset me, I just didn't think it was all that important. All my life I have denied it, pushed it from me — and I did not want it brought out. It did disturb me, but it happened so long ago and I was so young. Yes, it did happen, but I did not think I was going to have to relive that one incident before the entire world. I think too much has been made of the whole issue. That distasteful episode with my cousin wasn't what I would call abuse, not compared some of the real abuse I endured as a child.

No Knife Play

My uncle Charles Mitchell told Florida investigators that he watched me stabbing a board one inch thick with a very large knife. Then he said I threatened him with the same knife.

Bullshit! All of the above is a total lie. I would never do anything like that to him or anybody in my family. Charles Mitchell is a good friend of my dad's. I wouldn't be surprised if James Harold put him up to it.

No Child Molesting

I have known Cindy Dobbin for years. Omatha and I met her and her first husband Mark at church and became friends. She and her second husband Steve are the people who gave me the puppy I named Rocky, which I had to give away because my dad was abusing the little feller.

Cindy Dobbin is the one that called the cops fingering me as a suspect in the Grissom homicide. Steve and Cindy have told police and reporters a few truths mixed in with some real whoppers. The truth speaks for itself, but not everything they have said is as reliable.

I believe Steve has said some things about me because he was jealous. He always thought Cindy and I were having an affair, but we were just friends. Steve said that around Halloween of 1989, I told him I was a bad person, and I enjoyed stabbing people. That is false. I did not say that to him.

Steve said that I showed him a knife he described as "seven inches long, brand new looking, very clean with a serrated edge at the handle." That is false. The only knife I had at this time was a Marine Corps Ka-bar fighting knife, and I damn sure never showed it to Steve Dobbin. He made that up. Anyway, a Ka-bar doesn't have a serrated edge.

The way Cindy described one incident with her kids, I picked her son up on my shoulders and walked off down the street with him. She told investigators that as we went out of sight, she frantically called Steve to stop me. According to the report, she was fearful of me because of her suspicion of my "possible homosexual activities or sexual advances on children."

I strongly resent what Cindy implied, and there is absolutely no basis to support her fears. I notice she fails to mention here that the kids had been cooped up at home all day and they were getting rowdy.

Cindy and Steve were having problems and I asked Cindy if the boys and I could walk around the block. I thought it would help ease the tension and calm down Shawn and Aaron.

Cindy asked Steve and they agreed. The next thing I know, Shawn, Aaron and I are walking down the street and Steve comes running up to me like I was about to kidnap his kids. I mean, Hell's bells! My car was parked in their driveway. Where was I supposed to go? I wouldn't have done anything to harm those boys anyway.

If Steve and Cindy didn't want me and the boys to take a walk around the block, why the hell did they tell me it was OK when I asked? I didn't just walk out the door with them, you know.

I have never done anything against Steve or Cindy and when I read what they said about me, it pained me to the core. It really hurts to be betrayed by someone you thought was a friend.

Enjoy Sex

I just don't envision myself as these people are portraying Danny. Take for instance these girls who appeared in Donnelly's book. If I had one thing to say about that nursing student from England it would be ,"She is lying." Either that or

Donnelly is fabricating. Why? For one thing, I never asked that girl for anal sex. Also, I didn't then and I wouldn't now have a compulsive desire about cleanliness after sex. If a woman is clean and takes care of herself, I LOVE THE WAY A WOMAN SMELLS during and after sex. This stuff that is said about my sex life in Donnelly's book is nothing but BULLSHIT. I guess he uses these stories to build up his book and make it more exciting, but it isn't TRUE.

Then there's the psychiatrist Dr. Krop's estimation of my supposed difficulty in achieving orgasm. I understand why he came to that conclusion, because I often prolong the final moment to extend the pleasure. The girls I dated in Sarasota may have expressed this as "taking a long time to climax." It really hurts me to hear people say this and not really understand how it is with me sexually. Every time I seek orgasm, I reach that plateau effortlessly. I just like to prolong the pleasure. I enjoy sex immensely! It troubles me to hear someone tell the world that Danny has problems getting off because they have received inadequate information.

Not Gay

So this convict says I told him I could have any woman or man I wanted, and the reporter from the Miami Herald says, "Danny is gay."

You have no idea what such statements by these outright liars do to me. I AM NOT A BLASTED BLOODY QUEER! There is absolutely nothing about a man that seems attractive to me. I have NO HOMOSEXUAL TENDENCIES.

I am not — have not been, nor will I ever be — QUEER or HOMOSEXUAL or whatever you want to call it. Whoever says such things will not say so to my face, because so help me God! I'll punch their lights out or die trying. Just because a man is soft-spoken, does that make him a stinking queer?

Look! I was on V-Wing for over a year and a half. The place is literally crawling with filthy punks. I didn't touch any of them. Even though I've had guys confront me outright, going, "Aw, Danny, all I want to do is suck your dick," that kind of shit makes me sick. I'd just say, "Naw man, that's your thing. I'm not like that."

So if people out there want to bump their gums and say Danny's gay? Fuck 'em! Let the son-of-a-bitchin-bastards say so to my face or shut-the-fuck-up! I don't want to hear it.

Now to add insult to injury, my Lady gets a letter from some lowlife convict named Frank implying I'm queer and was sweet on him when I was on V-wing. This dumbass is trying to shake down my girl for some dough.

It would be laughable if it wasn't such a dirty, underhanded, outright lying scheme. If I could get my hands on this Frank So-in-so, whoever the fuck he is, I'd rip his heart out by the roots and make him eat it. Believe it!

This shit really upsets me, because I can't straighten it out myself. The jerk is beyond my reach. The investigator asked if I knew this Frank, but I don't know the dildo's last excuse for a heritage. I told him "NO," and that's the truth. I am unable to put a face with the name. If he was on V-wing while I did time there, I'm sure I'd recognize his face if I saw it, and oh, how I'd love to rearrange his features so his mama wouldn't know him!

Then he asked me if I had written any love letters to this Frank piece of shit. My answer: "NO! That's absolutely ludicrous!" And we had a good laugh. Regardless, even though it is humorous enough to stir a brief bout of laughter, I consider this attempt to blackmail my Lady a grave and serious matter and so does the prison.

This Frank dimwit is obviously running a scam. In my entire life, I have never sent a letter or note containing romantic innuendoes to a bloody ugly boy or man. NEVER! Damn the bastard! I hope we can nail a blackmail charge to his mangy hide. That would suit me just fine.

Let's get this straight. I AM NOT GAY. I don't care what John Donnelly or anyone else says. I HAVE NEVER BEEN GAY AND I DON'T WANNA BE GAY. So you can tell that sorry excuse for a reporter if I'm gay, his mother is a whore who sucks cocks in Hell!

I'm fed up with this shit. I can't face my

accusers and straighten them out. People I don't even know keep crawling out of the woodwork taking cheap shots at me and IT'S PURE BULLSHIT!

Damn it! I'm telling the TRUTH! I've never written any love letters to this Frank piece of shit. If he does have something, it's a forgery.

Now you believe what you want. But God as my eternal judge, you wait and see. This Frank mess is going to be revealed as nothing but a dirty scam.

Rolling v. Ryzuk

The Gainesville Ripper by Mary S. Ryzuk boasts of being "the complete and total story of Danny Rolling," but this book is nothing but one lie after another, mingled with public records blemished with secondhand unreliable statements by people just looking to make a name for themselves. It is so full of lies it should be labeled FICTION.

Ryzuk puts herself in scenes she has no knowledge of. Worse! If she can't come up with a scene, she makes one up! She couldn't draw from the source, so she fabricates and elaborates and takes liberties she is not qualified to expand on.

She relates conversations that did not occur. How dare that woman put words in my mouth! I have never even met Ryzuk, nor have I written to her. She doesn't know a damn thing about me, other than what she could slap together from the public records and what she could steal from the correspondence between myself and my fiancée. Ryzuk pretends to read my mind, but her version of my thinking is imaginary.

Anyone who buys Ryzuk's book in good faith that it is true crime is being ripped off. In reality, she doesn't know a blasted, bloody thing about how I feel or think! Factually said, Ryzuk's book is true GARBAGE.

To point out each and every fabrication in this book would be like dumping three different thousand-piece puzzles in one pile, mixing them up, then trying to piece together one true puzzle. It's exhausting to plow through line after endless line of bald-faced malicious lies. I think just a few examples will give you the general idea.

Most of Ryzuk's misinformation can be corrected by just reading this book. But I'd like to set the record straight on a few specific details for those who may have been confused by this so-called journalist who can't even get my name right. At least we have taken the time to honestly research our story and make accurate statements. Obviously, Ryzuk took little or no time whatsoever to research the facts, and her work reflects that unequivocally.

From the beginning, Ryzuk calls me Daniel. None of my people has ever called me that. It's not my name. In fact, I've never been addressed by that name by anyone until Ms. Ryzuk took it upon herself to do so.

Then she quotes my family as calling me Danny Boy. I have never been addressed as such — not by friends or family. My name is DANNY. That's what it reads on my birth certificate, and that is what my people have always called me. Not Daniel, not Danny Boy — just plain DANNY. She could have gotten my correct name from any of the crimes I've been convicted of or any other official records. They all give my name as Danny Harold Rolling. It's never been anything else.

Ryzuk describes me as a teenager fantasizing about murder. More conjecture. She has no idea how I felt at that time. My heart did not house murder until I was rotting in that sewage-filled prison cell at Parchman. True enough, I did masturbate and have violent fantasies at this time, but it was rape — not murder — that filled these moments. There's a big difference.

She claims that I got in trouble at school and had to repeat the third grade due to bad behavior. NOT TRUE. It was illness, not bad conduct. I was held back because I had mumps, measles, tonsils, and the croup. I had missed too many days and couldn't make up the deficit.

I was not in and out of trouble at school, as Ryzuk claims. I had some problems and my grades were low, but I didn't give school officials trouble.

When I entered the Air Force, I did get into trouble for marijuana and failure to obey a direct order, but Ryzuk describes an incident with a stolen bike that is a complete fabrication. Nothing like that ever happened.

When it comes to my ex-wife, her name is Omatha, not O'Mather. Another example of Ryzuk's failure to check the FACTS that are revealed in the official records.

Then Ryzuk tries to analyze our marital relations, saying I was impotent because I tried to control my wife and I couldn't do it. Bullshit! I've never had any problems with impotence! And I did not try to control Omatha. The only sexual problem we had was that Omatha couldn't achieve orgasm. She just didn't seem to enjoy sex. I tried to please her, but she was indifferent at best.

Ryzuk's descriptions of all my crimes are slapdash and full of errors. For example, take the Winn-Dixie robbery in Columbus, Georgia. She says I was busted by two deputies who just happened by. Here's how that one went: I had parked the Rent-a-Car at the far end of the mall parking lot. After the robbery I tried to make it to the getaway car, but there was a 3-foot deep marsh back there I wasn't aware of. The plan was to scale the 10-foot chainlink fence behind the Kroger and make way to the wash where I had parked the car, but the marsh slowed me up. By the time I did sludge my way back to the car, the place was crawling with cops and reporters. When I came out of that marsh, they had floodlights on me and TV cameras were all over the place. All I heard was the clicks of police slamming live rounds into their firearms and voices screaming, "Put the gun down! Put the gun down!" Does that sound like two cops just happened by?

She also knows nothing of my prison experiences. "He was a good-looking young man," she says, then she mentions a "vicious sexual component" and "fresh assaults he had not been able to repel at first." Lies! Total bullshit. God as my sovereign judge, I have never been sexually abused in prison. I did not get involved in that type of filth. From day one, I'd bust a muthafucka upside his mug before I'd allow a slimy dog to mess with me. And they all knew it. The same goes today. I'd rather kill and die than stoop so low.

Here is another one! Get this! She describes a trip I took while on furlough from prison. I have never been granted a furlough from any prison any time in my entire life. NEVER! She dreamed up this entire episode. It did not occur.

She says I escaped from a work detail in Georgia and went to a tent revival and slept in a pecan orchard. I did escape, but not from a work detail. It was from the county jail. There was no tent revival, no pecan orchard. And I was not, as she says, apprehended by Alabama authorities. I was collared by the Louisiana Highway Patrol just outside of Natchitoches, Louisiana.

Here is another prime example of Ryzuk's deliberate attempt to distort and falsify. She repeatedly calls my mom a brunette, because that fits her theory about the murders, but Claudia is and has always been a redhead.

Ryzuk claims I resented my mother. That is an outright lie! I have never been resentful of my mom. I loved her with all my heart. She was the best mom in the whole wide world, and I resent Ryzuk for saying different.

She has me blaming my mom for not protecting me from my dad. Let's get this straight once and for all: I have never blamed my mom for my dad's attitude, or for the problems in my life. NEVER! Nor did I feel she failed me in any form or fashion. In my eyes, my mom was the positive force in the family. She gave us boys her love. She cared for us as best she could. And my dear sweet mom has never been, as Ryzuk so cruelly describes her, whiny. I resent Ryzuk's attempt to distort the facts and place the blame for my crimes on my mom. Damn Ryzuk for casting her in this unflattering light when she has no evidence for it, and it's just not so!

Right here and now I want to spit in Ryzuk's face. The biggest and most dirty-handed lie of them all is implying there was something improper about the relationship between my dear sweet mom Claudia and myself. She doesn't put it in so many words, but she makes it quite clear that's what she's getting at. Ryzuk, you bitch! DAMN YOUR LYING MOUTH TO HELL! Anyone who ever knew Claudia Rolling will tell you point blank she was a very special person loved by many. She was the sweetest, most loving mom anyone could ask for, and as sure as there is a God in heaven above, there was never anything improper going on between Claudia and me. If we were

ROLLING 14

guilty of anything, it was caring so much for each other it hurt, because we both went through so much hell from James Harold. When he wasn't around, all three of us clung to the only source of comfort we had — each other. But we never even entertained such as Ryzuk implies. The relationship between Claudia and me never went beyond a mother's love and a son's admiration. There was no incest — NEVER!

Ryzuk's whole book is nothing but a pack of lies. I refute her sleazy slurs as FALSE.

APPENDIX C
THE STRUGGLE

Powerful images exist within the borders of "The Struggle." The theme to this intricate and emotionally expressive painting is the battle between Good and Evil, with mankind caught in the middle. The prize for this struggle — eternal life or destruction.

The crazed man suspended between Heaven and Hell struggles with the demons haunting his mind. He could represent all of mankind — then again he is a reflection of the artist.

The 4-band color strand stretching horizontally across the canvas depicts a divider of spheres of eternity. The backdrop is black as night.

The eclipse is the moment of truth — the darkest hour of the final battle in the struggle between Good and Evil, with the powers of the universe colliding with the positive and negative forces at work in the temporal realm.

The two angels represent the forces of Good as they do battle with the forces of Evil.

The angel below the color strand is locked in immortal combat with two demons. The higher and more powerful angel struggles with a poisonous viper, the epitome of Evil.

The Struggle

From behind fleshly veneer
A gasping soul appears
Born innocent, bloody and mild
Fate's toy, Destiny's child
Beams of light find
An empty, bewildered mind

Where am I? Who am I?

Thus the Struggle begins
Good and Evil within
And Sin, Honor's evil twin
First to crawl
Then stumble and fall
Down life's long hall
For some a noble course

Others fare worse

Forces of the Universe
Both positive and perverse
Traverse the bridge eternal
Where spirits holy and carnal
Cast lots for mortals

In the end
Into the Angel's arms ascend
Or to the Jaws of Hell commend

And the Struggle begins again.